# GARDENERS

# Gardeners

## ENCOUNTERS WITH EXCEPTIONAL PEOPLE

## Diana Ross

'When you have a taste for exceptional people you
always end up meeting them everywhere.'
Pierre Marc Orlan

**F**

FRANCES LINCOLN LIMITED
PUBLISHERS

Frances Lincoln Ltd
4 Torriano Mews
Torriano Avenue
London NW5 2RZ
www.franceslincoln.com

A catalogue record for this book is available from the British Library.

ISBN: 978-0-7112-2896-2

Printed and bound in China

9 8 7 6 5 4 3 2 1

# Contents

# *Foreword*

Somewhere around the start of the new millennium I began a dedicated search for people I would like to meet who had some kind of connection, however tenuous, with the gardening world, and who I hoped might be willing to talk to me about themselves and their work and, wherever possible, walk me round their gardens. I was fortunate that so many were, and doubly fortunate that almost all were prepared to give me so much of their time because I soon discovered that allowing a conversation to go where it will, and to trust that the story is somewhere hidden in the tapes – my lump of rock as it were – that accumulated as the day, sometimes days, wore on would ultimately reap greater rewards than attempting to stick to any prepared agenda ever could. Indeed, I agree with the little girl who, when told to think before she speaks, allegedly replied: 'How do I know what I think 'til I hear what I've said?'

However, my intended subject's connection to his garden has sometimes proved to be so very slight I have been obliged to search quite hard within my material for even the tiniest horticultural hook, or thorn perhaps, on which to hang the story. But find one I must because all the encounters here assembled were destined for publication in the subscription-only gardening quarterly *Hortus*, whose *raison d'etre* is to provide an outlet for garden writers wishing to express themselves at rather greater length than is acceptable to magazine editors nowadays, and I remain forever grateful to its editor and proprietor, David Wheeler, for his indulgence in this respect, although occasionally he did have to remind me to mention a plant *en passant*.

Perhaps this aphorism coined by the French writer Pierre Marc Orlan, 'When you have a taste for exceptional people you always end up meeting them everywhere', goes some way to explaining what seems to have happened, while the penultimate encounter in this book provides the best example: Professor James Lovelock, the inventor of Gaia Theory, has a positive antipathy to gardening as an activity, although it is fair to say I did not know this when I wrote proposing an interview. I am also indebted to a friend from New Zealand from whom I learned that the Maoris believe that the most important thing in life is people: 'He aha te mea nui? He tangata. He tangata. He tangata,' they say, which he tells me translates as: 'What is the most important thing? It is people, it is people, it is people.' Just so.

Having the opportunity to relive so many fascinating encounters in order to make my selection for this book has been the icing on the cake, although doing so has revealed a few obsessions and prejudices of my own I had not realised were quite so obvious at the time. It has also revealed one distinct bias: eight out of my chosen twenty are people well into their ninth decades, while a further eight are already in, or on the cusp of, their eighth. But then, if offered, my first choice would always be a Rembrandt self-portrait, or one of his mother, to hang on my walls.

I am grateful to nature writer Richard Mabey, whom I interviewed in late 2005, for his wise counsel with regard to any possible, or necessary, updating of the subjects we covered on that occasion: 'Of course,' he wrote in response to my email, 'I'd reply to you completely differently if we were talking now, but that's another story. . . . My own iron rule is not to tinker with pieces that were truthful at the time they were written.' And so, only where someone's circumstances have changed fundamentally since we met – for example, following the death of her husband, Lady Salisbury has become the Dowager Marchioness of Salisbury, and no longer lives at Hatfield – have I added an explanatory line or two to this effect at the end of the relevant piece.

# Roy Roberts

## GARDENER

It was for [Plas] Brondanw's sake that I worked and stinted, for its sake that I chiefly hoped to prosper. A cheque of ten pounds would come in and I would order yew hedging to that extent, a cheque for twenty and I would pave a further piece of terrace. I had indeed come to reckon all my small earnings in terms of forestry catalogue prices . . .

Sir Clough Williams Ellis, 1883–1978

By 1958 Sir Clough had been earmarking his hard-earned cash in this fashion for almost half a century. That was the year Roy Roberts turned up at Llanfrothen, the remote village in the heart of Snowdonia where Plas Brondanw is situated, because he was courting – or, as he would have it, 'sniffing around' – his future wife. He was twenty-one years old and about to leave the regular army that had been his life since he was fourteen. Unfortunately, he had little hope of finding a job in such a close-knit farming community and, once married, soon found himself with nothing much to do, so he took to wandering aimlessly up and down the gloomy lane that leads up from the village, past Plas Brondanw, into the mountains beyond.

As it happens, Plas Brondanw is not a typical garden of its period, not altogether shut in on itself, and only a low stone wall separates it from the road. One day, Roy Roberts spotted Sir Clough's gardener, Bowden, at his work and in due course got into the habit of dropping in for the occasional chat, even going so far as to lend the old man a hand from time to time to stave off boredom. Actions have consequences: Bowden retired eventually, and 'Roberts' – as Sir Clough always addressed him – found he'd landed himself a proper job.

As he recounts the story to me over forty years later, he thinks Sir Clough really wanted nothing more than a dogsbody, but it's hard to believe he hadn't spotted the man's intelligence and thought him a worthwhile investment, even if he might have to wait a bit for a return on his money because, Roy now admits, 'in those days if you showed me a carrot and an asparagus I could tell you which was which, but otherwise I hadn't a clue.' What's more, there was the topiary to be kept in shape, or, worse, created, when even the word, let alone its execution, meant absolutely nothing to a man who had spent his formative years painting some things, saluting others, and – the sum total of his gardening experience in the army – digging over his Colonel's wife's garden with a table fork, which was the tedious punishment devised for miscreants. Still, he reckons it beat being sent to prison.

Nowadays, with Sir Clough long gone, and the vegetable patch Roy had to master (but never learned to enjoy) reverted to sheep pasture, he is left largely to his own devices. Which suits him: he insists he never has taken any notice of what anyone tells him to do – a trait that must have made life difficult when Sir Clough was still his boss and given to handing out precise orders every morning before he set off for nearby Portmeirion, his celebrated fantasy village. I remember many years ago now a reviewer of a book about the aesthete Edward James stating that 'James was the kind of man who would tell his gardener what to do.' I wonder: is that as rude as saying he's the type who has to buy his own furniture? I fear so. But either way, if 'Roberts' is being strictly honest with me, for all the good it ever did him, Sir Clough could have saved himself the bother.

Interestingly, though, when it came to the baffling business of how to clip the topiary Sir Clough left his man to work it out for himself, only advising him to leave a rounded dome at the top of whatever shape he was after so that if it didn't work he could always turn it into a column. The result is a dazzling assortment of odd, organic shapes you feel must represent something, if you could only think what. But Sir Clough liked them well enough, apparently. What he didn't like – could be 'funny' about according to Roy – was straight lines: he liked his hedges 'dented'.

Unfortunately his gardener prefers them straight. He is still working on the straightening-out process he surreptitiously embarked upon years before Sir Clough died, and hopes to complete the task before he finally retires.

The problem is, Sir Clough continued to order yew, box, beech, and fir from forestry catalogues to the very end of his life, with the result, Roy calculates, that if you laid the material out flat it would cover four acres. But it is not laid out flat. For example, the Italian 'cypresses' – actually a type of fir that has to be painstakingly pruned to simulate the pencil-slimness of the genuine article (which could never withstand the rigours of the Welsh mountain climate) are 20 feet tall. Even the less lofty hedges pose problems because the garden is so steeply raked: to reach the centre of a 200-yard-long box hedge more than 5 feet across and about as high, he has to lean off a ladder teetering on the brink of a ha-ha wall with a 6-foot drop into the field beneath. He does it, he says, on 'a wing and a prayer'.

He has acclimatised himself over the years, but there was a time when, tied on to a ladder he'd roped to one of the fake cypresses, he would be physically sick from the swaying motion as he struggled to clip its flimsy tip in a gale. To get through the workload he must start clipping in June, and hope he's finished by Christmas: from dawn until dusk every day for six months of the year he sets up his Heath Robinson contraptions of apple crates and ladders, ties himself on, and gets cracking, whatever the weather. Lawn maintenance, however, requires good conditions, so when the rains holds off long enough for the grass to dry out sufficiently, Roy has to untie himself from his ladders, and haul out the mower. Which annoys him very much, but not as much as he imagines an assistant would. Unfortunately, a nasty accident fourteen years ago cost him three fingers, and kept him off work for eleven months, so the grass did not get cut at all, which is why, when he was invited to do a series for Anglia TV on topiary in Tuscany only recently, he turned the opportunity down because he feared the garden would suffer unacceptably. And now that it is open to the public, he dare not take the risk. 'Who's the first one they laugh at?' he demands, accusingly. 'The bloody gardener, that's who.' I have the feeling sometimes Roy Roberts wants things both ways.

So, a proud man, and as he tells his story I do begin to wonder if Sir Clough fully appreciated the fact: there were some awesome clashes, which suited Roy, who loves a fight, but not Sir Clough who hated confrontation. They coped by keeping out of one another's way; after all, there were not too many men around that remote part of North Wales able or willing to tie themselves to trees for weeks on end for someone else's sake, and few other options open to the man who was. Nevertheless, the camel's back was almost broken on one occasion when Sir Clough told 'Roberts' he had to paint 'a dead bloody tree' on the hillside outside the garden proper, in full, humiliating view of the village: Sir Clough liked everything not actually alive to be painted his trademark colour Portmeirion Green (in fact a milky turquoise) with lots of gold embellishment. Not to everyone's taste.

For all his self-professed bloody-mindedness, Roy Roberts turned himself into a fine gardener, but when I congratulate him on his achievement he won't have it: 'You could teach a monkey in that time! You learn, don't you? If you make a cock-up this year, you don't make it next. Plus you overhear people talking in the pub, and you listen. They'll only let on so much, but for someone who doesn't know sod all about it, getting to know the basics is something.' He believes that in any event the best way to teach someone is to let them loose: 'I've made some terrible mistakes, but I burnt them, or I'd say someone nicked it, or I'd go to the shop and buy it.' At first he 'bloody killed' half his plants by digging in fresh manure or lime, and if his boss noticed a plant was missing he'd tell him the sheep got in. 'Bowden never had that problem,' Sir Clough would grumble. Well, no.

A garden on a Welsh mountainside is ace slug territory, and Roy got hold of a good tip from his sessions in the pub – coat hosta leaves with soft soap. In fact, he no longer uses any chemicals these days, except on the paths, although he used to (like most of us), and once with potentially deadly consequences: 'A clump of nettles outside the kitchen door was bloody annoying me so I sprayed them with weedkiller. A few days later cook says, "She's quite bad, you know." I thought nothing of it. Next day she's worse, and cook tells me she can't understand it because she's had nothing but nettle soup.' 'She' was Sir Clough's wife Amabel, who was cultivating the nettles for culinary purposes. Roy sweated it out. Lady Williams Ellis recovered.

He had a chance to make up for nearly killing her when she became his boss after Sir Clough's death in 1978, and he became her chauffeur until her own death ten years later. They got on well: for one thing, Lady Williams Ellis disliked flowers to the extent that if anyone sent her any she would chuck them straight in the bin, according to my informant. Such eccentric behaviour impressed Roy, who doesn't care for flowers either. As a matter of fact, flowers really only serve to gild the lily at Plas Brondanw, where Nature herself plays the Vita Sackville-West role: at the end of each yew *allée*, a pair of imposing turquoise-and-gold-painted gates draws the eye to the wild majesty of the mountain scenery beyond, and by so doing incorporates its savagery into the garden's overall design, while at the same time wittily proclaiming: 'No admittance!' In Sir Clough's day, the few flowers permitted inside the gates had to be white: Japanese anemones, the odd azalea and the transient blossom on a group of wild cherries carefully planted to frame a view of Cnicht, the conical, often snow-capped, Japanese look-alike of a mountain at the end of the garden's main axis.

During the couple's lifetime, the garden remained altogether private, so any vegetables Roy managed to harvest were for the table, and his heroic work on the topiary was for their benefit alone. But after Lady Williams Ellis died, that changed. Presciently, in his autobiography *Architect Errant*, Sir Clough wrote:

> It is warming indeed to see the avenues I then planted growing so flourishingly and the whole place maturing in ever-increasing beauty. . . . If it is movingly beautiful also to my descendants I hope that they or one of them may be able to live there. If it is not wonderful to them, then I hope it may be enjoyed by someone else who will yet think kindly of those fore-runners who spent four hundred years, off and on, in making what they admire.

His descendants do still own the property but none of them chooses to live in the ancient house, and its future is still to be decided. In the meantime, the spirit of Sir Clough's second wish has been granted: since 1993 the gates have been opened at 9.30 every morning and closed again at 5.30, and visitors entrusted to put their money in an Honesty Box. Unfortunately, only about a thousand people each year do turn up: it is simply too remote. But to merit the road signs with the brown flower to alert the punters to its existence, the garden must already be attracting twice that number. This is awkward: without the signs it couldn't possibly – Catch 22.

Especially since Plas Brondanw possesses none of the amenities today's garden visitor expects; there is no lav, no caff, no shop, no dedicated parking; just the pub half a mile down the steep lane. The few who do make the pilgrimage are often faithful returnees (among them, garden photographer Alex Ramsay, Sir Roy Strong and David Wheeler all put it top of their list of favourite gardens). Unfortunately, being open every day has, Roy tells me, increased his workload immeasurably because in the old days if he didn't get round to doing something one year he could get around to it the next year. No longer. 'It's professional pride, isn't it? And so we are back to his point that the 'bloody' gardener will be blamed for any perceived imperfection, and he couldn't bear that.

As he sees it, and I would agree with him, another downside to letting the public in is the perception that a garden must have colour at all seasons, and lots of it. Many National Trust gardens have been diminished as a result, as has Kew, with its proliferating winter-flowering pansy bedding-out schemes. At Plas Brondanw, Sir Clough's granddaughter Mena is now Roy's boss and, desperate for visitors, has felt obliged to go the same route: a massed tangle of *Hydrangea paniculata*, phormiums and hebes flops about in a long bed originally designed as a simple carpet of herbs arranged in contrasting shades of green. Roy hates the hebes, and the way the hydrangeas fade to pink. He also hates the daffodils Mena has planted in 'his' grass, making it even harder to maintain to his exacting standards, and he absolutely loathes the crocosmias spreading like wildfire along the hedges. The family also introduced peacocks as an added attraction, but since I couldn't see or, more likely, hear any peacocks I wonder what happened to them. All Roy will say, deadpan, is that they didn't last long.

He describes the time quite recently when he saw a cherrypicker in operation on the topiary at Levens Hall and how he'd thought he'd like one of those, but discovered the machine cost £8,000. Fat chance, he thought, resigning himself. But he was in luck: the Health and Safety people somehow got to hear about this maverick gardener working all alone off dangerous ladders in the middle of nowhere without a mobile phone, and decided he should get his cherrypicker, once he had been taught how to use one and passed a test. Roy was duly sent on a course where it was assumed everyone had at least heard of COSHH (the acronym for a manual entitled *Control of Substances Hazardous to Health*). He, of course, had not: 'Cosh? What the bloody hell is cosh?' he demanded. But, as he says: 'You learn, don't you?'

I had wondered when I arrived that morning what the unwieldy contraption sprayed the regulation Portmeirion Green lying sprawled like an exhausted giraffe across the small courtyard at the entrance to the garden was for. It was of course the new cherrypicker, only twice the size ordered. (I learned later that its replacement eventually arrived, duly sprayed, but that it rarely gets an airing, and that Roy's only concession to COSHH is to keep the mobile handy when he's working on his ladders, because he sees the sense: 'Many a time I've been working high up in a tree and it starts swaying around and I think I'm bloody mad. I'm here very early in the morning and very late at night. It might be days before anyone noticed.'

But how the topiary gets tackled will soon be someone else's problem. I am curious to know what he intends doing with his time once he's retired, since he doesn't fancy growing his own vegetables and isn't one for company: 'I don't mind the odd night in the pub, but there's nothing more boring than holding a bloody pint in your hand unless you're going to have a conversation or a good argument.' Even on his day off, he confesses, he prefers to lurk in his refuge at Plas Brondanw, away from the noise of other people's lawnmowers, surrounded by the usual paraphernalia garden sheds accumulate, as well some they don't – fridge, cooker, radio, filing cabinet, two armchairs filched off a skip, electric shaver, and his collection of military memorabilia. (He retains affection for the institution that taught him all he needed to cope with life, including a number of creative ways to deploy swearwords.)

As for what he will do with himself, I might have known: Roy Roberts has a dream, a marvellous dream; he dreams of sailing a boat alone around the British Isles – notwithstanding the fact that he gets seasick up a ladder, and has never sailed a boat in his life. 'I haven't a clue', he shrugs, 'but I'm not stupid. I'd join a sail club and get some training. Then I'd say "Bye! See you!" to the wife and set off' – unlike his erstwhile boss, whose greatest love apart from Plas Brondanw and architecture was sailing, but who insisted on dragging his family along too, and once nearly drowned the lot of them. The errant architect's wiser, if no less romantic gardener, insists he wouldn't go out of sight of land: 'Don't get me wrong, it would have to be something I could live with. If the weather turned bad, I'd tie up somewhere for three or four days and I'd go home 'til it got better.'

And when he does set sail, what will happen to the garden? It is unlikely one man could cope with the workload, let alone the isolation, but gardeners cost money, so the family – all too aware that going the car park and lavatories route would destroy the *genius loci* – might yet be tempted. My own feeling is that while 'Roberts' remains the garden's guardian, Sir Clough's spirit can rest easy, and if sometimes in our conversation his gardener sounds less than reverential towards his late employer, well, no man is a hero to his valet.

Roy Roberts has now retired from Plas Brondanw, but has yet to set sail. However the garden is open daily, the Honesty Box remains in place, and there is still no caff or lav or designated parking lot. Plas Brondanw garden, Llanfrothen, Gwynedd is open 9.30–5.30 p.m. daily. £3.00 in the Honesty Box at the gate. For further enquiries, telephone Portmeirion 01766 770228.

# Tony Hall

## HORTICULTURIST

I am a plantsman and I look at gardens from the perspective of what's grown in them. To me the most exciting glasshouse in the world is at Kew Gardens. It is not one of the grand houses in terms of scale but it does represent a perfect blend of good plantsmanship and high technology. This is the Alpine House at Kew. Although it is small and off to the side it is the first place I rush to when I visit because it is always the most exciting place.

J.C. Raulston, Professor of Horticulture, North
Carolina State University (1940–96)

If you consider the fact that for almost thirty years the post of Manager of the Alpine Unit at Kew has been held by the same person, then the Professor's encomium – written in the late 1980s – may be taken as a personal tribute to a man whose plantsmanship and dedication to communicating his experience of how to grow these difficult little plants has gained him an international reputation. But if a boost to the esteem in which Tony Hall is held were needed, it was undoubtedly given when he unwittingly found himself playing a star part some years ago now in an ill-fated Channel 4 documentary about Kew Gardens entitled *Paradise Pruned*. The programme had been intended to be one of a series, but in the event Kew's managers turned out to be not quite so ready to allow the cameras access behind closed doors as the less inhibited staff at the Royal Opera House had been a couple of years earlier for that riveting series *The House*. Thus, what had been intended as an illuminating series ended as a tantalising one-off, with Tony Hall cast as the recalcitrant maverick, the lone voice defending the art of horticulture (and the importance of communicating this art to the next generation to ensure its survival) and the plants themselves – the

Living Collections – for their quality and scientific value. This willingness to stand up and be counted found him pitted against the Leviathan of a somewhat flummoxed but always dogged management body committed, as Tony saw it, to transforming its garden managers into computer operators tied to the office and out of touch with their *raison d'être*.

At one point in the programme, the Curator of the Living Collections beards Tony, who is half-buried under papers and reference books and fag ends, in his utter shambles of an office (in sharp contrast to the fastidiously high standards of hygiene and order he maintains in the plants' domain). He rebukes Tony for the amount of time he spends on his special interest (Juno irises), lectures him on how he must not abuse his privileges, and informs him of his need for further training in management skills – i.e. computers. Tony listens patiently as humiliation is heaped upon humiliation and when he gets the chance responds with exquisite politeness: 'Really? That fills me with dread. I am basically a gardener and an old-fashioned supervisor.' Mesmerised, I found myself marvelling at the man's dignity while fearing for his future. Meanwhile, the manager, baffled but not quite disarmed, tries a couple more shots – something about plants being easier to understand than people, and a finger wagging exhortation to Tony not to withdraw into his shell.

But the manager's role turned out to be only a minor one in the unfolding drama: sharing top billing with Tony Hall was former civil servant John Lavin, whose job at Kew is to negotiate with its unions on pay restructuring. Lavin spent his time on camera yelling down the telephone, or crossly ripping up his notes after a presumably unsuccessful encounter with the union bosses off it. He reckoned negotiating with the miners in 1984 on behalf of the government had been a breeze compared with dealing with Kew's 'stroppy, intelligent people, not militant but always asking why' – an admirable attitude, he admitted, but one that was beginning to wear him down. It showed. Conversely, non-union member Tony Hall was usually filmed in silent communication with nature as he got on with the business of looking after his plants, which, he observed in a dry aside, 'you don't have to talk to'.

So the frustrated television director got his revenge, and at the same time gave the case for the importance of a hands-on approach to horticulture a rare airing. I had been so captivated by Tony Hall's attitude, I arranged to meet him at Kew some months later and he began what turned out to be a poignant and remarkable story by remembering his own early years as a garden labourer and how, traditionally, gardeners have always been seen as 'the lepers of the horticultural world', always been treated like 'dog s**t'. He reckons that this attitude has only changed quite recently, with the media's apparently insatiable obsession with gardening celebrities. An image of Charlie Dimmock, whose star was very much in the ascendant at the time, hovered in the air between us, but we overcame the temptation to waste time discussing the phenomenon, time that would be better spent in the telling and recording of how Tony Hall had so unexpectedly, and belatedly, landed up in the world of horticulture at all, let alone at Kew

The fact is, music was the world in which Tony Hall had planned to live out his life ever since as a child at school in the 1950s he was offered an arbitrary choice – chemistry or the violin – and chose, equally arbitrarily (but, as events were to prove, with painful irony) the violin. The combination of an appetite for knowledge and a real musical gift the young Tony Hall discovered he possessed landed him, in 1961, at the age of seventeen, a coveted scholarship to the Royal Academy of Music. The future looked bright.

Unfortunately, fate had other plans: after a series of barbaric and ultimately useless operations in his early twenties he was rendered profoundly deaf, and in despair. It took a long time – over six years – before he stumbled into horticulture, and only then because he needed to find something to fill the emptiness. Reflecting on the enforced abandonment of his dreams and the bleak period that followed brings back bitter memories, yet such is his urge to communicate on any subject which affects him deeply he now not only lectures internationally on his work with alpines, he also gives talks on music to the staff and students at Kew, reading the scores of his favourite composers (ranging from Schoenberg through Vaughan Williams and Samuel Barber to Bach) while his audience listens to the tape or CD – a feat equivalent, I imagine, to a blind person managing to deliver on cue the words to an illustrated lecture.

The music establishment's loss has unquestionably been horticulture's gain, but how did this come about? And what made him choose Kew? This is the story: one afternoon he was weeding a path at the home of his erstwhile music mentor, Bernard Shore, and finding the experience oddly soothing. Bernard Shore, who had noticed his former pupil's absorption in his task, just happened to know someone whose son was Head of Richmond Borough Parks Department and so Tony Hall ended up a garden labourer in the Terrace Gardens without knowing the name of a single English native tree or shrub. Then one day a young man who had been employed as a garden labourer at Kew joined the team. Whoever he was, with his ability to spew out Latin names that could turn a tree into, say, *Betula utilis*, a shrub into *Rhododendron Pentium*, or a flower into *Anemone nemorosa*, he was the all-important catalyst that changed Tony Hall's life: with only the vaguest idea of what or where Kew was, he knew absolutely that if he wanted to learn, which he most emphatically did, he must get there. Having located the place, he got himself taken on as a labourer (a 'botanical horticulturist' in today-speak), learned a lot of Latin very fast, decided that wasn't enough, applied to become a student and – after a year away at Merriest Wood College near Guildford – was accepted. He was up and running.

He is modest about his achievement, reckoning that demands today are far more intellectually challenging than they were back in 1973, but adding the coda that 'of course, no one knows how to garden any more: they are all scientists'. To put it another way, a BSc. in Hort. or Ecology is, in his estimation, no substitute for a hands on apprenticeship. At one point he referred to Kew's botanists as 'haymakers' because, as he sees it, 'they spend all day studying dried plant material and wouldn't recognise a living plant if it stood up and bit them on the bum'. I mistook his irreverence for contempt, but when I say as much he is shocked: that is not it, not it at all. Then I remember: he might easily have gone the science route himself – indeed, his twin brother is a science teacher. Nevertheless, it was not hard to imagine that making fun of the BScs helps this beleaguered horticulturist, who is so fearful for the future of his cherished plants and whose own job description he barely recognises any more, release any build-up of steam. As he says, 'If you work at Kew, people think you waft about in a white coat with a paintbrush pollinating orchids all day long'. A lot of them do. Tony Hall, on the other hand, habitually dresses in trainers, bomber jacket and white silk scarf like an RAF pilot off on a wartime mission to flatten Hamburg.

Interestingly, alpines held no special interest for him when he was a student: 'Actually, I was very open-minded. I was like a piece of blotting paper. I absorbed everything.' So, having completed a stint in the tropical department working with ferns, which he enjoyed, and a spell on the tree gang, which he also enjoyed (although the experience scared him half to death: another by-product of the brutal ear operations has been a permanently impaired sense of balance and while everyone else at Kew dashes about on bikes, Tony's is a trike), the move to the Alpine House had simply been the next stage in his training programme. Except that he found himself stranded there for two years due to staff shortages. He was still there when the post of Unit Manager of Alpines became open, and although as a student he was not strictly eligible, he applied for the job and got it: in a little over six years he had transformed himself from unskilled garden labourer into head of one of the most prestigious units in one of the most famous horticultural establishments on the planet. It is not difficult to understand why he has since refused to move on up the corporate ladder: one more rung and, like his immediate boss, the Head of the Herbaceous Section, he would be out of touch with what he had come to Kew for in the first place: 'I would be hopelessly separated from the plants and my students, which is half the fun. I need them. I learn from them. It is a two way thing.' *À propos*, he remembers Dan Pearson as having been a superb student, someone who was, as Tony admiringly puts it, 'very careful of the collections, very practical' – in other words, a student of the calibre he hoped might one day take over his own job. But he realises a student of such quality would not want to remain at Kew; Kew, with its enclosed environment and less than spectacular financial rewards, is really only attractive to people who seek the security it can offer.

The Polish philosopher Leszek Kołakowski mooted that the basic human needs are freedom and security which, he pointed out, is unfortunate since the two are incompatible. The aphorism notwithstanding, Tony Hall has achieved a fair modicum of personal freedom by spending many more unpaid hours at his work than the thirty-six he is obliged to put in, concentrating in those extra hours on the Junos irises and making them his special area of expertise. He writes about them – about all alpines – as well as lectures on the subject all over the world. He is a judge of Alpine Garden Society exhibits at its shows, and sits on the Joint Rock Garden Committee (comprising the Scottish Rock Garden Society, Alpine Garden Society and Royal Horticultural Society). Often unpaid, or at best in peanuts, this generous gift of himself has brought its rewards: it has given him the opportunity to meet other specialist growers and learn from them while incidentally enhancing his own – not to mention Kew's – reputation.

And so he flies above the rest, as the solo violinist he once hoped to become floats over the orchestra. Otherwise, he rarely leaves the place – for the simple reason that he lives 'over the shop' (his flat is bang next to Kew Palace), and is so committed to the plants he never deserts them for long because 'things can go wrong very fast – or come right for that matter – and they fall sick or flower when it suits them, not us'. He walks his areas – which include the woodland – two or three times a day, even at weekends when he is off duty. 'Kew takes advantage' he shrugs, resigned. 'Their attitude is: if you are foolish enough to spend all that time with the plants that is up to you.' In fact, the only time he signs out with unfailing regularity is during Wimbledon fortnight when he binges on tennis, revelling in the gladiatorial spectacle it affords.

It goes without saying that the plants under this perfectionist's aegis get all the attention they require, but the Junos get that little bit more: nothing is too good for these small, rare, difficult, lovely, sweet-scented denizens of the high, dry, winter-freezing/summer-baking mountain ranges that stretch from the eastern Mediterranean to Pakistan. But however attractive their characteristics, he ascribes his special interest in the species to the fact that under the almost impossibly difficult growing conditions provided by Kew's banana-belt climate they present him with such a challenge: 'These little plants need to be understood. When they respond, it is a pleasure. When they don't, it is hell. In fact, I am pleased just to find them alive and kicking at the end of their rest period.'

One particularly rare and difficult species – *Iris postii* – took him twelve years to bring into flower from the bulb. At that rate of maturation I reckon there must be bulbs flowering on some desert slope in the Middle East whose seedling grandparents had only recently germinated when St Paul was still on the road. Another, *Iris edomensis*, whose flower is a stylish colour combination of veined brownish-purple and grungy greenish-yellow, with a flash of orange-yellow to lighten the effect, was among a number he had been repotting one evening when, most unusually, he succumbed to exhaustion and left the precious bulbs perched on top of the compost in their Long Tom pots overnight. A badger got the lot. Almost miraculously, however, Tony managed to identify them all by the remnants of their roots, and to persuade the chewed up scraps to produce more bulbs in due course. It took years, and a further five to coax them into flower. He reckons growing plants 'is 90 per cent care – mostly intuition and perspiration; there is only a very small intellectual side to it', which is a horribly off-message point of view at Kew these days.

Apart from foraging badgers, to leave a Juno iris unprotected in the aphid-saturated, botrytis-friendly atmosphere of the British Isles he considers too dreadful a squandering of natural resources to contemplate, so he uses chemicals, and mourns the loss of Benlate. 'But', he warns, 'I must stress this is my personal view. Kew has both a legal and a philosophical obligation to be ultra-safe.'

However politically incorrect his own methods may be, and however much he despairs of the management's attitude sometimes, Tony never fails to acknowledge his debt to Kew, repeatedly affirming his gratitude towards his now retired mentors, John Simmons and Brian Halliwell, and making certain I understand that Kew is, after all, primarily a scientific establishment, even while he bitterly regrets the lowly position the Living Collections hold in its pecking order. Indeed, this lament ran like a refrain throughout the interview, reminding me of something he said in the television programme: 'Keeping up the standard with fewer and fewer staff and more and more extra responsibilities is a question of rationalising the collections and asking the important question: "Why *am* I growing this?" rather than, as in the old days, "Why am I *not* growing this?" That is especially hard for someone like myself who has a curiosity and a thirst regarding growing new, rare, interesting plants. I think they're looking for managers. It is as simple as that. I don't think plantsmanship is as important as it used to be.' But while he is prepared to let the powers-that-be know what he thinks of this change of emphasis, he is always courteous (good manners and fair play feature high on his list of moral musts, while mediocrity and intellectual snobbery, along with all politicians post Lord Boothby, pubs, religion – he is a 'devout atheist' – and newspapers are abominated). He admits he was feeling at a very low ebb at the time the programme was being made, and that this had prompted him to go so far as to say to camera: 'Have I got a value at Kew? Sometimes I don't even feel that.' Letters flooded in from those who felt otherwise, the most supportive being from the heavy brigade including Chris Brickell, former Director General of the RHS, Tony Schilling, former curator of Wakehurst Place and Valerie Finnis, renowned plantswoman and a woman after Tony Hall's heart (Valerie Finnis founded the Merlin Trust, a charity which helps to encourage young horticulturists to travel and study plants).

I wondered if he had ever contemplated leaving Kew in moments of frustration. He had not: apart from the security it has given him, where else would he have access to so many interesting plants, and so many opportunities to hand on his experience to others? Nevertheless, he does despair at what he describes as the 'Disneyfication' of Kew; but then again, Director Generals come and go, and it is possible Professor Peter Crane (the new incumbent at the time of our encounter) may have different ideas; in fact, Tony is hopeful the man might bring some lateral thinking to bear on the subject. Either way, he knows Kew will be obliged to rely more and more on self-generated revenue as the years roll on, and while Sir Ghillean Prance, Professor Crane's predecessor, pioneered the Friends of Kew project that has turned out to be such a nice little earner, how to keep the punters coming through the gates he accepts must be the priority. Predictably, he deplores the bedded-out pansy schemes Kew favours, and simply hates the Princess of Wales Conservatory, indeed any dumbing-down, but is still hopeful the establishment will do more to encourage serious plantspeople to visit the Living Collections and encourage foreign scientists to avail themselves of Kew's valuable resources. And what if money were no object? (As if!) In that case, he would like to see Kew work to gain a reputation as a superb growing establishment: apparently specialist growers are invariably better at caring for plants than any botanical institute and Kew is no exception.

By chance, I came across an article by the botanist John Akeroyd in which he too makes a plea for the horticulturist to be recognised: 'I also hope' he writes, '[that] we shall see more respect and encouragement for the practitioners of gardening. [. . .] Newspaper and magazine articles praise fashionable and affluent garden designers *and anybody ever associated with Kew* [my italics] but few bother with those who actually turn over the soil.'

The *virtuoso's* job in a concerto is to make his instrument dominate the orchestra until he and it are – with a bit of luck – reunited at the finish. In

Tony Hall's case, as his literally maddening deafness progressed he was obliged to switch from the violin to the viola because he could hear, or at least feel, its lower frequencies. Unfortunately, however, it is far harder to make a viola heard above the clamour of an orchestra. His own voice is similarly low-pitched, resonating deep down in his thoroughly fumigated chest, which for him is an advantage because he can feel himself speak, and since he lip-reads perfectly he can also 'hear' the orchestra, as it were. The problem is: can it hear him?

Tony Hall is now retired from Kew, but has been retained as an Honorary Research Associate. He continues to despair of much that goes on at the establishment these days (including the new Alpine House which he considers an abomination: 'No longer are people enticed to spend hours admiring rare alpines/bulbs; they are just herded through on the way to the Princess of Wales Conservatory') but continues to haunt the place with his presence, nonetheless.

# *Roy Lancaster*

## PLANTSMAN, WRITER
## AND BROADCASTER

I've seen all the treasures of the world, all the exotica, and I've come
back to the British flora, to the moor with its handful of native plants,
and that has a calming effect. It takes me back to my roots . . .

Roy Lancaster

I turned into Roy Lancaster's drive one morning in midsummer, and
nearly hit a cluster of plastic bags full of plants standing on the tarmac.
Curious, I peered inside and, as one might expect of any plantsman (let
alone the doyen with only one third of an acre to pack his collection into),
the bags contained one of each of everything: one *Thalictrum rochebruni-
anum*; one *Canna iridifolia*; one yellow-flowered aquilegia; one *Dahlia*
'Bishop of Llandaff', and one *Gillenia trifoliata*. Behind the bags, an
unusual-looking hydrangea on the point of flowering was climbing ener-
getically up the north wall of the house. There was no time to take in much
else before I am spotted and, right there on the front doorstep, treated to
an inimitable Lancaster profile of the first plant that catches his eye.

Fascinated, but conscious of the very likely possibility that the entire
morning could slip away in this fashion, I beg for a moratorium: could we
perhaps settle ourselves somewhere out of sight of anything organic
because, inseparable though they may be, I had come hoping to find out a
little about the man behind the knowledge. So in we go, only to end up in
the sitting room whose windows look out over the back garden, and a
beguiling honeysuckle-like climber with large orange, apricot and cream-
coloured flowers growing up the side of the house sets him off again:

'*Lonicera calcarata*!' he exults; that's the only one in the country, apart from one I put in the tree at the front. "Calcarata" means "spur". The flowers have spurs – a unique feature.' It is also hardy, highly scented (of tuberoses, I decide) and produces red berries: a Lancaster gem. Then he remembers: 'In fact I was going to ask you when you arrived for God's sake not to let me ramble because I will follow wherever my mind takes me, wherever the story's leading. Someone came here once, and we started in the garden straight away and I ended up telling him where all the plants came from, and he hardly once said "Let me ask you this." I was just talking in a monologue, and when he'd gone I said to myself, That was *crazy*! That was *stupid*! He only heard one part of me.'

He disappears off into the kitchen to make coffee because his wife, Sue, was (most unusually) away for the day on a project of her own and as he potters about I can hear him singing a romantic ballad from, at a guess, the 1920s or 1930s. I decide to wander in after him but, full of apology, he stops me: he is not good at doing two things at once – which makes two of us but rather begs the question how, without this aptitude or a secretary, he manages his crowded schedule. (As the day wears on I realise that Sue is his secret, that her role in his life is all-encompassing.)

We begin by exploring the early years. I knew that he was born in Bolton in Lancashire shortly before the Second World War, that his interest in English native wildflowers began as a very young boy growing up in a world that did not extend beyond the mill town's rubbish tips and the moors within easy reach beyond, that his first job had been as a gardener with Bolton Parks Department, and that his love and understanding of English plants had broadened into an appreciation of more exotic species during his National Service years in Malaya. I also knew that after his return from the Far East he had trained at Cambridge Botanic Garden, and from there, in 1962, gone to work full-time for Hillier's Nurseries, ending up as Curator of The Hillier Arboretum before leaving in 1980 to turn freelance.

I hoped he would flesh out these bare bones for me; in particular, I was curious as to whether there had been someone special to direct the young boy – someone whose voice had guided his ambitious, adventurous spirit on its trajectory. His father? Or a mentor, perhaps? Not his father: 'My father was interested in gardening but he died when I was fifteen, before I'd even become interested in plants, and I can honestly say that I didn't really know him. I was a keen bird-watcher at that time. Birds were my first interest. I used to travel all over looking for birds.' However, he reckons he has always been lucky in the people he has met along the way, and the two first people in a long list to whom he listened were his school biology teacher, and the local museum curator. There was also his friend the Reverend Mr Shaw, who by his own example inspired his young protégé to keep detailed accounts of his wildlife observations: 'He was one of these famous vicars of old, probably the end of a long line of vicar-naturalists. He was an ebullient, larger-than-life character who drove around the borders of Lancashire and Yorkshire in old cars with leather seats looking for plants. Whenever either of us saw a plant that looked interesting he'd stop and we'd go back to see what it was.'

As to how the young Roy Lancaster managed to turn into a career an interest in a subject that at the period was still largely a leisure pursuit for gentlemen amateurs – before he could even begin to try, he had to be discouraged from his ambition to become a train driver. He remembers how he felt: 'That power! To be in control of that wonderful engine! I was an avid train spotter. And I can hear now the announcements on Trinity Street station, Bolton: The next train in is the 3.45 for Glasgow, Stirling and Inverness. My God! Where's *Inverness*?!' His teacher and the museum curator between them persuaded him to change his mind: 'I've tried to put myself in their place since and I've thought, well yes, I suppose if I were in their shoes and a kid of fourteen comes along who actually wants to know about birds – and later plants – I'm going to say Right! Come on! Let's at least be helpful!' The curator, whose name was Alfred Hazelwood (Roy is as good with people's names as he is with plant names), pointed out that it would be ten years before he could hope even to get onto the foot-plate of a steam engine, and that with his father gone he needed to bring home money for the family. Had he ever thought of becoming a gardener working for Bolton Parks? He had not, and remembers why: 'When we were doing our favourite subjects at school – ornithology, woodwork, whatever – I'd look through the window and see one of the teachers with a group of boys tramping behind him in the rain carrying rakes and hoes and things: it always seemed to be raining, and they always seemed to be cultivating vegetables. I thought they were stuck in the gardening class because they were the sort of people who had no particular interest in anything.' Nevertheless, he heeded Alfred Hazelwood's advice, which is how he came to overhear one of the local town councillors begging his foreman in the Parks Department to find a menial job in the gardens for his not-very-bright son. The foreman said he could, but warned the councillor that for anyone wanting to get on in life there was rather more to gardening than a willing pair of hands, an observation Roy Lancaster OBE, VMH, plant-explorer, writer, broadcaster, television celebrity, teacher and lecturer never forgot.

But he soon discovered it would not be easy to get on as a gardener in the élitist world of horticulture: in other people's perceptions gardening is not a profession. Fine. In that case he would call himself a 'horticulturist'. That was then; now he may call himself whatever he likes, and he likes to call himself a gardener: 'Because I trained as a gardener. I knew I could not earn my living from being a dream-maker or a storyteller. I had to have some skill I could offer. Gardening was such a skill, and it has allowed me to do my other things as well – the dream-making, if you like.' But before the humble horticulturist could metamorphose into a proud gardener he had some catching up to do: at school his two most hated subjects apart from maths had been history and geography, the very subjects that could supply answers to the questions he was beginning to ask himself: 'Where do plants come from? – mountains, rivers, forests, depressions. And what about history? All the people from royalty down to sea captains, pirates, ministers, travellers, adventurers! I learned those two subjects my way, a way I could easily digest, and it was exciting! It was adventure!' Adventure! Stories! Dreams! The boy from Bolton lives on.

The phone rings. Roy answers. It is his friend, the Japanese botanist and plant hunter Mikinori Ogisu, who Roy reckons is one of the greatest living authorities on Chinese and Japanese flora, and who was his guide on three expeditions to Japan. Sometimes his friend faxes, but more often he calls and as he likes to chat for an impressive half hour at a time Roy finds himself in a bit of a fix – longing to talk, but conscious of my presence, and anxious not to offend either of us. He asks Mikinori if he might possibly call back later, but frets on and off throughout the day: 'He's ringing me from Japan and I say do you mind ringing back later! But he knows me well enough. He's been to China again, and he'll have some things to tell me.' It was Mikinori who collected the seed of the honeysuckle now heading skywards outside Roy's sitting room window. Apparently he had been exploring the temperate forests 1,280 metres up Mount Omei in a remote, roadless area of Sichuan Province in south-west China when he noticed it flowering 25 metres up in the canopy and, assuming it was a tree in flower, decided he would have to come back on another occasion with a professional climber to collect its seed. Only then did he realise what he had stumbled across.

The phone goes again. Again he answers it. And again: not only no secretary, no telephone-answering machine either it would appear, but if I enquired about this lack it might look as if I were getting restless at the interruptions, which normally I would be, and since each one reminded him of another good story I was finding the situation perfectly bearable. (I learned from Sue later that they do indeed possess an answerphone, only Roy would never think to turn it on; she is not sure he'd know how.) In any case he enjoys talking to people too much – and writing to them: he himself told me about his inclination to answer immediately the handwritten letters that come in: 'If I was a millionaire I would spend a lot of my time sitting down writing letters to people. I love it!' Handwriting fascinates him: he can dream himself into the shoes of a favourite plant explorer merely by concentrating hard on the man's signature, while Sue deals with the brown envelopes.

Every now and then I find myself referring to Roy Lancaster's heroes and role models as 'plant hunters', but he prefers to call them 'explorers':

'People like Wilson and Kingdon-Ward – certainly Kingdon-Ward – Joseph Rock, George Forrest, may have been paid to look out for new plants, collect seeds, but if that's all their lives had been they would have been much smaller people.' In 1971, Roy was invited to join a plant-hunting expedition to Nepal – his first. But he was working full-time at Hillier's Nurseries in those days, and although it was possible his boss might grant him unpaid leave, he also might not. Yet he must go. He would go! Living vicariously was no longer hitting the spot. Harold Hillier was baffled. Why go to the Himalayas? What's new? Hasn't it been done? In other words, what is the use? Roy stood his ground: 'With respect Sir, *I* haven't been.' His boss gave in. Today Roy counsels youngsters who worry that someone has already been everywhere to think: 'But *you* haven't! That's what matters. You're different. How you react and what you make of the experience will be different from other people. You are an entirely different person from a Wilson or a Forrest or a Lancaster.'

I wonder if there is actually anywhere left uncharted for today's plant-explorer to investigate? Yes: forests in Northern Iran, in the Caspian area, as well as temperate rainforests in southern Chile remain 'unlogged'. I imagine he means in the sense of not yet investigated, but he means the logging companies haven't been into these areas – yet. Roy is not particularly bothered by today's stringent laws on plant-collecting; he is as happy to take photographs. What is hard to bear is the sheer, awful ignorance with regard to plant conservation that persists in some parts of the world: 'It gets up your nose when you know you could have your fingers wrapped for picking a fruit.' And he despairs at the thought of a rare and lovely spleenwort growing in the Yangste Gorges, whose only other habitat is some islands in the Atlantic: the Chinese officials connected with the dam project about to drown it into extinction insist that everything in danger has already been moved. 'Rubbish!' he snorts. 'Bureaucracy! If only we could get up into those crags!' Not quite a rant, but close.

Sue's absence means lunch out, so we drive over to the Hillier Arboretum for a bite, and a turn round the grounds afterwards. Gardeners, students, managerial staff, visitors, the song of a chiff-chaff, an insignificant little plant among the exotica ('That's the enchanters' night-shade. Little white flower sparkling like stars. Grows in woodland just like this. Long white creeping roots. It's a perfect pest in gardens.') all, equally, attract his full attention. Hard to believe the slice of cake and small glass of white wine he chooses for himself could be metabolised into so much sustainable energy. A thought: has anyone ever flummoxed him with a plant? Yes, and only recently: 'It was an umbel. Binny Plants in West Lothian gave me this plant – this seedling – and I said "What's this?" and they said "Well something like . . ." [and he mumbles, his mouth apparently full of marbles], and I said "Omigod! I need time to recover from that." Now every time I write it out for someone I spell it differently. It's from Greece.' (The correct spelling is *Molopospermum peloponnesiacum*.)

Our stroll takes us past a series of ponds bordered by damp-loving flora with *Gunnera manicata* and *Darmera peltata* predominant. He chooses the latter for the Lancaster treatment: 'It's called *Darmera peltata'* – and repeats the name slowly to be sure I've got it down correctly – 'and it's in the saxifrage family. Pink flowers come up before the leaves, then the leaves follow and make this lovely umbrella. Beautiful tints in autumn. Comes from the woodlands and wet places of northwest America. Often shares the same swamps with the big yellow skunk cabbage. A Pacific Coast plant. One of the first introductions of the plant was made by a man called Benedict Röezl. He was a bearded one-armed Czech who lost his arm demonstrating the machine that would separate the fibres out of the leaves of sisal. Unfortunately he got his hand caught and it pulled his arm off.' 'A one-armed bearded Czech?' I yelp. 'A one-armed bearded Czech' he corroborates, and continues: 'Now, you'd think after that kind of start in life he'd want a gentle profession. No! He decided to become a plant-explorer and he spent the rest of his life in Central America and Brazil hunting orchids. Apparently he was robbed no less than seventeen times by bandits. On the last occasion he was coming out of the bush; he was starving; his clothes were torn; he had scratches and cuts all over his body; and he was clutching a big pile of orchids. Normally they would have just cut his throat and robbed him but they looked at this guy and one of the men said: "What are we going to do?" And the leader said: "Well, he's got hardly any clothes and here he is clutching a bundle of weeds so he must have God's protection. Let's leave him." It's said he's one of the very few plant explorers who actually died peacefully in his bed at home; many of them came a cropper.' Roy found this account in an out of print book entitled *The Plant Hunters* by Tyler Whittle, which he recommends hunting down for the author's fresh way of telling all the old tales.

Meanwhile, visitors are hovering hopefully. My companion acknowledges them all: 'Good afternoon! Hey! You've got the sun out for you now haven't you. That's nice! Really warm on you. Are you enjoying it?' And for anyone who will listen, he throws in a Lancaster lecturette for good measure. He asks an old lady in a wheelchair if she has any favourite flowers. She looks bemused, so he helps her out: 'I like these primulas. They're from China, the Himalayas. A breath of mountain air!' Later, someone calls out cheekily: 'Oh, I know you! You don't look anything like Alan Titchmarsh! I had an uncle with one brown eye and one blue eye, like David Bowie.' Valiantly he tries to draw her attention to a nearby shrub in flower, but she is interested in his celebrity, not in what Roy Lancaster is here on this earth to celebrate.

Even so sociable a soul as Roy must, I imagine, feel the need to switch off sometimes, and he does: 'Switching off can be as simple as coming back to the garden on my own and sitting and just letting all that hype drain away – let the garden, the birds, everything about the garden just speak to me. The gardening experience takes in all the senses, and if it doesn't you've got a problem.' Walking with friends in the New Forest out of season is another way, and listening to music; music is crucial. In the car coming home he told me about his father who worked all his life in the mill, but who was also a gifted violinist – so gifted, he auditioned for a place with the Manchester-based Hallé Orchestra, and only didn't get it because he unwisely admitted to being slightly deaf. Roy regrets he doesn't play any instrument himself, but he does love to sing and whistle, and is a regular concertgoer. With his wages from Bolton Parks he used to buy old 78 rpm records being sold cheap after the arrival of the newfangled LPs: 'Sometimes maybe I could only buy one record; it might be the opening movement of something, and that's all I had, but I used to play it again and again.' His tastes are catholic: as well as Beethoven and Berlioz he collected the old crooners, such as Al Bowley, whom his son recently informed him was allegedly also a crook and a gangster. Roy was outraged: 'I don't care! Don't tell me that! I don't love him for the person but for the songs he sang, and the romance of him.' He sings along to a double CD of Bowley's songs in the car on his way up this or that motorway to this or that engagement.

Roy Lancaster enjoys his work greatly, but he is nevertheless trying to cut down on some of his commitments which – as with a bad nicotine habit – is easier said than done: 'I am slowly sorting some of these things out because it's now got to a stage . . .' He trails off, and remembers how one day he was expected at three separate committee meetings in three different parts of the country, and, exhausted at the prospect, ended up going to none: 'It's the journeys, the tiring long road journeys.' He usually drives, certainly if he is lecturing, because he doesn't trust other people's projectors and always brings his own. He also gets asked to do lots of what he calls 'freebie-type things', and his wise wife has suggested he limit himself to accepting no more than half a dozen such requests each year, on a first-come-first-served basis.

May, unsurprisingly, is the toughest month: apart from his teaching commitment at the English Gardening School, he is involved in an official capacity with the Courson Flower Show in France, the Chelsea Flower Show in London and the Gardening Scotland Show in Edinburgh. His itinerary as described sounds like one of those frenetic 'if-it's-Tuesday-it's-Brussels' charabanc tours'. But after three weeks of non-stop hurtling, he and his wife have managed to snatch a couple of days in a B&B in Edinburgh, although even that had to be hard fought for: 'I said No! No! No! [to all the well-meaning people who wanted to put them up] and we wandered around the Royal Mile, and we went to Holyrood Palace, and we had ice-creams. We were on our own; we could do what we liked; and it cost virtually nothing. It was great!' They ended up lying on the grass on

Carlton Hill overlooking Princes Street, and Roy told his wife (as if she didn't know): 'I cannot remember when I last lay down on my back in the grass looking up at the sky. And the sun's shining. I can hear the voices of the other people around and the only thing that's missing is the song of the skylark.' By way of explanation, he tells me how he used to love lying on the grass on the moors above Bolton 'listening to its song and trying to pick out that darn bird. It brought back all those memories.' If adventure, dreams and stories fed the boy, my guess is memories and people fuel the man.

Given such a relentless schedule, it would not be difficult to imagine the Lancaster garden might suffer the same fate as the cobbler's children's feet. Not so: 'Some people say I'm a collector, not a gardener, but just to collect and plant and leave everything where it is would be impossible – I'd have a jungle then, and that would defeat the whole object of my collecting.' So when the weeding got on top of him recently he contacted the local N.C.C.P.G. and proposed tea, a talk, and a trugful of plants for any members who felt like spending a day helping him out: 'Five ladies plus tools turned up. A great day!' And a great idea.

Roy Lancaster's lifelong love-affair with English native plants and his world-wide network of plant-collecting colleagues have resulted in an eclectic mix of the exotic and the commonplace in his own garden, so that I wasn't entirely sure if the buttercup creeping around in the background was an unwanted intruder (it was) or an invited guest such as the white-flowered variety of Herb Robert, and the white campion. His greenhouse is agreeably ramshackle, with a plethora of tender, seed-collected treasures spilling out of the open door. But the plant that has yet to flower will always be his favourite, an extreme case in point being the hydrangea (*H. schizophragma integrifolium*) I'd spied earlier, grown from seed collected in China. He's been waiting twenty-three years to witness its first flowering: 'You need anticipation; it's part of the magic: not this year, maybe next. They say old gardeners never die because they can't go just yet.' He takes cutting of large shrubs that have fulfilled their promise, which his friend the local butcher grows on for him, and he has just swapped a large specimen of the Panda bamboo, *Fargesia denudata*, for a lorryload of rhinoceros dung from the Cotswold Wild Life Park. There is something Utopian about these exchanges of goods for services rendered, and vice versa.

I hesitated to ask Roy his opinion of the BBC's blanket coverage of the Chelsea Flower Show, but he brings up the subject briefly himself: if only the producers could see their imaginative way to allocating him sixty consecutive minutes in the marquees to talk about a plant, or plant species, in depth. Instead, this year he was offered one mean little minute about what gardening means to him. He obliged, but regrets it: even more galling when he considers the amount of rot that gets talked about gardens, garden design in general, and Chelsea gardens in particular: 'People talk a lot of . . . a lot of . . . ' (I felt he was having a struggle to express himself in printable language) '. . . a lot of *hot froth* about the Chelsea gardens. To me a garden is an artificial thing, whatever you do. It doesn't matter how skilful you are. You may make a wild-looking garden but it's not as wild as the real wild. In a way, this justifies my interest and my passion for going out into the wild to see where plants choose to grow, rather than where we want them to grow.'

He might – does – enjoy a visit to, say, a Jekyll-inspired garden, even a minimalist modern creation, but the only gardens he could live with exist in his head: his 'dream' gardens. One appeases his collector's urge to possess, featuring as it does a series of valleys, or gullies – one for each continent – leading like the spokes of a wheel off a plateau in the mountainous terrain he prefers. His house would be at the hub, and every day he could decide which continent to visit according to what might be in flower. The other is perfectly realisable, and he describes it carefully: 'A busy garden, in a way – lots of interesting things to look at near the house, and a path – it would be a meandering path, not a straight path – to lead me out into an empty space with a hedge around, a plain hornbeam or beech hedge [for the birds], with nothing to fix the eye on, and my mind would empty of all the busy plant names. I could linger there and maybe that would be enough, but beyond that would be a wild garden, and I mean a *wild* garden: a piece of land, woodland preferably, that had never been gardened. It would be full of bluebells and red campion. Hopefully it would have brambles as a nesting site for nightingales.'

He admits he would be horribly torn if the only land available to him were native woodland: 'Would I fill it with foreign plants? Are you then ruining the status quo? You had a good thing going there until you started poking in these other things – a lot of people do this.' The observation makes me think of historian Thomas Pakenham's irritation with the world-wide fellowship of zealots he calls The Taliban, now busy-bodily ordering the chopping down of anything not native to its situation, and whether Roy has a point of view on the matter. He believes it depends on the circum-stances: 'In a garden, I think anything goes; you can have the whole world in a garden, because it's an artificial place. You create your own illusion, if you like; if you want to be surrounded – as I am – by the world's flora, or at least that part that will grow in our climate, fine. Wildlife is not going to fly into your garden and say "Ooh! Ooh! Oh! Oh! Here's a foreign acacia!" and fly back where it came from. It's not going to not nest in a Lawson cypress because it comes from Southern Oregon. I think people go over the top. But beyond the garden, beyond urban areas where I think anything goes within reason, I do like to see native trees in rural landscapes. It needs common sense, and it needs sensitivity: how far do you have to go back before you can say "Oh, well, that's a foreigner"? You see sycamore now in many rough wind-swept upland areas, like Scotland, and the Pennines, and it looks perfectly at home, but it's not; its reintroduction was in recent times – that is, several hundred years ago – but it was here originally. My old boss Harold Hillier pointed out that if you go back before the Ice Ages, before they destroyed all our rich native flora, tree flora especially, you'd have had sycamore, no problem. You'd have had metasequoias . . .' and he lists a number of exotic contenders. 'Man brings them back, but that's not an excuse to fill our native woods with these foreign plants.' He mentions a late friend who considered any purple-foliage trees inappropriate in the landscape, and Roy himself cannot stand that 'pinky, creamy, blotchy, sicky thing' (the variegated version of the balsam poplar, *Populus* 'Aurora') now ubiquitous in the west of Ireland.

Reflecting on the ravages of the Ice Ages reminded him that people are always asking him if he finds British flora boring in comparison with 'the wonders of the wide world' he has seen. He does not, and quotes T.S. Eliot's Little Gidding:

> We shall not cease from exploration
> And the end of all our exploring
> Will be to arrive where we started
> And know the place for the first time.

The lines sum up his own feelings: 'I thought Yes! Yes! YES! That's exactly what I feel: I come back to the British flora, to the moor with a handful of native plants, and that has a calming effect. It takes me back to my roots, to my younger days when I would dance over a new plant, which may be a common one to me now but then it was new. It's important for people when they look at a common plant to try to remember the day that plant was new to them: to try to recapture that moment when you wanted to dance.' And I was treated to a full-throttle rendition of 'Ruddier than a Berry', which his friend the vicar used to break into whenever they came across an exciting plant on their travels. The memory prompts him to ponder: 'Are you born with enthusiasm? Or do you catch it, like some kind of wonderful disease that is passed on from one to another?' He answers himself: 'Well, Mr Shaw had a big part to play in it.' And here we were ourselves, six hours and many exclamation marks on, back where we started.

*Travels in China, a Plantsman's Paradise* is available in in a new edition (Antique Collectors' Club, 2008).

# *Tony Schilling*

## CURATOR

Whatever you can do or believe you can, begin it. For
boldness has genius and power and magic in it.

Johann Wolfgang von Goethe (1749–1823)

Until ten years ago, Tony Schilling had always lived – except for one brief
interlude – in the south-east of England. Furthermore, he chose to
spend the whole of his working life until he retired in 1991 under the umbrella
of one organisation, the Royal Botanic Gardens, Kew, and for twenty-four of
those thirty-two years to remain in charge of one garden: in 1967 he was
appointed Deputy Curator of Wakehurst Place, the establishment's satellite
garden in Sussex. His name is revered in the highest horticultural circles as
that of the man responsible for transforming what had previously been a
private estate into the modern botanic garden it is today. So it came as something of a shock to his many friends when, in 1997 at the age of sixty-two, he
decided to leave them and all that was familiar behind to embark on a new life
with his third wife Vicki in the remote north-west of Scotland.

I heard of the migration north from a somewhat baffled friend of the
couple and the story caught my imagination, as had the realisation that Tony
Schilling would have already been at work on Wakehurst Place for twenty
years when the Great Storm of 1987 smashed its way through 'his' garden's
five hundred acres, and in the process brought down between fifteen and
twenty thousand mature trees in a few hours. No individual garden suffered
greater loss, and I wondered how he had coped at the time with the emotional
trauma of having his life's work trashed in such contemptuous fashion by
Nature in a bate. Yet, unbelievably, in one contemporary newspaper interview I came across he sounds sanguine: 'There are plusses,' he is quoted as

saying. 'We are going to end with views which even in our wildest management dreams we would not have the guts to do. We'd have been accused of being arboretum morons. It'll take two years to clear up all the damage, but we've got to think positively. It's no good damn well crying.' And if his stricken expression in the accompanying photograph betrays an inner desolation, it also highlights the man's strength of purpose.

When I eventually get to meet Tony Schilling in his mountain fastness, and hear the story at first hand, I learn just how much he had needed to ask of himself: those two years he'd predicted it would take to clear up the mess had turned into four and, point or no point, he admits his tears had flowed in the end: 'One of our garden constables came round the office door after we'd been sorting things out for several months and said Oh, Mr Schilling, we feel so helpless just watching your chaps slaving away. Is there nothing I can do to help? And I said No! It's fine. It's fine. Then he left, and I blew it.' He laughs. 'Hopeless! Everything just came out. I wasn't expecting it and of course at that moment someone rather important came to see me . . . Stupid!' Or simply human: at that same inauspicious period of his life he was also having to cope with the emotional wreckage caused by the collapse of his second marriage.

The stress took its toll: two years on he suffered a massive heart attack, yet still managed to complete the clearing-up process, with the heroic support of his staff and, among many others, volunteers from the United States who 'flew over armed with chainsaws'. But by 1991, he'd had enough so, having done his sums and decided he could afford it, and having taken care to marry Vicki before he announced his decision, to ensure she would receive his pension in the event of his death, he took early retirement. 'I thought there's only one person going to look after me and that's myself, so I upped and offed.' It was time for the rest of his life to begin.

I discovered what a rich hinterland of a life lay behind Tony Schilling's horticultural interests when I opened the bulging envelope he sent in response to my request for his CV, and found a tape of his riveting interview with Scottish Radio for its version of *Desert Island Discs*, along with a list of his hobbies, of which listening to serious music, selective bird-watching (not LBJs – 'little brown jobs'), mountaineering, photography, gardening and botanising, are only some. 'People think of me as a gardener', he explains when we meet, 'but I see myself as having a wider spread of interests than that so I thought why not just tell 'em? That's what made me say Yes when you wanted to come up here.'

Nevertheless, he had taken the trouble to itemise every significant date of his professional career, including a detailed record with page numbers of all the scientific papers and articles he has had published in prestigious horticultural journals; a list, with dates, of all the botanical tours, plant hunting expeditions and trekking parties he ever joined, or – more usually – led, along with a list of all the Royal Horticultural Society's Floral Committees he sat on, awards he won (including the Royal Horticultural Society's Victoria Medal of Honour in 1989), and societies he joined – all handwritten: as a technophobe he owns neither computer, mobile, fax nor answerphone. He keeps a record of every plant in the garden in half a dozen $6 \times 6 \times 6$-inch red plastic card index boxes, causing a friend to observe caustically that Tony Schilling's garden is not gardened it's curated. However, another friend shows it in another light: 'This garden,' he writes in the visitor's book, 'is not just a collection of interesting and rare plants mixed with native species, it's also a reservoir of happy memories and old friends.' Even the stray cat they'd named Pushkin when she decided to move in with them got her memorial: Tony planted two hundred puschkinias to mark her grave.

Unfortunately, on the first day of my pilgrimage it poured all day, and the garden was shrouded in cloud. However, this did mean more time to hear a born raconteur tell his story, beginning with the migration: 'We were fed up with the south for various reasons, mostly too many people, and we thought somewhere around Ullapool would be nice, so we came up a year in advance to make dead certain we wanted to come, did our homework, opened a bank account and a building society account, then sold the cottage, put the money into the building society, a change of underclothes and a few essential files into the car, and roared off into the darkness at half past three in the morning with nowhere to live. Marvellous! Everyone said "How brave!" and I said "No, how sensible" because we're first-time buyers, no ties. We took three days to get up here because we weren't in a hurry, and we enjoyed ourselves en route.' He who dares: they found what they were looking for almost on landing, and not only was it for sale, it was empty: 'Within seventy-two hours we'd shaken hands on it and we moved in within the month. If that wasn't meant I don't know what was.' Justifiably, Tony is delighted with the meant-ness of it all. I, on the other hand, am feeling faint from a mix of admiration for the way this careful planning had left them, paradoxically, free as birds to fly off, and leave the rest to chance, and, I fear, some nagging irritation I felt only a restorative slug of *schadenfreude* would cure. Could it really have been that simple? It seems it could.

My suffering might have been made even worse if I had been able to catch a glimpse of the view that drew the pair to their nesting site in the first place: on a fine day no fewer than four Munros (Scottish mountains above 3,000 feet and objects of worship to the mountaineer) are visible to the south and east, while to the west Ullapool appears as a number of tiny white dots on the foreshore at the narrow point where Loch Broom flows into the Atlantic. Unsurprisingly, a fine view had been top of the list of must haves, of which only one item had proved to be a romantic dream too far: 'I wanted dormer windows, roses round the door, that sort of thing and this is just a boring bungalow, but it's very nice inside so we're happy.' Discovering that crofting cottages may look cute but are badly built and suffer from rising damp was at least some consolation.

Tony Schilling first discovered his affinity with mountains at the age of twelve, when his father took him up Helvellyn one day: 'We watched the sunrise on Midsummer's Day and that was it. Finished! I've been leaping around the Scottish and Welsh hills ever since.' He even chose to celebrate his twenty-first birthday climbing in the Black Cuillins of Skye. A few years later, he managed to locate *Arabis alpina*, a 'squinny' little plant common to the Alps and Arctic Norway, but only found in the British Isles in one spot somewhere up above two thousand feet in those same difficult mountains. He'd set himself quite a task, as usual: 'Up three back two all the way, and it was raining. We found it growing right at the base of the cliff near the top of the ridge. A *miserable* little plant! Why did it choose to grow there, the stupid thing? Amazing. But I love plant geography. I like the ecology of plants. I like the phyto-geography, which is what grows where and why. I've written incredibly long, boring articles on such things as, for example, how *Betula utilis* changes very, very gradually from Afghanistan to south-west China, so that at each end its characteristics are very different, yet you can't find the join.'

He always knew he wanted to be a naturalist when he grew up – 'I was a real nature boy, frogs in the pocket, home for lunch at five o'clock and a good old telling off, that sort of nonsense,' but his school in north London didn't teach botany so he wasn't at all clear what he meant by this. Neither were his parents. However, he managed to find his way into the Parks Department of his local borough, which for the non-academic type who wanted a career in horticulture in those days was the first step on the long road that led to Kew.

Reading through Tony's CV, I attributed the fact that once he'd got himself to Kew he'd never left out of a need for the security a large establishment would give him to counter-balance an equal but opposite craving for discovery and, judging from this footnote to that list of hobbies, for tough physical challenges: 'In 1961 accomplished the fourteen peaks (over 3,000 feet) of North Wales in ten hours fifty-four minutes [*sic*], a distance of approximately thirty-five miles with over 20,000 feet of ascent and descent.' But why would anyone who loves mountains and tracking down their flora want to spend his weekend off doing anything so apparently pointless? 'Good question. I think everybody in life needs . . . well, at least if you're physically inclined, you need to push yourself to where you think your limit is just once in your life, and I had a dream – I sound like Martin Luther King – I had a dream of doing this for years, and I knew North Wales very well. I'd climbed all the hills before, otherwise I don't think I would have wanted to do it, because it's rather like rape and pillage – you don't stop to look. Which is quite criminal in beautiful scenery, but having known them well it became a challenge. That was one of my proudest physical achievements actually.'

As for my assumption, he reckons the security aspect was incidental. 'I didn't go to Kew and become a government servant deliberately, I just *happened* to go to Kew which just *happened* to be a government department, and it gave me huge opportunities I wouldn't otherwise have had.' It certainly did. In 1961, Kew allowed him six weeks unpaid leave to accompany a team from Aberystwyth University as its botanical adviser on a scientific survey of Arctic Norway; in 1965 it granted him a two-year secondment to Nepal to advise its government on the setting up of a botanic garden in Kathmandu; and during his years at Wakehurst Place he usually chose to spend his annual leave either taking trekking parties up as far as Everest base camp (five times), or else leading, or being a member of, botanical tours to Bhutan, Nepal, China, and the Eastern Mediterranean, from which he brought back plant material for the benefit of Kew. Now, he gives thanks for his Damascene moment at dawn on Helvellyn. 'I was thinking: if I hadn't got interested in mountain walking I wouldn't have got interested in arctic alpine plants, so I wouldn't have gone to Norway, and so on. The whole thing just clicked. And if I hadn't done that I wonder which direction my life would have gone instead? Who knows?'

An unanswerable question that leads to some philosophical reflection on the subject of luck: 'It's like a game of cards: if you're not handed the right set you can't do much with them but if you *are* handed the right set you can still make a mess of it. I've had one or two close shaves in spite of it all because Mother Nature's the boss. You can make every allowance you like but if you're in the wrong place at the wrong time . . .'

'Like the time you led a group of friends in search of plants and a spot of adventure on a trek in the Annapurna region of Nepal?'

'. . . and had a close brush with death? Yes! Sounds very dramatic, but it was. Was it Winston Churchill who said something to the effect that there's nothing more exhilarating than being fired upon by the enemy, as long as they miss? To outrun an avalanche by the skin of your teeth! Everything was so sharp afterwards. It sounds very sentimental and romantic but I was so glad still to be on this planet. Everything looked doubly beautiful – with a capital B.' He remembers a quotation from *A Slender Thread* by Stephen Venables: 'It is good sometimes to trespass high in the sky and live life with uncommon intensity experiencing something that gets close to the sublime.' (Stephen Venables was the first man from Great Britain to climb Everest without oxygen and, in Tony's pantheon of mountaineering heroes, a man to rank alongside the Hunt-Hillary team that first conquered the mountain.)

As a matter of fact, Tony Schilling appears to live in a permanent state of uncommon intensity: one night he'd lain in bed pondering for hours a hypothetical question he'd set himself: which of his three great passions – mountains, horticulture (including environmental matters), and music – would he give up if he had to? He began by considering a life in East Anglia, but that was too easy: he could turn the clouds in the vast East Anglian skies into mountains in his imagination, and so not feel deprived. He forced himself to begin again, this time from his actual situation because, as he points out: 'Here, I've got the mountains, I've got the environment, I can garden and I've got my music: which one would it be, and why? Probably, and this will amaze you, it would be gardening because I can get flowers and plants on mountains. It would be a different sort of gardening, but I'd still have my music. When I was in Arctic Norway on that first expedition it was long before Walkmans, so I used to *think* Sibelius. And when I went through both divorces and was absolutely fed up to the back teeth it was music I hung on to. Music is a constant emotional support. I can't read a note – I'm musically illiterate – but I know what I like and I'm passionate about *what* I like.' What he likes (and can analyse his reasons for liking) includes Ravi Shankar; jazz, modern and trad; and some pop music (Abba, Procul Harum, Dire Straits, Kate Bush). 'I amuse people because I've got such catholic tastes. For example, I like modern composers such as James MacMillan, and I love Shostakovich. He can be sensitive and highly amusing. There's a piece he wrote called *Hypothetically Murdered*. An absolute riot! And he can give you this tremendous power and crescendo, and then he can stop it absolutely dead, like a cliff, and go into utter silence. Then in comes a very quiet single violin. Agghhhh! Hair on back of neck stuff. Terrific.'

However, the fact remains he has not actually had to sacrifice the garden for his music, so I wonder just how much time that leaves him for botanising in the mountains. Not much is the answer: 'I have good intentions but the garden gets in the way. It's a case of *mañana*. But I can still dream, and relive the experiences.' However, if he perceives the challenge to be great enough he can be motivated: 'There's a plant grows just north of here on a mountain called Kumoor, and its one of the very few places in Britain it grows. It's an artemesia, one of the wormwoods, *Artemisia norwegica* subs. *scottica*. I've actually been up and found it. It's a miserable little thing, but it's fun because it's exciting.'

But if Tony doesn't venture into the mountains as he much as he used to, he likes to stay close to them: he hasn't been south of Inverary in eight years. Even so, since he could well have added 'talking on the telephone' to his list of hobbies, he reckons he still knows more than his friends about what's going on in his old territory. And if he won't go to them, they must come to him, and many have, including his long-time sparring partner, the late Christopher Lloyd whose sharp-to-the-point-of-cruel sense of humour Tony enjoyed – for the most part. His friend's name happened to come up in conversation just as Vicki announced lunch, so we had the best possible accompaniment to a good meal: great gossip. Here perhaps I should add that Vicki did not wish to be interviewed although, as the woman who helped Alan Mitchell found The Tree Register in 1988, and responsible after he retired for turning it into a charity (of which HRH The Prince of Wales is its Patron and Tony its Honorary President), she is as much a force to be recognised in the horticultural world as she is in her husband's life.

But it wasn't all gossip: I dare to mention my frisson of envy for the courage they found to cut the cord and go off as they had like that. 'If you have a dream, live it!' Tony advises sternly, pointing out that in any case we all bring our happiness – or our misery – with us, so that, for example, if he and Vicki had to live in Watford, they'd be just as happy. He hesitates for a nanosecond (appalled, I imagine, at the idea of Watford) but rallies: 'We'd have to be, otherwise we'd be miserable, and I don't want to be miserable!' But Vicki reckons that what her husband is talking about is not in fact happiness, but joy: 'Joy is what sustains us on a rainy day. Happiness is ice cream with waffles.' Tony is delighted with her definition: 'Oh yes! She knows my weaknesses. We had ice cream and waffles *twice* last week. Wonderful!'

Actual rain is still tipping down outside, and my eye spies enough garlic and onions drying out on a windowsill to supply Sainsburys (except that

Tony's are trussed as artfully as if for display at the Royal Horticultural society's Autumn Fruit and Vegetable Show), which makes me think Action Man has plenty to keep him happy when he's stuck indoors. As for the joy that sustains him through metaphorical deluges, I conclude that this stems from an unswerving belief that whatever life throws at him his cup remains half full: even the need for emergency triple heart bypass surgery in 2002 he perceives as a reason for gratitude – gratitude for the quality of service the National Health Service in Scotland provided, which saved his life.

The weather improved the following day, and the view from the bungalow revealed itself to be as majestic, and humbling, as I'd imagined. You could sit out there on the Schilling terrace all day simply being, or you could if you weren't Tony Schilling: 'People think gardens just happen! The trouble is they don't stay as you want them. You've got to decide when to step in and how much, that's the art we were talking about earlier. You paint a picture and you put your brush down and you frame it and stick it on the wall. You write a book and it gets published. But a garden is in a state of continuous flux.' I wonder if he sees himself as something of a perfectionist? 'In certain directions, yes. I'm a perfectionist such as you wouldn't believe in this garden at the moment because the weather pattern has been so horrendous. I have high standards. People call it an admirable trait, but to me it's quite natural. What's the point of third-rate? Doesn't come into the book. I'm a hard taskmaster. And I drive *myself* hard, and that's why I never felt bad about driving staff hard.'

By the time we'd completed the outdoor tour, I had so many pages of transcript of our conversation in, and about, the garden and its aesthetic, and such long lists of its flora and who'd given him this or that, or where he had seed-collected the other, I would need another four thousand words (and a return visit to absorb the atmosphere in solitude) to do it justice. But then again, the best person to write that story would be Tony Schilling himself. Perhaps he will, one day. Or perhaps he won't: friends have urged him to write about his work at Wakehurst Place, but Tony only willingly undertakes a project if his heart is engaged, which in this instance is no longer the case. Unusually, he sounds, almost bitter: 'I gave more than was healthily reasonable or sensible to Wakehurst's management, so I doubt I will ever be tempted to put it all to pen. I'm flattered, but unswayed.'

Although so close to overload, there was still one question I needed to ask about those two years back in the 1960s that Tony had spent with his first wife living among the Nepalese people. He had already beguiled me with a number of well-polished and amusing stories about dangerous leopards and Nepalese princes and such, but I was curious to know how the overall experience had affected him at a deeper level. 'Well it changed my life. It was my first experience of a Third World country and I came back at the end of it thinking totally differently. I thought, if anybody ever comes up to me after this and talks about poverty I'll tell them they don't know what they are damned well talking about, because there isn't any compared with what I've experienced. Somehow, although they've got virtually nothing, they have dignity and whatever they've got, however little, they will share it with you. Very humbling. I looked at a pop-up toaster in a shop window in Dorking when I came home, and I thought that's not necessary! What do you need those for?

Remembering the Nepalese people's patient acceptance of their lot serves to stoke his rage whenever he hears anyone complaining about the NHS: 'I mean, I've had very good experience of it anyway, but I've seen what people go through out there. We had a little boy in the Langtang valley dying of gangrene, and he refused to come down to the clinic with us. We said: "We will pay for you, we will carry you, we will do everything." But he said he was frightened of malaria in the low valleys. He said a Buddhist monk had come through the village and told him it was written he would die this year. Totally philosophical. We had to leave him, and I walked up the path crying my eyes out.' I can see that the memory of that moment is threatening to unleash once again the tears of the man who used to be known as the Iron Man of Wakehurst, or, behind his back (as Vicki discovered), by the team of bolshie tree surgeons he was having to get tough with over some point of discipline, as the Ayotollah. 'I wasn't very popular at times,' he concedes, laughing, 'but that doesn't come into it, you have to do what is right.' I wonder if perhaps being able to experience tears and laughter in about equal measure is what joy is all about.

# Christian Lamb

## PLANTSWOMAN, AUTHOR
## AND TRAVELLER

'God help me, I've often tried to think what it is that makes me know I must have that particular plant. But I've never thought of myself as a collector because I never did want to have every single variety of daffodil or every single variety of camellia.' I am not sure I recognise the distinction Christian Lamb makes here between her own irresistible craving to acquire this or that particular plant across a wide range of species, and what she perceives as the true collector's need to possess the whole set of one single family – sports, cultivars, the lot: either could stand up in a twelve-step meeting and announce, hand on heart, 'My name is so and so, and I am an addict.' Which is not to imply that either type – if there is a distinction – would ever wish to conquer the habit. Certainly, Christian Lamb exults in her own in her entertaining and exhaustively researched book, *From the Ends of the Earth*, in which, among a wide-ranging mix of associated matters, she explores through their personal letters the adventures of the plant hunters responsible for discovering in the wild all the species she has amassed in her third of an acre of Cornish garden.

But my reason for wanting to meet Christian Lamb had not been triggered by a wish to try to help her unravel the perceived mystery of what informs her choices, because I believe she largely answers this question herself in her book. No, my curiosity was primarily aroused by the fact that she was eighty-four years old when this, her first book, was published in 2004. In these hard-nosed days of the youth-and-celebrity-obsessed book industry, how *had* she pulled it off? Also, I wanted to meet the woman who, with no previous experience of public speaking apart from addressing her local yacht club and Women's Institute on the subject of camellias, had coolly approached the Garden Club of America to suggest that its West Coast members might like to hear her lecture on her hero, Sir Joseph Banks. Perhaps her being an elected Fellow of the prestigious Linnaean Society had influenced its decision to accept her offer, or possibly a glowing testimonial from someone at Kew had had something to do with it. Either way, once up there on those platforms she was on her own.

Christian Lamb was happy to satisfy my curiosity, the only problem being when – because, as she told me over the telephone, 'I am always frantically busy – can't afford to hang about at my age – so I always try to fit fifteen things in where only eight will fit. My garden's exactly the same. In any case, I can't bear having nothing to do.' She is currently frantically rushing to finish her second book recounting her experiences in the Wrens during the Second World War. But a window conveniently opened up in early April, directly after the Cornwall Garden Society's spring flower show weekend, when the camellias and magnolias should be in full spate. Perfect.

My destination turned out to be a small village on the coast due south of Bodmin, and somewhere over 170 miles from London, a journey Christian told me would take me four hours. Four hours? She was adamant: four hours is all it takes her to drive from her Cornish door to that of her Chelsea bolthole. I decided to allow seven, and in the event needed most of any slack to negotiate the last eight miles of tortuous single-track, high-banked road from Bodmin, with the final assault on her property taking up the rest: her only access is a ninety-degree turn off the lane to the village on to a steep, frighteningly narrow unmade road wedged between an unforgiving Cornish wall and a twelve-foot-high stone-faced escarpment behind which house and garden hunker down out of sight. I scraped my way to the summit, fully expecting that part of my reward would at least be a spectacular view of the English Channel, but instead found myself face to face with another twelve-foot barrier, this time a hedge of camellias in full flower.

Which is how Christian likes it: having begun the process of transforming an ordinary family garden into what she describes as her 'living plant museum' after her husband died seventeen years ago, she can now incarcerate herself within her green stockade and not be bothered by the tourists (the Eden Project is only a mile or two away): 'I'm completely cut off from the outside. I can't see out, and nobody can see in.' But truth to tell, when Christian and her newly-retired Naval Officer husband decided to settle with their young family in the village in the late 1950s, she had not, even then, she tells me over lunch, felt inclined to get too deeply enmeshed in village life: 'I said to John, in the Navy you had to know people because of promotion, but now we are down here, let's not get frightfully involved with people we simply hate and we'll have to go and have lunch and high tea and God knows what.' Neither did she much enjoy the chosen family pastime of messing about in boats: 'We decided the children must do something in the holidays and sailing was cheap, so we bought a ghastly little boat. I love the sea but as for sailing, I'd never even thought about it. In any case, the worst thing to have in a boat is a Naval Officer – they've no idea how to sail a boat; they only know how to tell somebody else how to do things. Hopeless! We had frightful rows and the weather was always ghastly, so eventually I struck and said, "You can take the children out, I'm going to sit on a rock and read my book."'

This *modus vivendi* suited Christian very well until the children left home and she needed something to do to fill the hours, so decided to help a friend restore a large, once notable but, post-Second World War, badly neglected garden, and in the process turned herself almost by accident into a recognised authority on camellias – and eventually into an insatiable addict: 'My friend had a wonderful collection and we kept sending things up to Kew. Some of them had been directly introduced to her garden and still had their original labels, so you can imagine that was very exciting. Now, I can identify most camellia species by the leaf – not all of them, but quite a few. No point in writing any more books about them because millions of people have written millions of books about camellias and they all say exactly the same thing. As far as the new hybrids that appear all the time are concerned, well, some of them are brilliant but most of them are ghastly. I wouldn't dream of growing any of the bad ones but every now and then I find a new one I really want to grow and I jam it in somewhere – or get rid of one I've gone off. That happens.'

An addict with a grandiose taste in exotic flora and only a very small plot to hand must indeed have problems keeping her habit fed, but before exploring that question and the garden itself, I was curious as to how she had found the confidence to deliver an untried lecture to knowledgeable groups of total strangers. In this instance, her late husband had been the one to coach her in the art of public speaking: 'John was a very good after-dinner speaker – they are taught to public speak in the Navy – so I said to him I know you hate plants, but you'll have to listen to this . . .' and began her delivery. He was aghast: 'You can't read it!' he protested. It was Christian's turn to protest – 'what do you mean, I can't read it?' – but not fazed: 'So, back to the drawing board. That's when I got my tape recorder: I practised into the tape recorder and played it back. Sounded dreadful. Had to do it again about five hundred times until I got it more or less right. But of course I didn't know how to have notes and work the projector. What a muddle!'

A possibly envious friend assured her that any fool can deliver a lecture: all she needed was a good beginning and a good end because nobody ever listens to the rest, and with this doubtful thought for comfort Christian duly set out to conquer California. 'I am rather good,' she admits modestly, 'at organising things I want to do and I thought to lecture in America sounds so frightfully grand, but I was never nervous. The only thing, I thought to myself: I must never ever, ever even think – let alone say – 'I'm mad! What am I doing up here?' or I would have collapsed at once, so I just pretended I was talking normally, and never looked at anybody in the audience. I thought they must know how bad I am, but I'll be on to the next place by then.'

Emboldened by her success, she thought she'd try her luck on the English lecture circuit: 'I rang up NADFAS [The National Association of Decorative and Fine Arts Societies] and said, "Would you be interested in a lecture on camellias?" and they said, "Well, yes, perhaps we might" . . .' Christian interrupts herself: 'Didn't I put that in the book . . . ?' She did, so we segue to the subject of travelling (of which she has done a great deal in her pursuit of her plant hunter heroes), and how to make the most of travelling alone in a group: 'You can probably spot the bore at the airport and keep out of the way. I don't speak to anyone for quite a long time – if you make friends they cling to you – and I make sure I'm always last in to dinner so I have to sit in the only space left. I also take piles of books in case I hate everybody on the journey. Usually I hate them all at first, but very often I make quite good friends in the end.' Only once did she land among a bunch of entirely uncongenial folk, a situation she describes chillingly as being rather like going to the same bad dinner party every night for a fortnight.

But something was puzzling me: time and again, Christian would attribute her late success in life to luck: 'I am the abject amateur in every direction', she announces at one moment, and at another: 'You know, I've never done anything sensible, never written a book until last year when I wrote my first'. As for her connoisseurship, she admits people do consult her as an expert 'but,' she insists, 'if you look up "expert" in the diction-ary it says something like "to have studied", so I don't really feel I can be an expert without any kind of degree, and I do feel very uneducated.' I did wonder if she were being just the tiniest bit disingenuous here, and she was: 'I don't mind being seen as an expert in something! Exactly! It's quite amusing really. But nobody in my family or anywhere else knows; it's only down here in Cornwall where I'm considered to be an expert.' For some, that would be enough.

However, it is a fact that Christian's beloved older sister had gone up to Oxford, and Christian assumed she would be following in her footsteps one day – until, that is, the Second World War broke out and she joined the Wrens instead, married her Naval Officer, and had had her first child before it was all over. It wasn't until after her husband died that she decided to make up for this perceived lacuna in her education by signing up for an Open University course on the Age of the Enlightenment, and in so doing acquired more useful material for her Banks lecture, and relearned the art of how to write a decent essay.

Which was handy when it came to writing her book, but not much use when it came to getting it published: none of the publishers she chose from *The Writers' and Artists' Handbook* even acknowledged receipt of her manuscript. Undeterred, she changed tack: 'I thought perhaps I'll try an agent. Same result, so after about two months I rang up one, told her my sad story, and she said I don't think you want an agent, what you want is a literary consultant. I said, "What is that? Tell me!'" Good question and the answer in a nutshell is someone you pay to advise you on how to whip your manuscript into shape, and get it published. So Christian set about finding herself a literary consultant, who in turn handed her over to a suitable editor who was himself both a gardener and a traveller. She was up and running: 'Well, you see, I had needed advice so badly and I couldn't find it. He wrote me the most frightfully good constructive criticism and became very much like a tutor at the university. He said, "You're going to have to work very hard on this but I see a lot of good in it." He made various flattering remarks and then just told me what to do, how to alter it. I thought: "Well! Goodness me! I've learnt such a lot!'"

Eventually her mentor decided it was time to deliver her manuscript to a publisher he had in mind – a self-publisher, that is. As a matter of fact I learned only recently that A.E. Housman self-published *A Shropshire Lad*, but Christian was mortified: 'I had thought that to publish it yourself was rather shaming, but he said there was nothing shameful in publishing it myself because some subjects are too specialised to get published.' Mollified, she winged off her precious manuscript, only to have her high hopes dashed when she visited the publisher to talk things through: 'I said have you read it? "Read it?" she said. "Good heavens no! I don't read the books I publish. I'd never get anything done if I did." And I thought how awful this is!'

Now Christian needed to bring all her considerable networking skills into play to help her find a Chinese printing company willing to print her book at considerably less cost than her enemy had quoted, and with the photographs spread throughout the body of the text just as she wanted. Her book – her baby – was eventually delivered five years after its conception. As usual, Christian puts her triumph – it received marvellous reviews – down to luck, but concedes when pressed that the whole project had taken 'a lot of slog and a lot of money'. Actually, she would have easily recouped her outlay if she had, as counselled, limited herself to the one print run of

2,000 copies. Unfortunately — and uncharacteristically — she ignored this advice and commissioned a further 5,000 to be run off. When these didn't all sell her daughter advised her to make a ritual bonfire of the remainder, and get on with her new book, but Christian decided instead to set up her own website to shift them because the thought of giving up on anything — 'Not until I'm beaten to the ground.' — is anathema.

It is not difficult to appreciate the energy and effort and self-belief it must have taken Christian to get herself accepted on the American lecture circuit, and to get a first book published that doesn't slot easily into any specific category on Waterstone's shelves, but I have a struggle when it comes to understanding the amount of skill and ingenuity it must take to persuade some of the planet's trickiest flora to grow hugger mugger as she does, much of it pinned hard back against the perimeter fence to leave a little space for the free-standing exhibits. Incidentally, the plant equivalent of being banished to the basement to make space for a new acquisition is to be given away to a friend. Paradoxically, it seems the only species to have their places guaranteed in Christian Lamb's museum are the ones that refuse to flower or die on her and get replaced over and over again until she succeeds in understanding their needs. On second thoughts, perhaps not a paradox after all, but the crux.

This is Roy Lancaster territory (in fact, it was Roy Lancaster who recommended both the book and its author to me in the first place) and I find myself reduced to asking banal questions, such as how many hours does Christian have to put into actual hands-on gardening. Answer: 'None, if I can help it!' OK, what about plant propagation? 'No I don't do much of that. I make Bill do that.' She reminds me that as she has written all about her relationship with Bill the gardener, so we don't need to go there. I wrack my brains for a question her book doesn't address; perhaps there was some pattern to the planting layout I wasn't qualified to recognise — by continent, perhaps, or hemisphere? I might have known: 'No, I really don't do it with anything else in mind except how the plant looks or, if I've got something I must grow and it's got to go somewhere, where the hell can I put it?' We pass a prime example. 'This is a rather splendid tree, a little michelia [*M. fuscata*] which is a sort of magnolia and it has to grow underneath something. Very temperamental. It hasn't got any buds at the moment, but it will have in a moment. They smell of bananas and cream. Most lovely little thing. I bring it into the greenhouse and put it out again. This is another variety but this [*M. yunnanensis*, origin south China] is much less temperamental. I had it too close to the hoheria [origin New Zealand] so I had to move it and I bloody nearly killed it. But every year I took off all its buds and trimmed it back so now it's not a bad shape and I shall let it flower this year. Clever little thing!'

Inside a miniature polytunnel lurking in the shadow of the camellia hedge, Christian is nurturing specimens of the Chatham Island forget-me-not (*Myositidium hortensia*). This little gem of a plant ticks all her boxes with its fabulous blue flowers, handsome leaves, relative rareness and fussy habit – perversely, it refuses the relative comfort of a cold greenhouse, yet is not hardy. It also likes its roots embedded in a mix of seaweed (the manager of a hotel in Tresanton once paid her in seaweed for giving a digital presentation of her book to an invited audience) and pure sand since it grows wild, or used to until it became extinct, on a small group of tiny islands situated in the middle of the Pacific ocean on the 'wrong' side of New Zealand. In other words, not easy to reach from England, a fact that has not deterred Christian from trying – and failing – twice, or from thinking she might try again. The thing to bear in mind is that, even if she does ever make that final difficult leg by small plane from New Zealand, she won't actually see the plant growing there on the beach. But that's the addict for you.

We move on a foot or two: 'That's *Jasmine mesnyi*. Comes from China. Found by this splendid fellow William Mesny who came from Jersey, ran away to sea when he was twelve, joined the Chinese army, and became a general. A very good story.' It is: it's in the book. But Christian has arranged for us to have tea with her friends Liz and Anthony Fortescue at Boconnoc and there we have to leave it. I do rather quail at the idea of having to contemplate two connoisseurial Cornish gardens in one day but there's nothing for it because, she announces blithely, 'I want to show off my grand connections!' And grand they are: the Boconnoc land was bought by William Pitt the Younger's grandfather, and the estate has remained intact in the family ever since, through the female line. Nor need I have feared overload: we drive through soothing miles of some of England's finest remaining areas of ancient woodland before we reach the garden's heart, and a sighting of any camellias.

After tea and banana sandwiches, we set off by jeep to contemplate the new pinetum her friend Martin Wood is creating for the family using the same varieties planted by Fortescue ancestors in the mid-nineteenth century, but laid out now according to a stylised plan in a clearing in the surrounding coniferous woodland. While Min (as he he likes to be known) and Christian bandy plant names, Liz Fortescue and I ponder the heartening thought that it's never too late: women can spend as long as they feel they need sitting on a rock reading a book, and not end up out of the loop. And I am indebted to Min for identifying for me Christian Lamb's possibly greatest gift. 'Christian,' he decides after some thought, 'sets out to do things which don't appear to be possible out of the utter conviction that they can.'

Driving back through the still leafless woods with their lichen-covered branches dripping moss and epiphytic ferns, Christian announces that we'll be eating in, which is a relief, but also a worry: if it has been a long day for me, Christian's has scarcely been shorter. She'd been working on her Wren book all the hours she'd been waiting for me to turn up. Given her punishing schedule, I wonder how she finds the time or the energy to do any housework. She doesn't – she never wastes energy on anything that doesn't interest her, and she was able to assure her anxious house-keeper, who was going away for a few weeks, that she has no cause to worry. 'Don't worry', she told her, 'It'll all be there for you when you get back. I shan't even dust.'

*From the Ends of the Earth* and *I Only Joined for the Hat*, Christian Lamb's book about her life in the wrens during the War, are obtainable from her website, www.christianlamb.co.uk

# Thomas Pakenham

## HISTORIAN

I slipped a tape measure round the smooth, silver-green, lichen-encrusted bellies of the trees and listed the measurements in a notebook. As I taped each tree I gave it a hug, as if to say 'good luck tonight'.

*Meetings with Remarkable Trees* (1994)

As though apology were needed, Thomas Pakenham begins this account of his fears for his trees' future by saying 'Now I don't usually hug trees . . .'. The trees he is referring to are nineteen ancient beech trees in the park at Tullynally, the Pakenham ancestral estate in Co. Westmeath, Eire. A fearsome storm was forecast for the early hours of 6 January 1991 and Thomas, being a practical and methodical man, as well as an agonised romantic, took all the measures he could think of to preserve his beloved trees – if not actually, then at least in recorded detail. (And if any were to succumb, he would be sure to count their rings: in one of his tree books the writer expresses his frustration that not everyone on the planet is as interested as he in trying to establish a tree's exact age.)

When we meet at his London base in Notting Hill Gate he elaborates further on the powerful emotions old trees stir in him – and young ones too, if he has nurtured them himself: 'I think there is a certain amount of agony and ecstasy in any romantic venture; the pain of seeing great trees that have been your friends, that have been friends of your family, blown down and smashed "like fallen warriors on the battlefield", as [John] Evelyn describes them in *Silva Britannica*. That is a very acute pain. In our case – our case being a family who has lived in the same place for three hundred years – it's been a great theme, these great tree smashes. They must have been whamming down for three hundred years because the trees when the family first arrived there would have been old trees, as well as young ones. But everybody felt it in 1987, didn't they?' However, he concedes that if you haven't experienced the intense joy of possession you avoid 'a pain you wouldn't have thought of'.

Only recently, I had heard someone on the radio observe that self-made people aren't, as a rule, romantics (in what connection I can't for the life of me remember), and I wondered if Thomas Pakenham considers ancient lineage a prerequisite for the possession of a romantic soul. By way of an answer, he recounts an incident in Phineas Finn, Trollope's novel about a self-made Irishman: 'The party go to see a great estate belonging to this awfully boring, deeply Presbyterian, supermarket owner from Glasgow who, if you remember, gets the girl that Phineas wants to marry and whom all the Liberals – the Gladstones of the day – are sucking up to because he's so rich and is going – not unknown today – to give the Party all this money. The first comment as they approach the house in their coach is: "Of course you can do a lot with money, but you can't buy old trees." It's the same thing, isn't it? He gives himself away because his park is freshly planted. It's a slightly snobbish sentiment but it's also a romantic one. We are talking about a very old tradition of pleasure in trees; a sort of pleasure and sadness, aren't we?'

In fact, almost before I had taken my coat off, or found a corner to settle in among the piles of papers and books littering floor and furniture alike, he had been off at a gallop with a dazzling account of the history of the English in Ireland, and his own position in that society today: 'I've always led this Anglo-Irish life. People use the word Anglo-Irish in various ways . . . but the original way in which the word was used in the nineteenth century described what were called "County" in England. Mainly Protestant, but not exclusively. By the end of the nineteenth century they were crumbling fast and hardly exist in that sense today. Well, I regard myself as one of them.' To give me some idea of what I might expect, I had, as it happens, asked a number of people their opinion of the man I was going to meet, and someone who knows him personally described him quite simply as Renaissance Man; the rest, who don't, were almost equally divided between those who exclaimed 'Oh yes! Thomas Pakenham! The man who writes those marvellous books about trees,' and those who said 'Oh yes! Thomas

Pakenham! The man who wrote that marvellous book about Africa.' (*The Scramble for Africa* that took him ten years to write, won a raft of awards, and has since been reprinted thirteen times in paperback.) But a third group does exist: those who recognise him foremost as the author of *The Year of Liberty*, the story of the great Irish Rebellion of 1798.

Half an absorbing hour whizzes by without so much as a plant's name being mentioned, let alone a garden, and since we have not established how much time he can give me, I begin to fret and to try, rather clumsily I fear, to shift the direction of his discourse away from Irish history, and into something more or less connected with horticulture, by commenting on his expertise in three so very different areas, by which I mean – but do not actually spell out – history, dendrology and photography.

And so I quite fail to persuade him to take off his historian's hat: 'Can I answer your question about how to reconcile three different subjects which appear different – Ireland and the abortive rebellion of 1798, the Boer War, and *Scramble*? The answer is that each one was a colonial story, or semi-colonial and each one was a crisis involving Britain and a dependency or colony.' He goes on to explain that the first book involved Britain and Ireland alone – and the events of a single year; the second, Britain and two British colonies – and a time-span of almost three years, and *Scramble* dealt with an entire continent – all the great European powers, plus Belgium, over a period of more than thirty years. In other words, as he cheerfully admits, he may have made his task harder for himself each time – 'possibly a megalomaniac streak there'. Nevertheless the progression from small to large is a logical one, and there is always this link between Britain and her colonies that appeals to his Anglo-Irishness.

Clearly, the man enjoys a challenge, which might account for his decision to learn how to use a professional camera and take his own photographs for the tree books, but I decide it might be risky to explore that avenue before we've got onto gardens and/or my time is up. In desperation, I suggest perhaps Tullyally's ancient park absorbs his attention more than its garden. Bingo! 'I've come to gardens! Could we get on to that?' 'I think we should,' I say, solemnly. 'I think we should,' he repeats, apparently oblivious to my tone, and sets off most promisingly: 'I was almost completely ignorant about garden plants, meaning shrubs and herbaceous things, until 1993. I can date it exactly.' Which reminds me: almost always, for no reason that I could identify, Thomas Pakenham specifies the date each photograph was taken for the tree books. 'You are absolutely right; you spotted that. I love dates! I'm a chronologist. It's how I think of history, in terms of dates.'

But before going into the details of his Damascene moment in 1993, I get taken on a journey that begins back in 1961 when the young Thomas inherited Tullynally and its burdensome death duties. A fascinating journey it is too, only one that has apparently nothing to do with gardening and everything to do with the exigencies of looking after a large, cash-strapped estate, and learning how to farm it when you haven't been brought up to such a life because your childhood was spent in North Oxford, and you'd read Ancient History for your degree. Indeed it wasn't until a change of Irish Government policy towards tenant farmers in the 1980s freed him from the day-to-day business of farming that he could find the time to express the aesthetic side of his nature: 'Now I was on the side of the garden and the woods, and against the farm. I argued at our meetings: We can't cut that tree down, it's essential for the landscape, instead of being tormented. I changed sides in a way.' And so he brings his story neatly back to its starting point, 1993.

I should have been more trusting: such is the man's gift, I had found *The Scramble*, for all its complexity and immense length, hard to put down. But then again, he has an equal gift for brevity when it's appropriate: on a single page in the picture-led tree books he manages to evoke the personality of his subject, record its biographical details (the more arcane, the better) and still find space to bring himself into the metaphorical picture, just as his tiny figure is usually to be found in the tree's actual portrait on the facing page. A journalistic training is the answer: Thomas Pakenham was at the start of a promising career in Fleet Street when he unexpectedly inherited Tullynally at the age of twenty-seven: 'I was a gossip columnist at one point, and that makes you interested in communication; it's the opposite of an academic training. If I'd been a lecturer at university teaching African history I would have had the opposite approach, wouldn't I? Analytic and rather narrow.' He reckons he was lucky (as he tells them, luck usually looms large in his stories) to have been working as 'the junior office boy' on *The Observer* in its golden age. We agree: writers should really be paid more for less, which puts Thomas in mind of the French writer Blaise Pascal, who apologised to his correspondent for the length of his letter because he hadn't had time to make it a short one.

This stint in journalism also stood him in good stead when he overshot the publisher's deadline for the second tree book by more than a year, and was obliged to set himself a tough goal if he were ever to finish it: come what may, two tree stories per night, which sometimes proved a 'grim struggle'. But not always: his wife told him he looked more as though he were getting ready to settle down with a box of chocolates on the sofa than at his computer to graft away into the small hours. And if anyone who's read *Remarkable Trees of the World* wonders why the writer visited every continent except South America, he ran out of money as well as time.

Time for coffee, and it'll have to be black because there's no sugar or milk. While Thomas is off making it, I ponder the paradox of the brilliant academic mind that often seems to thrive in chaotic surroundings (think John Bayley and Iris Murdoch) and pass the time jotting down the titles of a row of books on one bulging, sagging shelf of many, in case they provide a clue to their arrangement that is not immediately obvious. They do not: *Farm Planning* rubs covers with *Venice, A Traveller's Companion*; *Poets in the North of Ireland* is alongside *Clive of India*; *Flora Britannica* by Richard Mabey cosies up to *Court Painting in England*, which in turn hobnobs with *The Back-Relief from Pain, Greek and Roman Art, Stained and Decorative Glass, Africa, the Art of a Continent*, a guide to Prague, *The Holy Bible* and a John Le Carré novel. John Buchan isn't far away, juxtaposed with *Exploring Long distance Paths, Dress Regulations for the Army 1900, The Atlas of Medieval Man, Fruticetum Brittanicum* by A.G.L. Hellyer and a few beautifully bound but battered leather volumes of the sort you come across in the libraries of terrifically grand houses. Only books on the subject of trees have a discrete space on the shelves, and of these, I learn, the four most referred to – the only ones he really needs – are the collected works of Bean, *Hillier's Manual*, John Evelyn's *Silva Britannica* and John Claudius Loudon's *Arboretum et Fruticum*. Reduced to choosing one, he believes it would be Evelyn's.

Treacle-black coffee to hand, Thomas slips back easily into his story: '. . . then in the autumn of '93 – why 1993 is *the* date – I went with a party of twenty professional and amateur plant collectors to Yünnan on a very well-organised botanical expedition, and for the first time I was confronted with the fact that I couldn't just be a tree person, that would be ridiculous: here were these wonderful philadelphuses and deutzias and astillbes, and all these wild-collected woody plants, but they were shrubs, they weren't trees. I wasn't going to say I only collect trees and I only plant trees. It was as simple as that. I collected 150 packets of seed and learnt two things, at least: the difference between a deutzia and a philadelphus and, crucially, how to grow them because we didn't have a professional gardener. It was one of the happiest times of my life, growing plants from seed that I'd collected in the wild myself, and to watch them from the egg as it were – to watch them grow from this little green mist on the tray in my own little propagation house.' His success rate was predictably high, prompting an idea: 'I thought I would do something original. You may decide it was a gimmick and I'm still rather ambivalent about it myself.' His idea was to plant up three separate areas each containing only plants grown from seed he had collected over one specific period of time from one particular region in the Himalayas. Feeling his rules were perhaps a tad pedantic even for him, he has since modified them to allow plants propagated by anyone who was on one or other of the three separate expeditions to be included, if his own efforts with that particular plant proved unsuccessful.

This led us to the subject of plant collections generally, about which, again, he is in two minds: 'Sometimes you stumble on something really rare which is only found in that one region and in the schoolboy sense of the collector of cigarette cards or toy trains you've got something really special . . . but then again – I keep using this word 'ambivalent' – it's boring to say it, but I've always thought of the word 'collection' as a rather dirty word; I've always thought of it as something slightly miserly as well as boring. I think of a garden as somewhere that should be beautiful, not full of rarities interesting only to the collector. I hate going round collections where there's no thought of arrangement and you've just got specimens in a row. I'm well aware of the pitfalls of buying out of catalogues a lot of very rare things and sticking them in the ground and saying, "Look at my *Podocarpus maximus*! Isn't it fascinating?" when it's really very boring, only rare.' I mention Lord Cavendish's own ambivalence around the matter of cataloguing his collection of rare trees at Holker Hall in Cumbria: so great is his love for them he is even dubious about listing their names on a database in case to do so would smack of the cad who keeps a record of his female conquests. But Thomas has no such anxieties – rather the reverse: when the taxonomist at Glasnevin Botanical Garden in Dublin offered to print out the labels for his collection, and suggested putting TP before the date – for example TP/1993.001, he was delighted: 'I own, I rather exulted. I thought, actually I rather like that. Yes! I like the swagger! Of course I could have used TY for Tullynally if I were more self-effacing, but obviously I'm not.'

The phone rings. It appears Thomas has gone off with his wife's keys and she is furious. As we set off in the pouring rain at a fast trot to return them to her, I get the distinct impression this is not the first time. Trying to appear at ease when I'm most definitely not, I bring up the subject of patience – how gardening requires so much patience, and could this be why it is a hobby more usually associated with older people? By way of response, my companion quotes John Evelyn off the top of his head: 'Evelyn talks about the mystery of why very old people plant trees which they'll never see, but you said it's only then they have patience, and I think Evelyn answers his own question by saying: "Only then are we sensible enough in old age to plant trees." As further illustration, he then recounts what he describes as The First Tree story or, if not the first, the second, depending on whether I believe Homer pre- or post-dates the Bible. Pass. But whatever its chronological position in history, it is a good story: Odysseus is home from the wars, at last. He's killed everyone at court, murdered all the rivals for his long-suffering Penelope's hand, and made love to her once he's managed to prove he is who he says he is by showing her a scar on his thigh he's had all his life. Now it's time to say hello to his old Dad who is at home, in his garden, planting and tending his trees. Only Dad doesn't recognise his son, or the scar . . .' My sodden notebook fails me: I'll have to beg for a reprise at our next encounter, which we've already agreed we're going to need. In the event, however, I didn't have to beg when the time came; he already had the book open at the appropriate place when I arrived:

> First he shows the scar, then he says: 'Or these trees. Let me tell you the trees you gave me years ago. Here on this well-worked plot I begged you for everything I saw, a little boy trailing you through the orchard, picking our way among these trees and you named them one by one. You gave me thirteen pear, ten apple trees and forty figs and promised to give me, Look! fifty vine rows.' [Then Homer says] The trees are living proof. Laertes knees went slack. His heart surrendered, recognising the strong clear signs that Odysseus offered him.

Meanwhile, back to the present and mission accomplished, as we jog back along the wet pavements I learn how closely the writer was involved in absolutely every aspect of the design and layout of his tree books – his babies: that discussions over the first book alone had involved more than sixty separate visits to the publishers, and that he provided all the engravings from his own collection, as well as some from his precious copy of *Silva Britannica*. The huge rewards he has already reaped – and continues to reap – in both the financial and emotional sense (to have touched so many people around the world is tremendously gratifying) do no more than accurately reflect the prodigious effort that went into their creation. I witnessed the effect myself when I was at Kew one afternoon trying to identify his Desert Island luxury (*Quercus castaneifolia*, the chestnut-leaved oak planted in the 1840s during Sir William Hooker's reign): an Australian tourist spotted me carrying *Meetings with Remarkable Trees* and, thrilled to bits, asked me if I would I take a picture of her beside her own chosen tree, just as the author does.

But the human figure is not, as I had imagined, placed there for scale: it is there to humanise the picture because, he explains: 'Trees are social; they live with us, and if you insist that they are natural history – and therefore there shouldn't be anyone around – you are actually falsifying the picture. I have strong views about that. My guide is: What do artists do? They think more about it than anybody else. Artists toil away all their lives working out these problems, and if you look at topographical painters you see the amazingly ingenious ways they use a person, horse, dog, sheep to humanise the landscape, as well as creating patterns in the picture, of course. I've had a horse or two, and I've used bicycles, and cars but, much as I like them, I've never had sheep in my pictures.'

So what had actually decided the writer to take his own photographs in the first place? Money, or rather its lack, is what: when the powers that be at Weidenfeld and Nicolson (publishers of all his books, as well as most of the rest of his phenomenally creative family's) saw the grainy black and white photographs he'd brought along to illustrate his idea for the first tree book, they were doubtful to say the least, but felt they owed him for all those best-selling history books. Nonetheless, it proved a tussle: 'The history of the first two volumes – and I think of the two of them very much as a pair – is that the first wasn't expected to sell many copies, and the publishers were deeply sceptical. What was I, an historian, doing fooling around with trees? And who would ever buy a book like that, because I wasn't a botanist, I wasn't a horticulturist, and I wasn't a forester? How could it ever succeed, and what was the book about anyhow? It didn't seem to be a book on gardening or botany – didn't seem to fit any kind of niche.' He reckons he was lucky (that word again): the company had been bought by Orion, whose head was Anthony Cheetham, and Anthony Cheetham happens to be a tree man with his own arboretum in Gloucestershire. Nevertheless, the accountants weren't going to be to handing out large dollops of cash in advance: Thomas would have to pay all his own expenses.

Which was a blow, but not a deterrent: 'I enquired from a friend who was a very good photographer whether he was interested. He said he was, and we went to Kew and he took a picture. He said: "Well, now you have to decide whether you hire me, but before we go any further I ought to tell you that people like me don't come cheap," and I said: "You mean it'll cost fifty pounds a picture, will it?" He said "Five hundred a picture, and a lot more if it's a wet day and we have to come back." I was completely baffled, but then he said: "Why don't you take them yourself? Any fool can take reasonably good pictures if they have a very good camera."'

So that's what he did: he bought himself a Linhof – the very best there is for the job in hand – and set about learning how to use it. But with no technical knowledge and absolutely no experience, all he had to rely on was a naturally developed visual sense, and his will. He is both terrifically proud of the results, and charmingly modest: 'If I say it myself, one of the pictures I'm pleased with – because it was a sort of fluke in a sense – is The Great Hedge of Meikleour, on the way from Perth to Braemar. It was raining and I waited with my Linhof in the middle of the road, with all these cars coming past me, trying to get a pattern of cars with their lights on because I wanted it to be spooky. So I was using these cars not just to show how high the hedge was but also to create a slightly sinister atmosphere. Take out those cars and the picture falls to pieces. But to show you how ignorant I am, and what an amateur I am, I thought this won't really work because it's raining, and it'll be a very dull photograph – very flat – and I want it to be more three-dimensional and have more kick in it. So I went back and took the same picture on a sunny day and it was absolutely boring; it's one of those occasions where the murk in the air worked really well. A more experienced photographer would have seen this straight off.' On another occasion he waited patiently (albeit in a car with a heater) for three whole freezing days in the snow for the shot he wanted, his point being here that as an amateur indulging his hobby he could afford to wait it out, whereas a professional could not.

I asked garden photographer Andrew Lawson for his opinion of Thomas Pakenham's skill with the camera, and he decided that what makes the photographs so special is the love the man feels for his subjects. So, an amateur in the true sense of the word. Naturally, I relay this to Thomas, and his face lights up: 'Oh! really? Did he say that? Well, that is very nice. I haven't said that, but I'd like you to say it. It is a labour, but it's a labour of love! I'd like that. I think that's a correct description.'

Clearly, then, love is the key, but I am warned I must not forget the luck element: 'Luck plays an immense part in all aspects of a project like the tree books – the luck of the light, the luck of the encounters you make: you meet somebody by accident at the airport. He asks you what you're doing. Your plane is late. The hours drag on. You get quite jolly. You show him a photograph. He looks at the photograph, and roars with laughter: "You're in the wrong place; that's not where to go, if you want to see a baobab." He draws you a *Treasure Island* map on the back of the ticket and three days later you're groping around trying to find this great tree and it's much better than anything you would have encountered otherwise.'

But he also had his fair share of bad luck, as he sees it: one day he was somewhere in the Australian outback in a hire car when he chanced upon a dangerously full stream he would have to cross to reach a particular group of baobabs growing on an outcrop of sheer rock somewhere over the horizon. He was alone; he had no food or water bottle; he hadn't seen another car for hours, and he had no idea how far he might have to hike with his heavy camera to locate his objective. Reluctantly, he decides against trying to ford the stream because he is due to fly back to London the next day, and won't make the plane if he gets stuck. Or dies, I suggest: in other words, perhaps this story has more to do with prudence than bad luck, and I own for the first time in our conversation that I don't really believe our lives are governed by luck, or its absence come to that. Somewhat to my surprise, he agrees, even conjuring out of the air a quotation to support this view: 'I can quote you John Luck . . . John Locke! It may not be in the *Book of Quotations* but I stumbled on it in the book he wrote about education. He was William III's doctor, most famous of course as a philosopher, but he also wrote about education, and he says this: "In this world happiness, or the reverse, is for the most part of our own making." *For the most part*: in other words, for the most part we do decide; we have free will; we decide if we'll make ourselves miserable by being cussed or make ourselves happy by being pleasant, but I do think it's also true that we make our own luck.'

Trees are not so blessed. Old trees especially are at awful risk from Man's caprices, not to mention Nature's. Indeed, *Remarkable Trees of the World* is as much a lament as a eulogy: at one end of the economic graph Thomas Pakenham's precious giants – indeed all trees – are at the mercy of the logging companies, and at the other of the eternal poor who chop them down for firewood or farmland. As to the venerable beech in the park at Tullynally numbered among those that received a good-luck hug in 1991, it survived that night to become the star of the first tree book, but was fatally wounded in another ferocious blast in 1999. Its passing is mourned with great poignancy in *Trees of the World*.

Finally, there is what Thomas calls The Taliban, and the last half-hour of our second encounter is taken up with his baffled rant against the fashion these days for condemning all flora not native to its location. In Ireland the *fatwa* includes beeches: whoever decides such things has deemed them 'alien invaders', despite beeches having arrived on the island over 800 years ago. Worse, they are one of only four Irish forest giants, the others being elm, oak, and ash. Elm of course succumbed to sickness years ago, and now a soil-born disease unwittingly transported here by man threatens oak. So, if beech does not get its sentence reprieved . . .

Thomas Pakenham's last words to me are an anguished plea: 'I'm involved in the Irish Tree Society [he is Chairman], and one of the issues now is that The Taliban are cutting down beech trees. I don't know if you can work this in, but anyhow you know my views.' Time had run out for us that afternoon. How much remains for Ireland's beeches, I wonder? Their fate may well be in the hands of this remarkable man, who will surely do his best for them.

The titles of his tree books:

*Meetings with Remarkable Trees* (Weidenfeld & Nicolson, new edition 2003)
*Remarkable Trees of the World* (Weidenfeld & Nicolson, new edition 2003)
*The Remarkable Baobab* (Weidenfeld & Nicolson, 2004)
*In Search of Remarkable Trees: On Safari in Southern Africa* (Weidenfeld & Nicolson, 2007)

# Hugh Johnson

## WINE WRITER AND
## GARDENING JOURNALIST

I thought: I don't want ever to write about wine again . . . but trees . . .
these elms . . . you should be ashamed of yourself: you don't really know
the difference between an elm and an oak. Then I thought to myself that's
what I'll write about. I don't know who it was who said if you want to
learn about something write a book about it, but it's absolutely true.

                                                                Hugh Johnson

Hugh Johnson's account of what decided him in 1971 to write his encyclopaedic book on trees reveals the man's nerve right enough, but
not the awful grief that fuelled it at the time. 1971 was the year the already
widely celebrated author of *The World Atlas of Wine* moved his family out
of London to Great Saling in Essex. Unfortunately, it was also the year
Dutch Elm disease hit Great Britain. The village of Great Saling was
famous for its elms and a number of its finest stood in the grounds of
Saling Hall, the Johnsons' new home, but by the time his book, *The
International Book of Trees*, was published in 1973 half the Saling elms were
dead, and the rest were dying.

However, I did not know any of this as I drove down to Essex through
Docklands early one dank Saturday morning in January. All I did know
was that it was Hugh Johnson's usual practice to write an in-depth book
on a subject that interested him, not because of *all* he knew about it but
because of how *little* he knew. And I knew this because I had borrowed
from the Lindley Library a battered copy of *The Principles of Gardening* –
the third of the Hugh Johnson encyclopaedic books – and in the introduction he quotes Beverley Nicholls, who said: 'I know that unless I write a

gardening book now it will be too late to write it at all for shortly I shall know too much . . .'. A quick trawl through the *Principles'* 110 sections revealed a text packed with facts yet entertainingly written, and further lightened by lots of small photographs on every page.

My instructions were to turn left at the pub with the orange and turquoise palm trees when I reach Great Saling, but if the pub's garden makeover serves joyously to reinforce my south-west Londoner's prejudices about Essex, the timeless atmosphere that pervades the Johnson property practically next door put the kybosh on them. In fact, I'd been reliably informed there were no Hall houses left in Essex because they'd all been burned down by their villainous owners for the insurance money, yet Saling Hall can trace its ancestry back to the tenth century, although it did receive its own makeover in 1699 when a Dutch-gabled, pink brick façade was added. This is the face that greets the visitor on arrival and is reflected in the calm waters of a duck pond large enough to pass for a lake in the miniature landscape park the Johnsons must pass through to reach their front door. The little park also boasts an ancient moat, and the village church is right there in the picture too.

Hugh Johnson meets me on the drive, and launches straight into his tale: 'You see where the oaks and pines are now? They are planted on stumps. In this front park alone we cut down twelve trees of more than fifteen feet girth. When we first came to view the house in 1970 we saw these vast elms over ninety feet high filling the sky. Superb! We came into this elm world and gazed up and thought: "My God! This is everything we have ever looked for." We moved in, and the news about elm disease came almost by the next post.'

The Chinese character for 'crisis' combines two symbols, one signifying 'danger' the other 'opportunity'. And, Hugh, having decided against his first impulse to head straight back to Islington, turned his own crisis into an opportunity: 'I went into all the science of the disease, and bought the kit to inject the trees with fungicide. I spent a huge amount of time and quite a lot of money doing that. In the middle of the village opposite the pub was the biggest elm [*Ulmus nitens = U. carpinifolia*] in the world –

according to Elwes and Henry's *Trees of Great Britain and Ireland*, published in 1906, it was thirty-five feet round and 115 feet high in 1840. So of course I tried to save it, worked on it for about fifteen years, even put collecting boxes in pubs.'

We pay our respects to the actual tree that had first alerted Hugh to his ignorance: 'Among these magnificent elms was a tree that didn't die. It was only in the end that I had the wit to realise it was an oak. Probably 350 years old. Needs cleaning up again. It's rather scarily over the road but I do keep an eye on it. Imagine fifteen of those – only they were elms – in the park at the front.'

Fortuitously, 1973 was designated Plant a Tree Year and Hugh, with his book just out, became very 'charged up.' He helped found The Tree Council in 1974, and thought up schemes to encourage people to look at trees, to appreciate trees, and, of course, to plant them. Cruelly, the drought years of 1975 and 1976 followed right on behind: 'So all these newly planted trees were dying. All the good will had been lost, and the elms were still dying, and the farmers were burning stubble. Do you remember? The sky would be full of smoke, fields in flames, the hedgerows in flames, the trees burning. I remember standing in front of a tractor in a field just over there, shouting at the tractor driver.'

Which seemed a suitably apocalyptic moment to end the story's first chapter and retreat indoors because it was freezing out. Indoors is all polished stone floors, cavernous fireplaces, ancient wood panelling, and a pervading air of peace. We settle ourselves in the quintessentially English sitting room with its chintz covers and geraniums in pots and little vases filled with scraps from the garden: *Lonicera fragrantissima*, *Mahonia japonica*, *Garrya elliptica*, winter jasmine, aconites, snowdrops, *Prunus autumnalis*, primroses (very early, surely?), *Arbutus × andrachnoides*, and the winter heliotrope, *Pertasites fragrans*. While I fiddle with my equipment, Hugh busies himself with the fire and informs me that the chimney had reputedly smoked badly for the first 400 years of its life, but has been cured of its bad habit by the simple expedient of hacking out half a brick depth at the back, and putting in a fireback. I am impressed, imagining it must have taken rather more lateral thinking than he gives himself credit for, or someone else would have cured the problem centuries ago. Nevertheless, though willing, he couldn't help me solve a technical problem with my tape recorder because he never uses one himself, or even a notebook come to that: at the very outset of his literary career (which began when he became a travel writer after reading English at Cambridge) Hugh made a conscious decision to trust to memory and first impressions – and accept Wordsworth's dictum that 'Poetry is emotion recollected in tranquillity'.

Such self-imposed discipline helps explain why his fact-packed books are nevertheless so readable: 'I like crunching facts into nuggets, yes. Brevity is one of my virtues. But you've got to show the reader that you are still there. I think to myself we're getting a bit serious here. Let's have a story. Let's rephrase that . . . I was only in my mid-twenties when I took on a very big subject and got away with it, so I thought, well, the way that I approach things does work. My enthusiasm, my feelings come across, so I'll do it for other things. After all, I was learning about wine. I didn't know the first thing about it at the time. I think,' he adds, 'the most interesting thing about life is learning.'

Hugh Johnson was Editor of *Queen* Magazine in the late 1960s, which meant when the publishing firm Mitchell Beazley approached him in 1969 with a view to publishing a wine atlas he had firm opinions on how it should look: 'I said we must make book pages as accessible as magazine pages: people always look at the picture, then they look at the shortest thing there is to read to get the flavour, which is perhaps the caption of the picture, or the headline, and when they are convinced by all that, then they start on the grey matter – the actual text. *The Wine Atlas*, with its spread-by-spread approach – which incidentally my wife Judy designed – changed the face of publishing. I rather immodestly say it was a complete publishing revolution. So of course I applied it to *Trees* and of course I applied it to *Gardening*.'

For the record, the *Atlas* has sold over three million copies, and counting, is in its sixth edition and has been translated into thirteen languages. The tree book has sold 750,000 copies and been translated into six languages. *Principles* (out of print), first published in 1979, sold 250,000 copies, and was eventually redesigned and reissued as *Hugh Johnson's Gardening Companion* in 1996. Each book kept him at the coalface for eight hours a day, every day, for two years. So how did it feel when he reached the end of one? 'Release. Freedom. Depression. What next? In about that order.'

It's time to hear what happened next in the tree story, and in Chapter Two I learn that, once the dead elms had been dealt with, Hugh decided he would create an arboretum at Saling in their place. Some years later he made another in central France, and eventually a third – or an attempt at a third – beside the sea in North Wales: 'I'd always dreamed of a forest that overlooks the sea, which of course is a rotten idea because the wind is full of salt.' Instead, on the same piece of land, he now dreams of creating in the shaft of a disused gold mine 'the world's best grotto in a mighty tunnel, which invites a certain amount of imaginative planting'. As for the French property, that was sold a few years ago: 'It was too much. Saling is not a latchkey place. This is a very "homey" home.'

Cue for a glass of Moselle and then lunch beside the Aga and my first chance to meet Hugh's wife Judy, who's kept herself out of sight all morning, and their daughter Lucy, who's dropped by. Over leeks-from-the-garden quiche, and quince-from-the-garden cheese, glass of something red, delicious handmade chocolates, and coffee, there's lots of wine chat, and then this intriguing revelation: practically the whole family, including most of the cousins and almost all the in-laws, are artists of one kind or another and every single one of them was born under the astrological sign of Pisces. The three of them break into a chant:

> Compassionate, sensitive Pisces
> May flinch when confronted with crises.
> His personal chink is a fondness for drink
> And a longing to sail on the high seas.

That would explain the forest-beside-the-sea dream, and the number of 'water features' Hugh has managed to fit into Saling's twelve acres. Reckoning it up later, I made the tally one moat, one cascade, and one duck-pond at the front; two pools, one water jet, one pond with 'Japanesey' cascade, a further pond, one swimming pool, and one Belfast sink full of water at the back. *The Wine Atlas* speaks for itself, and the reference to the Piscean's suffering under stress only emphasises the poignancy of the tree story, and the man's courage in the circumstances.

Hugh Johnson is, however, arguably as famous in the horticultural world for his Tradescant's Diary column in the *The Garden* as he is in the viticultural milieu for his *Wine Atlas*, and over coffee he talks about how 'Trad' came to be born. Again, we are back in the 1970s when the RHS was on its financial beam-ends, and in a deep crisis of its own while Hugh, conversely, was by this time on a roll: 'I'd just written my tree book, and I had got to know Sir George Taylor (Director of Kew) when he was on the RHS Council Publications Committee. He said [morphing effortlessly into a Scottish accent]: "You know about magazines. What shall we do with the Journal?"' Sir George told him the Society was beginning to think it couldn't afford to go on producing it, at least not monthly, but Hugh warned him: 'You'll lose all your members. They'll forget they belong. You've got to make it more interesting; make it the reason why they do belong.' 'But how?' queried Sir George.

Hugh knew how: 'I'd worked out the sort of magazine they could have, adapting the journal, putting a coloured cover on it, calling it *The Garden*. I told him it could be financed by selling advertising. The shock! You can imagine the conversation that went on. I then spoke to my publishers, who had just made a packet out of my wine book and were doing very well with *Trees*, so I said: "How about starting a *magazine* company?"' They agreed, and 'Trad' made his debut on 6 June 1975 in the first issue published by New Perspectives under Hugh's editorial directorship. Between the pair of them, they brought the stuffy old journal to life. And to alert members to what a treat they were in for, he blazoned the names of the contributors to that inaugural issue across its colourful cover: Arthur Hellyer, Anne Scott-James, Graham Stuart Thomas, Christopher Lloyd, and Elizabeth David. Quite a haul.

However, by 1979 membership of the Society was already beginning its inexorable rise, and Hugh felt obliged to reflect the interests of its new readership in the magazine – in other words, to bring it 'down market', which he hated having to do. So, with American backing he helped his friend the late David McLintock launch *The Plantsman*, a 'green stocking' publication intended to compensate for the removal from *The Garden*'s pages of 'the sort of scholarly, unhurried, lovingly minute studies of plants which are the true meat of specialist horticultural literature.' The stylish little magazine had a plain paper cover and, inside, simple line drawings and lots of Latin, which turned out to be far too esoteric for the RHS, who decided to take it over and bring it visually into line with its glamorous big sister, which it had already decided it would rather publish itself. And that was that.

But 'Trad' continued to appear in *The Garden* every month until 2006 when, for reasons best known to the magazine's editor, the column was axed. Actually, Hugh had long feared 'Trad' was out of its time, but hadn't the slightest intention of giving it up unless obliged. When that day arrived he decided to out his *alter ego* – interestingly, while Hugh tends to refer to his three major books as, respectively, 'my' wine, 'my' tree, and 'my' gardening book, 'Trad' has his own persona – and transfer the column under his own by-line to *Gardens Illustrated* magazine. Apparently there were always a few subjects 'Trad' felt best avoided – the deplorable standards of municipal planting, for example – because whenever he did the hate-mail arrived in sackloads: 'I'm a snob. I'm elitist. I don't know anything about public gardening. Who am I to say anything about it? So I stopped. Not worth the fight.' Ditto anything to do with shooting, although he did once risk asking readers if anyone had a recipe for squirrel pie. I doubt he'll have trouble of that kind with his new readership, and my own guess is that future students of garden history will one day consult 'Trad' for his idiosyncratic insights into gardening fashions and gardeners' preoccupations in the late-twentieth/early-twenty-first century, the way social historians mine Pepys' diaries for what they reveal about the social mores of seventeenth-century England.

Sir Roy Strong advised 'Trad' always to tell readers how many gardeners the garden he is describing employs. Good point: At Saling two, usually. Two, plus Hugh when he's not on the high seas. (Judy's role is to play the appreciative witness, although she was herself the National Gardens Scheme's Essex County Organizer for over twenty years, and sat on its Council as Chairman of Publications for ten – the 'Yellow Book' was her business.) Unfortunately, the ex-chauffeur-come-reluctant gardener who worked for Saling's previous owner had downed tools soon after Hugh and his family arrived: 'He didn't like the level of activity expected of him. I asked him to dig out some ground elder, and he went on strike, so when I saw a young man about my age wheeling a pushchair down the road one day I approached him,' The young man turned out to be a factory worker from Braintree who in due course came to work for Hugh full-time, and today Eric Kirby and his wife are the lynchpins in the Johnson household, along with Aileen Foulis who's been working in the gardens for over ten years.

Once, as a last resort he advertised in Teddy Goldsmith's new magazine, and he still hugs himself at the idea of advertising for 'staff' in *The Ecologist*, as though it were *The Lady*. But he did get a reply – from an untrained, twenty-year-old hippy type called Christopher employed by Blackheath's Parks Department. Working on a hunch, Hugh took him on: 'He was *very* intelligent, and as soon as he moved in [to a caravan in the grounds] he started borrowing my books. I was on my own learning curve – not yet writing *Principles of Gardening*, though I'd got it in mind – so we swapped books and talked about everything all the time.' Chris Bailes is now the curator of the RHS garden at Rosemoor.

He also succeeded in recruiting his neighbour Ken Akers, whose day job was the painting and decorating of royal residences but whose hobby was growing alpines to show standards. Ken lived in the lodge that had originally belonged to the Hall and Hugh would watch him at work in his greenhouse. One day he bearded the man: 'Ken, what you really want to do is garden, so why don't you come and garden here?' And he did. He remains Hugh's neighbour, but is now a freelance garden designer and lecturer. (There were also failures, one involving a tribunal and having to pay out a lot of money to someone.)

We go out on site again for the final chapter in the tree story and as we walk through the conservatory Hugh notices some nasty-looking brown blotches on the leaves of a precious *Buddleja asiatica*. Aphids. But the temperature is kept too low for nematodes to be operational so what will he do? He thinks he'll forget he's seen them, and thinks again: 'But I shall probably use some foul and possibly illegal substance.' Which reminds him: do I know anything about bio dynamism? Only that it works. Why? 'Because the wacky owners of a vineyard on the Loire claim their wine's fine quality is the result of their burying a cow's horn filled with "magic" compost in the soil when the moon is in Saturn.' True? 'Mostly.' However, it always does to be sceptical– he was also given a homeopathic-sounding recipe for keeping rabbits off his land: Shoot one rabbit. Burn its skin. Grind to a powder. Add a pinch to plenty of water. Sprinkle around. Rabbits won't bother you again. Did it work? 'No.'

With only an hour or two before dusk and twelve acres to cover we will have to dash. First stop, a small clearing surrounded by trees – a secret garden that Hugh describes as being very 'tulgey' in summer. 'Tulgey?' 'It means "leafy".' It's from Lewis Carroll:

> And as in uffish thought he stood,
> The Jabberwock, with eyes of flame
> Came whiffling through the tulgey wood
> And burbled as it came!

In the clearing, two sturdy but child-sized chairs made out of elm wood – which I learn is indestructible, even in water, so was traditionally used for building docks – and a number of tree paeonies looking as dead and dejected as only tree paeonies in winter can. In the background, an old, black-painted barn with a peephole cut out of its side at eye level to reveal, in summer, a jet of water rising up out of one of the Saling ponds in some woodland many feet below. Despite the 'naturalness', the casual Englishness, of the scene, there is a definite whiff of Japan about it.

The change in levels at a certain point is sudden and steep, because half the garden is situated in what was a gravel pit in Victorian times. The seven-foot bank between the two levels is planted higgledy-piggledy with massed box shrubs in assorted sizes clipped to resemble something vaguely organic – perhaps boulders that have worked their way down some alpine glacier and piled themselves up in a great heap at its end.

Beneath this bank lies a wide expanse of mown meadow: there are more open green areas at Saling than you might expect in a would-be forester's garden, and Hugh explains that while, yes, the garden is all about trees, nevertheless he likes space, adding: I am not a label collector, and I listened to the best authority [Humphry Repton], who said: "Plant the hills and flood the hollows".' In a corner of this Repton-influenced area, snug under the steepest part of the box bank, Ken Akers created a shallow pool into which water slides down over natural-looking rocky outcrops. On his travels in Japan Hugh once stumbled upon its virtual double. Two 'rather good' (that is, 'period') Japanese stone lanterns he was given stand sentinel among the box boulders, adding to the Japanesey feel of the space without shouting 'This is a Japanese Garden!'.

Ultimately, however, the trees have it, and each one, or each group, has its own story. At this time of year, inevitably the evergreens dominate the picture: a *Phillyrea latifolia,* the hardy olive well-positioned at the base of the bank; a substantial Monteray pine (*Pinus radiata*) Hugh was photographed planting as a two-foot stripling thirty years ago to grace the pages of the *Radio Times*; a mighty Cedar of Lebanon that was toppled in the storm of 1990, set back on its 'foot' by the local farmer, survived the ordeal, and is now thriving; a fine *Calocedrus decurrens* – the incense cedar – Hugh brought back in his sponge bag from the States as a rooted seedling; and a tall, slender, tiny-leaved evergreen nothofagus, *N. solanderi*, dancing, as my guide puts it, a *pas de deux* with a graceful gingko perfectly matched for size. But dancing too close. One will have to be sacrificed for the other eventually, which hardly bears thinking about.

But Hugh cannot emphasise strongly enough the importance of design in a naturalistic garden: 'When the trees grow beyond your vision of how high they should be then you have to start thinking again: editing out; cutting down. I am aware of the visual lines, the energy lines of this garden. I could draw a map of this garden with arrows where the forces go and I'm not being mystical.' Only, occasionally, sentimental: one tree – a scented American balsam, *Populus trichocarpa*, has been given special dispensation: too tall, too large altogether for its position, it should be for the chop but isn't because Hugh remembers it as five feet of unrooted stick he shoved unceremoniously into the earth thirty years ago, and hasn't the heart.

We come across a miniature forest of young oaks standing straight and tall and very close together because trees like company, and again Hugh invokes Repton: 'Dotting a few starveling saplings on an open lawn would never do any good.' Beyond the oaks, a group of young beech have been planted in a protective circle round a thirty-foot elm that is being carefully watched, but which could still and almost certainly will succumb any day to the disease that killed its parents. Hugh points out the exquisitely fine herringbone-pattern of its end branches etched against the wintry sky and I realise just how great has been our loss when they disappeared from the landscape.

At the far limit of the garden, on the wall of a temple dedicated to Pisces (what else), hangs what appears to be a decorative arrangement of whitewashed scallop shells embedded into plaster. They are scallop shells all right, but they haven't been whitewashed, they've been fossilised, and the 'trophy' is in fact a twenty-million-year-old piece of chalk. So, branchlets shaped like fish bones; all those ponds; the house's very name sounding like a water sport, and now antediluvian scallop shells: the Piscean references continue to accumulate.

But we've come full circle, back past the inspirational oak and the mossy remains of the elms in time to contemplate one last watery feature before the light fades altogether: the willows' reflections in the moat. There is also time for one final What Next? 'I want to be published as a writer, not just as an encyclopaedist. There is a big difference. There are things I want to talk about without this obligation to mention everything. It's become a chore, a total chore but *The World Atlas of Wine* is to certain people an important book and I'm not going to abandon it, so I've taken on Jancis Robinson – the best wine writer of her generation – as a partner.' This wise move has left Hugh free to write the books he wants to write, and last year saw the publication of the first of these: *Wine: A Life Uncorked* (a title he loathes but his publishers insisted). Now he is at work on *'Trad' Looking Back* (its working title): 'After all, I wrote it for thirty years, and I've got this garden that has taken thirty-something years to make. I've got all my old diaries, and I've got my photographs. It's time to reflect.'

Saling Hall garden is open once a week for the National Gardens Scheme. Private visits welcome on weekdays only. Written applications to: Saling Hall, Great Saling, Braintree, Essex CM7 5DT.

Hugh Johnson's 'Trad' column can now be found on the internet, at www.tradsdiary.com.

# Geoffrey Dutton

## ACADEMIC

Ah, but a man's reach must exceed his grasp,
Or what's a heaven for?

Robert Browning (1812–89)

G eoffrey Dutton (known in poetry circles as g.f. dutton, and in the scientific arena as (retired) research molecular biologist Emeritus Professor G.J.F. Dutton, DSc, LLD, FRSE), white water swimmer, and mountaineer, is perhaps best known in the horticultural world as the author of *Some Branch Against the Sky*, a dense, scholarly, but wonderfully wry and readable account of the exigencies and joys of making and maintaining a garden he started to create forty-five years ago on the extreme, exiguous edge of the south-east Scottish Highlands, where a climate about as determinedly inimical to the successful cultivation of anything you'd ever be likely to want to grow prevails. He also wrote a series of articles on the same subject back in the late 1980s and early 1990s for the Royal Horticultural Society's magazine *The Garden*, and a more easily digestible account entitled *Harvesting the Edge*, omitting all Latin names (except, perversely, on its cover which is festooned with them) and including a plentiful sprinkling of his poignant, yet occasionally disconcertingly sharp, verse in lieu.

On the train up to Scotland last spring to meet the professor in his mountain fastness, I happened to be reading *The Worst Journey in the World*, Paisley Cherry-Garrard's nail-biting account of his own harrowing experience as a member of Scott's heroic but ill-fated scientific expedition to Antarctica in search of the South Pole and, among other things, the nesting site of the Emperor penguin. In it I came across this description of Dr Bill Wilson who died in the tent alongside his old friend Scot:

[Dr Wilson's] diary is that of an artist, watching the clouds and mountains, of a scientist observing ice and rock and snow, of a doctor, and above all of a man with good judgement. You will understand that the thing which really interested him in this journey was the acquisition of knowledge.

It struck a chord: Professor Dutton evidently possesses a similarly wide range of interests and qualities that complement one another and, indeed, somewhere in his writing, he remarks on this himself: 'I could in fact argue that making this garden is writing a poem, and walking the paths, reading it'. And when we do meet, he tells me how annoyed he gets with people who insist on defining the pursuits that never bore him any fiscal reward as 'hobbies'. 'Grrr!' he expostulates, 'Just because they didn't put as many groceries on the kitchen table as Science did – not that that put many!' And in a letter politely supplying answers to a list of mundane questions I never got around to asking on the day of our encounter – for example: 'Do you supply your own water? (Yes). Do you have a television? (No). Do you generate your own electricity? (When the National Grid fails, which is frequently) – he took me to another level of understanding of what gardening is all about in this succinct postscript. 'Gardening' he writes, 'is a synthesis of explorations – Craftsman: physical dexterity and stamina for maintenance. Scientist: intellectual – selecting viable plants and keeping them healthy. Artist: imaginative – providing visual and "mental" satisfaction. Intelligence: to keep all these in balance; neither trivial, i.e. pastiche, nor rhetorical, i.e. blatant.' (Those who would limit gardening to the category of mere craft, please ponder.)

Since I intended renting a car in Edinburgh to reach my remote destination, the professor had supplied me with meticulous instructions to get me round Edinburgh as efficiently as possible, which meant on the appointed day I found myself crossing the Forth Bridge, still swathed in a ghostly early-morning mist, in no time, and eagerly anticipating my first experience of the Great Hedge of Meikleour somewhere up the road ahead. I was not disappointed: although still bare of leaves and lacking as a result its reputed air of menace, the long line of massive, elephant-grey trunks standing like a well-drilled circus troop beside the road was an impressive sight. Once in Duttonland, my instructions were even more precise, and included descriptions of landmarks well before, and far beyond, his garden gate. A belt and braces man, I felt.

I arrive on time but very nervous, and proceed to mislay my car keys twice within minutes of arriving. Unfortunately, my host, a puckish figure, sporting a white floppy sun hat and his trousers tucked into stout wellies, materialises at the height of my panic. 'You're human,' he shrugs when I confess I'm flustered. Doubting such a possibility, I ask him if he ever loses his own. 'All the time,' he replies, which is encouraging. Nonetheless, as the day wore on I did began to think my guide's laconic observations about our human limitations were disingenuous: Geoffrey Dutton sets nothing less than heroic standards for himself, his plants and, in this instance, me: our walk turned out to be a long one – over four hours without a break. An epic poem.

I have opted to do the interview as we walk and soon realise what I have let myself in for: Geoffrey Dutton speaks fast, in soft, sibilant tones with a slight stammer, a faint Scottish accent, and a propensity for pronouncing Latin differently from me. Add to this the fact that the sometimes vertiginous, occasionally slippery, always narrow paths of his garden were designed to be trodden single file in monkish contemplation meant my tape recorder was usually pointed at his back; that the birds are out in force proclaiming their territories in ecstatic outbursts; and that The Burn tumbles in a ceaseless, crashing cacophony down its rocky gorge situated a little left of centre of the deep-pleated ten-odd acres we are traversing up, down and sideways at a smart lick, and I reckon any self-respecting sound recordist would have simply packed up and gone home.

All I can do is trust the professor will cast enough pearls to make a necklace, even if my equipment doesn't manage to pick up more than half of them, and also that he was wrong about my mortalness. One thing I particularly want him to explain, and hope to catch his reply, is what he meant in a poem of his entitled 'Joy'. In the poem the narrator describes the sense of satisfaction he gains from shooting a flock of bullfinches that have just spent a week ripping his precious (because so often ruined by frost) Japanese cherry blossom to bits for the sheer, anarchic hell of it. It ends: 'twenty-seven bullfinches/In one week of sun. The best,/almost, with that particular gun.' He doesn't sound quite as sweet and loving about nature as . . . 'I am not sweet and loving about nature,' he interjects. 'I am part of nature.' So do you get annoyed with, or feel sympathy for, birds when they wreak havoc in the garden? 'Neither. I just reproduce the human situation.' I mutter something about his humour being terrifically dry, but am called to order on that score too: 'It's not humour, it's just what's going on; not that I'm beyond shooting a few song birds and rabbits. Blackbirds are a damned nuisance, but I've got to live with them and they've got to live with me.' Somewhere in his writing he points out that a sense of order is paradoxically vital in a natural-looking – or marginal – garden and that 'untidiness is confusion', yet there they were, under our very noses, hooligan hordes gleefully grabbing beakfuls of unseasonally dried-out moss from the carefully-maintained grass paths for their nests.

Geoffrey Dutton's bark is, however, far louder than his bite and another of his poems, also about birds, ends: 'I cannot understand/ why I am pleased/ when they feed from my hand.' And this extract from *Harvesting the Edge* equally well captures in prose his attitude in the marginal garden:

> Because you interfere only when you have to, and with least disturbance, you learn to study the life of plant and animal, ally and competitor; you realise your human responsibility and power of compassion, on this vigorous battlefield; how to carry safely, and use to the minimum, your saw, snare and gun or your new chemical weapons, which are so crude compared with the delicately murderous molecular armoury concealed about you in fiercely rivalsome root, leaf and blossom.

But before I get ushered into the garden via an unobtrusive wooden latch gate opening off the narrow road that winds its way over barren moorland to seemingly nowhere, I am given a bird's-eye view of the Dutton domain from the blasted heath above, where, unsurprisingly, a wind farm is scheduled. A pity from the aesthetic point of view, but otherwise a sound project, surely? My guide lets out a derisory snort: it will, he argues, cost more to construct than ever it will claw back in revenue. He believes we have all been manipulated by the politicians with regard to sustainable energy projects, ever since Mrs Thatcher took on the miners back in 1984.

How on earth had I formed the impression Geoffrey Dutton was an ecological warrior of the New Age, Friends of the Earth, variety? He is not, neither does he pretend to be, and from rereading *Some Branch Against the Sky* it is plain with hindsight that the professor, for all his compassion, is prepared to go to whatever poisonous lengths a human being will if danger threatens; in this case, threatens his painstakingly nurtured shelterbelt trees and the carefully sited clumps of clipped beech and sculpted western hemlock (*Tsuga heterophylla*) planted ubiquitously to foil at a lower level the insidious wind, and further protect all other flora within his jealously guarded territory. I almost step on a mole trap inside the deer and rabbit-proof fence, which reminds him to tell me the foxes hereabouts are huge and grey and growl at you. He even deems the sweet little red squirrel a pest. What about something less esoteric – slugs, say? 'Oh, yes' he says, deadpan: 'huge things – bigger than anyone else's.'

On our way back down the road, still outside the garden proper, we'd passed a stand of young birches which I had assumed was self-sustaining native woodland. But no, without protection, little vegetation in the Cairngorms survives the predations of deer and rabbits; everything that manages to raise its head above ground level has been helped to do so by man. I am clearly somewhat out of my botanical, not to mention intellectual and psychological, depths and continue to make a number of naive observations as the day wears on, and many more in our subsequent correspondence. Mercifully the professor has a forgiving nature, and/or is able to mask any understandable impatience with his well-honed gift for irony. This, for example, is his reply to a postcard I had hastily winged off in pursuit of a letter posted before I realised the answers to my questions were all to be found in the index of *Some Branch*: 'Your postcard,' he writes, 'is reassuring.

You have read the book now. (I confess I had doubts, especially from the innocence of some of your questions!) I had composed a reply, giving all the answers detailed in the book, and only sweetly inferring such a useful coincidence, and no less sweetly assuring you the index would suffice (I was proud of the index, forced on an ever-reluctant publisher – "Who the hell ever wants to look anything up? People don't bother these days . . . ")'.

One thing I did manage to work out off my own bat when doing my researches was that 'marginal' gardening must be the mirror opposite of J.C. Loudon's definition of a word he coined for his own purposes: 'gardenesque'. Gardenesque, according to Loudon, means the cultivation of plants as different from the surrounding habitat as possible. Conversely, a 'marginal' garden, as defined by Professor Dutton, 'is one minimally differentiated from its surroundings, and so requiring minimal effort to make and keep up'. Which may be so, but one sceptical reviewer of *Some Branch* decided to do the maths, and to challenge the writer on the second half of his claim. For my part, in the early stages of the walk I had little evidence, at least in its herbaceous contents, to make me question the first half of that definition either, because nine-tenths of the understorey planting had not yet dared poke its head above the parapet. Even when it does, I learn from my guide, it is sure to be hit by a late frost and turned to 'jelly'. However, the indigenous wood anemones are out in force, running in rivulets beside the paths and spilling out into great pools wherever space allows, with the already emerging fresh lime-green leaves of the native wood sorrel (*Oxalis acetosella*) poised to take over when the anemones leave the stage. Once the growing season gets under way, of course, these paths are going to require a lot of maintenance, because – as the professor points out in *Some Branch* – this is a garden, not a wilderness, and the paths create important horizontal spaces in the overall concept. Indeed, on our wander he shows me some of the small stone huts he has constructed at strategic points specifically to house his fleet of hand mowers. Their roofs have been planted with grasses and moss and lichen methodically embedded into the walls, so the trap is neatly set for innocent visiting Americans, who assume them to be the ancient relics of a bygone civilisation.

As we walk, we bicker amiably about what constitutes gardening, I maintaining, for example, that the siting of a pair of carefully clipped evergreen shrubs at the feet of a silver birch (*Betula pendula* and *B. pubescens* being the two natives) in a clearing with an incomparable view of the hills beyond is gardening, my companion that this is an example of what he defines as 'guiding': 'gardening' is what townsfolk do. (He considers working in the greenhouse to be gardening, and he detests it for being tedious, repetitive work that does not push the boundaries of a plant's tolerance or sufficiently challenge his own search for knowledge and understanding; even so, he does own one.) Next, I spot some giant hogweed just emerging from its winter dormancy, exquisitely sited dead-centre in front of a huge, lichen-splattered boulder on the top of which a Chinese rhododendron has (apparently equally imaginatively) settled itself. When I insist this careful *placement* is gardening, he lets it go. Indeed, in *Harvesting the Edge,* he actually advocates using hogweed as an 'unclippable' vertical, its ghastly reputation notwithstanding:

I know hogweed is preached against: it can provoke unpleasant reactions in susceptible persons who embrace it half-naked while sweating, and it poisons anyone who eats it as rhubarb. Here among reasonably normal people it has been an entertaining and harmless monster.

Eventually we come upon an intruder invading the anemone's sacred space and it receives a rough poke from his ski-stick: 'You see – by grubbing them out I discourage those characters, and I encourage the anemones by patting them on the head and saying "Aren't you lovely?"' Next, a spreading patch of omphaloides (blue-eyed Mary), as pretty as a picture but not the picture he was after, gets dealt with: 'You've got to wrench them out when they start colonising the anemones. That's guiding, you see?' My turn to let it go. Unfortunately, an obviously freshly watered, clump of *Hacquetia epipactis* flourishing on a bank in the embrace of some moss-covered tree roots sets me off protesting again. Unabashed, my adversary admits he couldn't resist buying 'the funny little beast' (any more than I could when I spotted it on the nurseryman's stall) and that – 'God, yes!' – you have to feed and water certain introductions because 'a garden has not courage to be a desert. I don't wait for the lights to go out: I water. This marginal stuff is fine, but then you are always led a little further on, you see? And then when you have more time to meddle you get more plants in that require helping over dry periods, that's the trouble: marginality is a sliding scale.' His word 'meddle' comes from Gertrude Jekyll, herself no slouch when it came to natural-looking woodland planting and who disapproved of interfering in places she considered best left alone. In *Some Branch* he owns his guilt: 'I cannot plead innocent to such experimental tendencies,' but reckons the woman he evidently admires wasn't above such things either, 'though the tinkering, as befits the site, is less than what went on at Miss Jekyll's Munstead Wood.'

I notice a number of rhododendrons with some of their limbs mysteriously wrapped in black sticking plaster. The reason is simple: 'Because they are poorly. It's worse now when you can get 74 degrees in April and in another month it can go down to minus . . .' Five or six? I hazard. 'God, much more! Which are you using, Centigrade or Fahrenheit?' No idea – both sound pretty chilly. 'We've had minus ten Centigrade in May. We've lost a lot of them with these early warm springs.' Seeing so many wounded soldiers reminds me of a no-nonsense guide at Hillier's Arboretum bluntly telling our group that when it comes to relative tenderness in a plant you fancy you must decide whether you want to be in charge of a garden, or a hospital.

Next we pass a fortunei rhododendron perched in a gap in the shelterbelt, and perfectly placed for a view through its twisted branches to the often snow-covered mountains on the horizon. 'You see? No soil at all, just rock; it lives up there and it flowered magnificently last year. Looks as though it's been there for generations. The east wind howls through here, and the flowers are all going to go black when the frost hits them before the summer, but they'll come up again. It keeps it tight.' Rooted as it is in solid rock, it rather poses the question of how he ever managed to get it planted (if that is the word) in the first place. 'Well, you have to lever them in when they are small, and you've got to look after them in among the junipers, and you have to make a cairn with the stones that come out.' Phew! That reviewer was right to be sceptical.

The broken, tortured, stems of the gallant juniper are all around: 'You can't beat it, it's so alive. Beautiful, but you can't persuade it to...' his words get lost in the environmental din, but essentially: you can't transplant juniper apparently. Also, it gets so battered and broken by snow it can't be relied upon for important visual statements, which is a pity since Geoffrey Dutton reckons its foliage and berries are incomparable. In *Harvesting the Edge* he paints a heart-rending picture: 'Juniper,' he writes, 'collapses rigidly and suffers torture of the rack as frozen snow around it melts and refreezes, dragging it irresistibly down and fracturing bones. Yet juniper has survived such abuse for millions of years . . .'. He describes how – if they are small enough – he tries to dig them out of the snow, or – more poignantly – how he reaches down and settles snow about them 'so they are at least buried in the Heroic manner.' We pass some seedlings that are all different shapes because, as a pioneering species – no wonder he admires it so – it must keep exploring different patterns of growth to find the one most suited to survive the conditions it has to endure, and the professor gives the very smallest a helping hand in their struggle, by using Baxter's soup cans to protect them from voles.

Every so often on our trek a *Treasure Island*-style map is produced to show me exactly where we've got to on our meandering climb towards the garden's apex and its 'wow factor', the Big Waterfall. But even without map or guided tour, you couldn't miss it: the paths and precise positioning of choice shrubs and trees make sure of that, and incidentally ensure the garden's hidden treasures don't get trampled on, although I unwittingly commit a solecism myself by stepping blithely on to what I thought was forest floor when it has in fact been as densely and intricately planted as the most sophisticated herbaceous border. Yet still I fail to get it, proclaiming enthusiastically my infinite preference for unstructured, 'wild' gardens over the formal type, and my companion has to disabuse me: for all its asymmetry and apparent naturalness, his garden is as formally structured as Hidcote. But if you didn't know . . . I murmur lamely. 'That's the whole point!' he remonstrates. 'The whole point of civilisation is to make it appear as if it's not necessary.' The paths open out from time to time, drawing the eye to a designated viewpoint beyond the garden and then close in again like, he suggests, the rhythms in a piece of music or a poem. He calls these moments 'epiphanies' or 'unexpected revelations' and I find myself insisting – again – that this is gardening, and gardening at its very highest level.' 'Yes, it is difficult,' he concedes.

Whether gardened or guided, a palpable aura of peace (noisy birds notwithstanding) pervades the space, which does not, its creator is at pains to point out, imply inaction: a sense of peace, or restfulness, indicates balance. To understand the truth of this observation I only have to peer through the wire fence on the garden's north border at the horrid commercial conifer plantation beyond, in which ineffably sad, hopeless lines of light-deprived, dead or dying telegraph poles march bravely off into the impenetrable depths of the interior. There could be no epiphanies in *this* forest and it makes the professor very cross, especially when he thinks about how skilfully the Scandinavians manage their own forestry projects. In fact, he approves all things Scandinavian, including the simple construction of their unpretentious wooden houses, and the way their equally unpretentious royal families manage to be kings and queens and princes without a class-ridden Establishment to keep them in business. According to Geoffrey, it was the Saxons who introduced snobbery into our culture. However his wry humour is not reserved exclusively for their descendants, pointing out that it was the Celtic crofters who, having been so enthusiastically cleared out of the Highlands by their own lairds as much as by the hated English landlords, went off to Canada and promptly cleared out all the Indians.

That beastly black forest does serve one useful purpose: it emphasises the skill and care and love lavished on the flora on the professor's side of the fence, in areas marked variously on the map as Pine Wood, Primrose Meadow, and Heather Table. This is the least cultivated part of the garden, but the pines still have their under storey planting of deciduous and evergreen shrubs, and a handsome lichen-spattered ice-age boulder lying in the close-clipped heather has a lone Scots pine perfectly juxtaposed between it and the far horizon. Japanese visitors find it hard to comprehend that the positioning of the rock, if not the pine, owes nothing to man and everything to a glacier. Similarly, the broken, tortured, trunk of an old juniper bush in another part of the garden has wrapped itself unaided round a rocky outcrop, reminding the oriental visitors of an ancient Shinto shrine.

Nevertheless, apart from the rocks that are excavated for planting-hole purposes with an assortment of tools normally associated more with the coalface than the garden, boulders do occasionally get moved around for reasons other than the purely practical. For instance, he lugs them about the Gorge to enlarge the pools and to satisfy his aesthetic ideal, although these tasteful reconstructions don't last long: when it's in spate The Burn cheerfully rearranges them all to please itself. My guide gives a hollow laugh at the very mention of 'stream-side' gardening, yet there it was – a pure white, double primrose flowering insouciantly at the water's edge, for all this were a water-rocks-and-rhododendron confection at the Chelsea Flower Show. But since Geoffrey Dutton would never have placed it in such a vulnerable situation himself, it must have been hurled there in a storm, and placed itself.

It is hard to imagine the awfulness of an Eastern Highlands winter on a fine spring morning, and I half wish I'd come in January: The Waterfall might be frozen and I'd be in for a treat because, when it is, out come the crampons and the ice-axe and up its hundred-foot drop the professor hauls himself, for fun. Or used to: these days (he will be eighty-three this year) he has trouble with his back, although you'd never guess, and he does call it 'convenient' back trouble which he calls into play when he wants Elizabeth, his wife, to give him a hand: 'She says she's the labourer. She's very good at that. She's got artificial hips.' Joking aside, I imagine his days of dangling off the end of a rope to plant Chinese rhododendrons on the slopes of a gorge that can hold its own for drama with any in Bhutan are probably over, but then again . . .

The garden has never been open to the public (other than by appointment to specialist groups) for the same reason g.f. dutton does not write verse expressly to be spoken at rallies or readings: 'Because my whole life has been an exploration. If you just give people what they want to hear (or in the case of gardens, see) you haven't progressed at all, although your pocket is probably heavier.' Apsley Cherry-Garrard described exploration as the physical expression of the intellectual passion. Given the rigour of the professor's own intellectual passion, and the demands made on his visitors by its physical expression, I imagine if the public were allowed access it would result in rather a lot of them tumbling headlong into the gorge off the Himalayan-style suspension bridge he built himself to span it, or off one of the precipitous paths leading to the garden's apotheosis, and then Health and Safety would get involved, and all further exploration would be curtailed.

Owing to the hire car company's tiresome inflexibility, I realise I am going to have to leave before we've completed the tour, and that there's only time to snatch a bite of the feast Elizabeth has prepared. As I pack myself back into the car, I mention my anxiety about how much of our conversation I feel certain must have been lost in the ether but the professor has the answer: 'Make it up,' he advises, and so the day ends rather as it had begun with me in a panic and he at his most laconic.

On the long drive back to Edinburgh there is time to reflect, and I conclude that if the experience of walking such a demanding garden with such a challenging companion over a four-hour period without sustenance has left me physically depleted, it has equally left me mentally charged-up. I even know how I want to end the story: I must give my erstwhile companion the last word I did not always allow him in our encounter and quote his own sardonic yet moving assessment of his life's work, as expressed in the penultimate paragraph of *Harvesting The Edge*:

'This garden will, I think, "ruin well". Unlike the monumental tyrannies of the hapless Speer, it was not consciously so designed; but the site, that has seen so much, will see to that. Left ten years, a century – 'undeveloped' of course if that be possible – a succeeding owner could guide it back to much the same garden as it is now, from what would still be the same soil, exposure and topography and pretty much the same wild vegetation. In which case a fine opportunity exists, for translation: of this garden as poem, made over into someone else's personal language. A pity I shall miss it.'

Owing to failing health, the Professor and his wife have had to leave their home on the edge of the wilderness. The garden's future remains in doubt.

# Lady Salisbury

## STATELY HOME GARDENER

Hatfield . . . the name evokes two opposing ideas: the perfectly ordinary little suburban railway station that was the scene of such a tragic accident a few years ago directly faces the fabulous splendour of the gold and black gates guarding the entrance to the historic property across the road, and from the station car park you can just glimpse the chimney pots of the great house silhouetted against the sky above the screening trees. As I stood there looking up, the chimneys transformed themselves in my imagination into the battlements of a fortress castle in the Carpathians; the suburban houses clinging hugger-mugger to the side of the hill (now a mountain) became primeval forest, and the railway tracks a river up which I had floated on a barge.

It was a beautifully cold, crisp, clear, bright day in late February – which was fortunate because I was at Hatfield to interview the Marchioness of Salisbury about her lifelong love affair with gardening, and the weather had been dire for weeks. I had asked if I could arrive early (the garden is closed to visitors in the winter months) and spend an hour walking round outside before the actual interview to refresh my memory from my only other visit some years ago with the European Boxwood and Topiary Society. An hour to appreciate what Lady Salisbury has been doing to Hatfield's forty-two acres over the past thirty years without a guide might seem ambitious, but I had assumed she would be too busy to accompany me, and that all I could do was my best.

I discover that having too much to do is no deterrent, however, and no sooner have I arrived at the front door than we are setting off on a tour of the garden that, with a break for lunch, takes over four hours, and even then we have to hurry. I decide to abandon my ever-so-carefully prepared list of written questions, allow myself to enjoy this rare opportunity, and trust that Lady Salisbury's story will unfold naturally as the day goes on.

For example, since we begin by looking at a new, as yet unfinished garden on the South Front it reminds me to ask whether Lady Salisbury works her designs out on a computer, or at least graph paper. She doesn't: 'No, I don't really draw anything. The Head Gardener and I walk about and mock it up a bit. I think I did a very rough sketch [in this instance] and we measured it out to see how it would fit in, and imagined how it might look.' Nor has there ever been a master plan: 'We do things bit by bit, as and when. It is always a question of time and priorities.' Only recently she found herself leafing through some gardening notes for 1977 headed 'Things to be Done Immediately', of which at least half remain pending.

It is a much-lamented fact that the original plans of the garden designed in the early years of the seventeenth century by Salomon de Caux for Robert Cecil have all been lost, but I imagine this lack of evidence in the archives allows Lady Salisbury greater creative freedom. She agrees while at the same time admitting she does long to know exactly how the garden would have looked: 'Even if I can't pretend to recreate what they had, my aim is to try to create something that is in harmony with the house because there it is, this great Jacobean palace that is really very unchanged, and it seemed to me the garden was so grossly out of harmony with the house it didn't seem to go with it at all. I suppose you might say it had been very Victorianised. My father-in-law, who was a very good gardener and had a wonderful eye for what would really look good with this house, had put down some York paving but there was still this *sea*, this complete *sea* of orange gravel everywhere and it still looked like a very Victorian layout laid on top of what had been an elaborate early seventeenth-century formal garden. I think if one can just get a feeling that it's happy, that the garden doesn't jar you. One doesn't know if one has managed to do that at all. One just has to creep along and feel one's way. I'm always putting things in and then pulling them out.'

Mindlessly, I mutter the cliché about artists having to allow themselves to make mistakes, but my guide points out reasonably that where a creative project the size of Hatfield is concerned you don't want to make too many mistakes: 'As well as the expense, it means another two or three years before one can complete what one's hoping to do.' At Cranborne Manor, the other ancestral family seat in Dorset where, as Lady Cranborne, she lived and gardened and raised six children from the time of her marriage in 1945 until the move to Hatfield in 1972, she reckons her task was made easier by the mellow beauty of the house itself, and the quality of the garden's existing (masonry) bones. Maybe so, but the *couturier* who drapes his frocks to best effect over the elegant skeleton of a lovely model has still to dream up his confections in the first place.

At Hatfield, where most of the bones are broken, and in the absence of any plans to consult (although a contemporary written account of the garden by a Frenchman does exist) her formidable task has been to reconstruct an actual skeleton, and the predominantly evergreen Boboli Gardens in Florence have been one of the inspirations behind some of her work. In the gin-clear light that morning, and without the distraction of any summer-flowering perennials to beguile us, her achievement can really be appreciated, with the topiarised specimens of yew, ilex, box, holly, hornbeam and beech showing to perfection against the fresh spring green of the grass that has replaced the offending gravel. Even most of the paths are laid to grass, emphasising the fact that Hatfield is a privately owned garden gardened by someone not prepared to compromise for the sake of practical expediency. Nevertheless, from time to time we have to negotiate roped-off Work in Progress areas, because 'if they [the public] fall down, well . . . We have to be *terribly* careful, and very often adapt things. We know all the rules!'

With so much evergreen plant material dominating the winter scene, something is needed to balance the composition, and *momento mori* come in the shape of herbaceous seed heads left hanging around in the borders like bird-friendly scarecrows, if that is not an oxymoron too far. Conversely, as harbingers of spring, no sight is more touching this morning than clusters of the exquisite little *Iris danfordii* bravely flowering in the dry gravel at the foot of each powerful, thrusting trunk in the famous *Quercus ilex* avenue.

Lady Salisbury keeps her own set of gardening tools in one of a pair of recently restored pavilions nearby, and seeing them hanging on the wall sets up a yearning: 'One feels a longing to get one's fork into the soil, but one can't until one's carted all the dead things off,' she sighs, reminding me of the German/Australian writer, Elizabeth von Arnim, who, as a young woman in 1903 had written (only twenty years before Lady Salisbury was born) about the lengths she had felt obliged to resort to to get her hands on a spade:

> In the first ecstasy of having a garden all my own, and in my burning impatience to make the waste place blossom like a rose, I did one warm Sunday in last year's April during the servants' dinner hour . . . slink out with a spade and a rake and feverishly dig a little piece of ground and break it up and sow surreptitious ipomoea and run back very hot and guilty into the house and get into a chair and behind a book and look languid just in time to save my reputation.

Elizabeth von Arnim would have cause to envy Lady Salisbury: while we are examining her collection of alpine plants in their specially-prepared raised beds, she talks about her lifelong love of these precious little plants and how she has been growing them since childhood: 'My sisters and I had our own little gardens and we used to study catalogues for hours (aged ten!). We used to collect alpines. I was always passionate about wild flowers ever since I was a small child – belonged to the Wild Flower Society, spent much time out looking for wild flowers, and painting them.' Unfortunately, the Second World War put the kibosh on her plans to study botany; if she had, she believes there would be less need for the forest of labels in her alpine beds that make them look 'like Flanders' war graves'. 'It's hopeless,' she despairs, 'I can't remember anything now. I'm completely untrained, untutored. I would love to have studied, and then I would very much like to have gone to Kew. I would like to have been able to do that, but the War made that totally impossible, and I married immediately afterwards.'

Lady Salisbury is Vice-President of The Royal Horticultural Society, Vice-President of the Garden History Society, President of the Museum of Garden History, was a trustee of the Chelsea Physic Garden for twenty-five years, and is a professional garden designer currently working on projects for clients in Ireland, England, Italy and the United States. Her role as Prince Charles' mentor, and the practical help and wise counsel she gave him in the creation of his own garden at Highgrove is well documented, and we barely touch on the subject, except *en passant* when contemplating an experimental black and white planting scheme in the South Front terrace borders, because something similar is being tried at Highgrove, but this she says is pure chance – or the *zeitgeist*.

I am curious to know if Lady Salisbury finds it hard to turn things down sometimes but if she does she is unrepentant: 'My husband says I don't say no enough, but, if there is a real interest, and a feeling that something ought to be supported and if there's anything one can do obviously there is a temptation to say yes. But you have to temper things a bit with what there is to be done here, because this is really quite a business now, being open to the public, and we hold a lot of events here. We have wonderful people to organise it all, but one has to be involved, and one *is* involved – helping to arrange it, and with ideas, and so on. I've always been someone who worked with her hands and did things herself. I suppose in a way it comes from very early training, and all that work I did in the War in military hospitals. I think there are two classes of people: some can delegate and some can't. It is in your nature perhaps. People say [in connection with her design business] "Why don't you get an assistant?" But I decided an assistant would be far more work. I'd have to tell them what I wanted them to do in the various gardens. Some people are quite happy to sit in a chair and tell someone else to go and do it for them, but I'd far rather go out and do it myself.' Again, Elizabeth von Arnim's frustration in this respect comes to mind:

If I could only dig myself! How much easier, besides being so fascinating, to make your own holes exactly where you want them and put in your plants exactly as you choose instead of giving orders that can only be half understood from the moment you depart from the lines laid down by that long piece of string.

Perhaps a compulsion to dig is what defines the true-born gardener?

Insofar as the planting at Hatfield is concerned, Lady Salisbury only bows to historical correctness in the Knot Garden situated in front of the Old Palace, and then simply because plants introduced to England in or before the early seventeenth century look so absolutely right there. For the same reason, she has also planted up the surrounding grass banks with contemporary flora – white muscari, *Fritillaria meleagris*, primroses and cowslips, *inter alia* – although, she admits 'they may not have had them in the grass, but they might well have done, particularly the white muscari. You don't hear about the blue. They may have had it but it's the white one that's recorded. I love the white one; it goes so well with the primroses. Sadly, the fritillary doesn't do awfully well on the bank because it likes damp, and I'm afraid the banks drain too well in summer.'

Going back to the work on the South Front parterre: it is a good example of how Lady Salisbury brings all her talents – her plantsmanship, her design sense and her gift for intelligent guesswork in the absence of any hard historical evidence – to bear on her projects. First, she decided to excavate the existing terrace down to the level of the park, because that is where she deduced the original garden, or court, would have been. She was right: they hit the old topsoil 6 feet down. In due course, a raised walk will be established round the perimeter of the sunken parterre, and the box at each centre will be clipped into, variously, a stylised *fleur de lys*, a shamrock, the Tudor rose, and oak leaves: 'Because,' she explains, 'we have a house in France, and because I'm half Irish and spent a lot of my childhood in Ireland; the Tudor rose for obvious reasons; the oak leaves because Hatfield is so redolent of oaks, and I'm building up a collection of them.'

We move on from there to consider another new enterprise, a half-planted avenue of hornbeam (*Carpinus betulus* 'Columnaris') which will eventually lead the eye to an ornamental seat at its end, and guide people's feet into the Wilderness Garden, the idea being to try to persuade visitors to stay on a path: 'Otherwise you get wander paths completely worn all over the place. We'll keep it grass, though.' Then on to the *latest* latest project, and another example of Lady Salisbury's willingness (or deep need) to make whatever changes to the *status quo* she feels necessary to get the garden to feel just right: 'Here,' she explains, 'I want a very gentle transition from the formal [Scented] garden, and I thought billowing cloud-clipped box would lead more naturally into the Wilderness, which is all just ornamental and forest trees.' We pass some tall specimens of box destined to become an equally billowing arch, one day. 'But by that time I'll probably be dead,' she observes unperturbed, 'You plant for future generations and *hope* they won't rip everything out, yet they very likely will.'

The appallingly wet winter has put this particular project (which involves dividing a wide border in half and laying a York stone path through the middle) on hold for months. It is a sorry picture, only cheered up by the sight of dozens of heeled-in hellebores gallantly flowering their heads off in their temporary accommodation: 'They are wonderful! Irresistible! I like the single ones best, but there's something enchanting about those double smoky ones. Hellebores and snowdrops seem to be the fashion flowers of the moment.'

'Now,' she warns as we approach the Holly Walk, 'I'll bring you to a ghastly sight.' She's right: the ground looks like a ploughed field the hunt has just ridden over, again partly due to the weather, but also to Lady Salisbury's search for the perfect solution. I wondered what had induced her to make such drastic changes to an area that had looked to my eyes quite mature and wonderfully dramatic when I saw it last, but she has her reasons: 'Have you ever seen the Borromini Arcade in the Strada Palace in Rome? I thought it would be such fun to do the same here. Sadly the columns [of clipped holly] were almost there, but by the time we'd done this very accurate levelling of the ground and got the widths between the columns exactly right we knew we had to cut them down and start again. Originally this area was black asphalt put down by my great-grandfather-in-law, Prime Minister Salisbury, who never could get any exercise and he weighed eighteen stone. He had a tricycle and he made little paths all over the park with asphalt and he had a boy who rode on the back of his tricycle with his hands on his shoulders and he'd jump off to open the gates. It was *so* ugly by the time I got here: decayed black asphalt full of weeds and cracks and holes, but my husband viewed it with great sentiment because he and his brothers used to have such fun roller-skating on it. It took me quite a long time to persuade him to get rid of it.

Having rather charged through the Scented Garden (her first project when the family moved into Hatfield but no longer up to muster so also in a state of flux) there is just time to nod at the West Parterre and cast an eye over the Knot Garden before dashing back through the 250-year-old Lime Walk to lunch at a table in a window of the house looking out over the East Front garden. For a while, a mallard drake strolling nonchalantly across the terrace deflects our attention to wildlife but we soon find our way back, via Lady Salisbury's love of music and art, to her repeated lament for the lack of any kind of formal training, and a nagging sense that the war and getting married and raising six children was no excuse for this lack because, she points out 'You see so many people who married and had a family and have done lots of things and still managed to do Open University or learn a new language or some-thing.' Maybe so, but perhaps not, I suggest, while also running a house the size of Hatfield.

Somehow we get on to the subject of truffles and how she is experi-menting with growing truffle oaks at the family property in France, and from there to the fact that New Zealand has apparently done a lot of scientific research on truffle-growing. Since neither of us can throw much light on what New Zealand and France might have in common geologically, we set off on the second leg of our tour, beginning with a stroll through the East Front garden that was partially restored by Lady Salisbury's parents-in-law after the War. However, their decision to plant 'John Downie' crab apples at the centre of each box-edged bed was not a success, so Lady Salisbury has replaced them all with yew topiary surrounded by the style of relaxed perennial planting she favours, now in its 'friendly scarecrow' guise. We are heading for the Wild – or Woodland – Garden, and on the way pass down an avenue of fruit trees (all rare varieties brought over from France for Robert Cecil by John Tradescant) planted alongside the faintly sinister maze, and under an arch in a tapestry hedge designed to mark the transition from formal to wild. Once upon a time, the Wild Garden was a typically muscular Victorian Gothic affair – mostly bare earth and holly and yew trees. Today, it is simply planted with wild roses and laid to grass around the so-called New Pond – actually the size of a small lake, and there in Robert Cecil's time. The Woodland Garden itself lies beyond the lake and was only transformed into a garden after the detritus of almost a hundred trees brought down in the storms of 1987 and 1990 had been cleared away. Now, a wide mown path meanders through the long grass under the oaks where hundreds of thousands of snowdrops have been planted, along with a few species tulips for a splash of colour later on, and a very restrained selection of flowering woodland shrubs – *Ribes sanguineum* 'White Icicle', *Cornus mas*, *Daphne bholua* 'Jaqueline Postill' and *D. laureola* – as the under-storey planting.

Nearer to the house, the little species daffodil *Narcissus pseudonarcissus*, along with *Cyclamen coum*, and *C. hederifolium*, have naturalised under the beeches and hornbeams and the exquisite simplicity of these areas reminds me to ask what had convinced Lady Salisbury to garden entirely organically years before Rachel Carson wrote *The Silent Spring*, or the Henry Doubleday Foundation even existed. 'Well, you see, having a very young family, it didn't seem to me very sensible to let your babies crawl about on this lawn covered in Verdone which blows up the dandelions, and kills the birds and the insects so probably wasn't doing one's children much good. Equally, DDT, which everybody was spraying everywhere, even on their vegetables and fruit, and all those awful pesticides, I thought probably it was better to keep to the natural things, and from that moment we went entirely organic. I was written off as a total crank, of course. All my friends said: Why don't you use this *wonderful* DDT and this *wonderful* Verdone? But it just seems to me to be common sense, more than anything. I joined the Doubleday very early, in the 1950s; I was one of the founder members. Someone gave me Rachel Carson's book when it came out [in the 1960s], and it just confirmed everything I'd been thinking.'

So it was appropriate that our last stop should be the kitchen garden. Here, nematodes, acid soap and whitefly traps are brought into service against any pests in the greenhouses otherwise, I learn, it is simply a question of mulch, mulch, mulch and dress, dress, dress. But what about caterpillars on the cabbages? 'You don't, she explains patiently, 'necessarily have fewer pests when you are organic, but you don't kill the beneficent insects. You have a different attitude. You are more tolerant.' Which leads to her despairing observation that these days people seem to seek perfection in everything: 'Perfect babies, even!'

Whatever ground we have not managed to cover – physically or metaphorically – will have to remain untrodden: it is time to vacate Paradise, and as the great gates close behind me so a train draws into the station and within twenty minutes I am back at King's Cross preparing to descend into the hell of the Northern Line at rush hour.

Following her husband's death, Lady Salisbury has become the Dowager Marchioness of Salisbury, and no longer lives at Hatfield. There have been some changes to the garden since she left, the most significant being that it is no longer managed according to organic principles, and the famous Hatfield Snowdrop Weekends have been abolished.

# Elizabeth Jane Howard

## NOVELIST

I live in a beautiful place with a meadow and an island on the river that runs beside it, which I have turned into a kind of nature reserve. There has been room to plant many trees and bushes, to naturalize wild flowers, snowdrops, bluebells, primroses, cowslips, anemones and Fritillaria meleagris. The island has a pond on it, and is now the home of reed warblers, owls, hedgehogs, a grass snake, herons, mice of many kinds, rabbits, frogs and newts and sometimes even an otter. I am trying to get hellebore, many kinds of ferns and trillium to flourish. Roses have ramped up the very old apple trees on the island, and last year a pair of swans built a shaky mansion for their eggs. I grow witch hazel, spindle, camellia, lilac and all kinds of buddleia for butterflies, and having used no pesticide for thirteen years has paid off. There is food for everyone. The seasons – at least three of them – give me acute pleasure: the changing light, the bony winter trees starting to leaf, and the wild plum with its fat green-white beads that open to little fragile white stars. Every day when I walk round something new has happened and this goes on for months – goes on, of course, for ever.

*Slipstream: A Memoir* (2002)

T he writer decided to leave London for the countryside in 1990, because she couldn't find a house with a decent-sized garden in north London that she could afford. She was sixty-seven years old, she was alone, and she would be leaving behind a network of friends in the city where she had been born and always lived. Nor did she choose somewhere in easy reach of her old haunts or even somewhere familiar, such as Sussex, where the young Jane Howard and her extended family used to spend their holidays in the 1930s and 1940s. Instead, she chose the little town of Bungay perched on the south bank of the River Waveney – the river that marks the boundary between Suffolk and Norfolk, and the river in which her island is set. Diss is the nearest town with a rail service to London, but Diss lies sixteen miles away to the west. People don't commute from Bungay

I had gathered most of these facts from reading Jane Howard's memoir, along with that captivating account quoted above of the wildlife garden on her island. I longed to hear more about her life as a country-woman because I sometimes dream of becoming one myself, am also single, and also on the cusp of old age. But there is a difference: I don't dare, which is why I particularly wanted to meet the woman, now in her eighties, who could write:

> One of the good things about living longer is that we have more time to learn how to be old. It's clear to me now that inside the conspiracy of silence about age – because of the negative aspects of the condition – there is the possibility of art: that is to say that it can be made into something worth trying to do well, a challenge, an adventure. I don't want to live with any sort of retirement, with nostalgia and regret wrapped round me like a wet blanket, I want to live enquiringly, with curiosity and interest for the rest of my life.

I wrote asking if we might meet and was rewarded with an invitation to lunch on such and such a day in September. I wrote again to ask if I might turn up in the morning, as these interviews take time. With very good grace she agreed, choosing not to mention that this would mean sacrificing a day's work on her novel, but warning me not to dare to pitch up before 10:30am. In the event, I get to Bungay before nine and go in search of a suitable spot to settle myself in, but with no Starbucks and the hotel in shutters, I seem to be out of luck. I eye the church. Bound to be locked. It isn't. Bungay, I decide, might be a very nice place indeed to move to. A brief tour reveals old red-brick alleys leading to Flemish-style cobbled courtyards strewn with the rusting, unidentifiable detritus of country life over the centuries you'd pay a fortune for in the Portobello Market, and the landscape visible across the river on the Norfolk bank, complete with pollarded willows and cows grazing the water-meadows, would have delighted Cuyp.

On the dot of 10:30 I find myself in front of a long, low, double-fronted, stucco-faced early-eighteenth-century townhouse with clipped box specimens lining the short path to the front door. A tall, white-haired, woman with penetrating dark eyes greets me with an appraising glance but few words, and proceeds to lead me through the low-ceilinged entrance hall, past an open fireplace and a couple of massive sofas, into a kitchen displaying all the signs (wooden draining board, butler's sink, gas cooker – NB: no Aga – and some dangerously sharp-looking knives arranged according to size on a magnet near the chopping board) of belonging to a real cook. Which is the case: Jane Howard wrote a cookbook in the late 1980s with her friend Fay Maschler. Straight through we go, and out into the conservatory where her gardening anthology entitled *Green Shades* is lying on the dining table for my attention. Red and pink zonal pelargoniums in terra cotta pots are massed on the windowsills; cymbidium orchids not yet back in flower are resting in shady corners; pots of basil and cherry tomatoes sit on the terrace in front of a ramshackle greenhouse.

We clear a space for ourselves at the table and I accept with gratitude the coffee on offer while, in the husky tones of the lifelong smoker, Jane tells me as she rolls herself a cigarette how she has to rest in the afternoons these days because 'pain eats your energy like anything', pointing out the wry irony of her situation: 'Unfortunately, when I began to have the time for [gardening] I didn't have the physique, which is bad luck really.' Her good friend Penelope Lively also had to give up gardening, and for the same reason – chronic arthritis: 'She can't bend, poor dear; I can't kneel, and she can't bend.'

Jane couldn't possibly have anticipated the chronic pain, but in all other respects she planned for her new life with great care, choosing Bungay because her old friend, the painter Sargy Mann, already lived there – right next door, on hand to help her through the difficult early weeks when the shock of moving made her ill, 'like an old shrub transplanted' – and the house itself for its size: 'I think people often make the mistake of having too small a house, so they can't have people to stay. I think you have to have a nucleus of friends who will come and stay with you. My work is very solitary, and I suppose one likes to have friends. But I really prefer the country, and I think I have most of my life.' When I mention my own occasional yearning, her advice is wise: 'Think very carefully beforehand what you'd want to import, as it were, in terms of people. I've only got one lot to come and live here.' Which is not to say that she hasn't made new friends locally, but rather that her old friends are important so she cossets them to make sure they will want to come down often. Perhaps there's a paradox here: the more you like company, the more enjoyable life in the country can be, if you are prepared to make the effort – or should that read *because* you are prepared to make the effort?

Four and a half acres is a lot of garden at the best of times, and now that Jane can't do much herself she needs more help, more than she feels she can afford. In her memoir I noticed that money, or rather its lack, gets more than a passing mention. I wonder, if she hadn't been obliged to earn her living would she have still wanted to be a writer? She would: 'It's hard and lonely and depressing and difficult but you just feel worse if you don't – you feel guilty if you are doing anything else, really – so that's why I write. Writing comes before gardening for me – just – but gardening is much more beguiling.'

As are bulb catalogues: meticulously labelled trays and dishes and baskets of spring bulbs were assembled on the sitting room floor – about a thousand, she reckoned. Once, there would have been double that amount waiting to be planted but as nowadays somebody else has to plant them for her she restricts herself, or tries to. The 'somebody else' is her linchpin, David Evans: 'He takes care of the island and the meadow. He's a very good naturalist and he's good at managing land. He does what's important but there's a [financial] ceiling beyond which I can't go, and he knows that. He doesn't just work for me. He does have other jobs.

*Elizabeth Jane Howard*

It is a lovely day, warm and still, and we set off for our walk through the formal part of the garden, which is enclosed on either side by high brick walls and measures roughly 35 × 70 feet – about what Jane had been hoping to find in London – and, incidentally, all she believed she was offering for when she put in her bid for the property. We don't linger: our goal is the island at the other end of the meadow that has just been cut, and through which we stroll more slowly, stopping to pat the trees she most values in her collection. They appear to have one thing in common: they are all above-averagely slow to fruit or flower or even grow much. According to Jane, this is to state the obvious: 'The least interesting trees grow very fast, and the most interesting ones don't grow very fast. You just have to wait for them.' She reads my mind: 'Well, you never plant trees just for yourself. You are lucky if you get something out of them. You have to balance it. You can grow things that are quicker to enjoy, but the ones that matter to me are the slow ones, usually.'

A fifteen-year-old mulberry growing in a small orchard at the entrance to the meadow has taken off, and its oozing fruit yields satisfyingly to the touch, while the walnut has managed to produce four nuts, and is duly praised: 'I'm rather proud of him. He's trying extremely hard. Only one last year – his first.' The *Davidia involucrata* standing apart at the centre of the meadow has finally flowered, but the gingko hasn't made much progress, and she has another five years to wait before her fifteen year old *Liriodendron tulipifera* can be expected to flower. Then there were the oaks, some in the meadow, more on the island: Jane inherited a special affection for the species from her paternal grandfather, who in his lifetime planted thirty thousand or so at his home in Sussex, and has planted a number herself – red oaks, holm oaks, Turkey oaks, English oaks. We stop to pay homage to a cut-leafed beech, not yet as tall as a man. It will be the third she's planted in her lifetime.

On the sunny banks of the river on the north side of the meadow, and along the old town drain on the other, Jane has established the instinctive plantsman's eclectic mix of flora: for example, a tree peony banished from the garden proper because it was sold to her as scented, but isn't; a handsome specimen of the oak-leafed hydrangea; a solitary cardoon; a number of winter-flowerering shrubs including the red-flowered variety of hamamelis and wintersweet (*Chimonanthus praecox*); hundreds of rose bushes, now smothered in hips. Bulbs, of course, thousands upon thousands. And camellias. Jane loves camellias: 'I've left camellias wherever I've been.' Unfortunately, here in Suffolk they don't flourish, though not from want of attention. We pass one sad specimen – and many more on the island – that had had the rank grass carefully pulled away from around its roots, and been fed large dollops of compost: 'We've done everything we can for her,' she laments. 'I must stop. I'm not going to plant any more.'

We come across a huddle of beehives belonging to a neighbour who rents the space: 'Hello, bees!' she calls out. I must have looked as astonished as I was feeling. 'You should talk to them,' she explains, 'and you shouldn't get in their flight path when they are on their way to work.' Which sounds only sensible, but I am finding it difficult sometimes to reconcile this incarnation of Jane Howard with the sophisticated beauty invoked in her memoir who had half the cultural elite of London and Paris at her feet in the 1940s and 1950s, and who was later famously married for eighteen years to the incorrigibly metropolitan Kingsley Amis. But people are complex, a fact of which I am sharply reminded when in a momentary lapse I ask Jane if she likes men, and receive a salutary rap: 'I don't think generalisations are worth hunting for,' but then softens the blow by owning up to unconditional love for all cats. I remind myself that she was married to the naturalist Peter Scott when she was only nineteen: if she had remained married, she would then have lived out most of her life very differently, not in London and Paris but at the Slimbridge Wildfowl Trust on the Severn Estuary.

We cross onto the island by way of a low wooden bridge almost hidden in the long grass. Climbing roses suspended from the trees hang down over the water while ducks paddle beneath looking innocent, but I am told these ducks are yobbish creatures who snap the heads off the fritillaries growing in the meadow for fun and nibble away at the edge of the island, causing it to erode and Jane to worry; another major expense is on the cards if the river conservancy people won't be responsible for stabilising the banks. We follow a mown grass path around the perimeter of the island. On one side, the fast-flowing water glinting in the sunshine is always within view; on the other, dense undergrowth where willow herb and agrimony and meadowsweet, nettles and rank grasses flourish. The deliberate introductions – for example a wild crab planted because its fruit make the best jelly – have to be pointed out because of course you couldn't guess. Many of the island's self-sewn trees – the alders, willows, and wild apples – have had honeysuckle, clematis, and/or roses planted at their feet. Some still have their labels attached. A guelder rose leans out over the river, its clusters of lustrous red berries translucent in the sunlight. They remind my guide of Edwardian ladies' hats. The common names of plants come easily to her mind, so no longer being able to remember their Latin equivalent is not a bother, but we shared a senior moment over one of the few plants – *Ceratostigma willmottianum* – I felt didn't quite fit with the ethos behind the island planting. In the end, I managed to nail its first name, Jane its second. But I was wrong about the shrub's incongruity: according to Graham Stuart Thomas, its cobalt blue flowers are as attractive to hummingbird hawk moths as they are to gardeners.

I imagine it must be tempting to plant and plant, and go on planting. It is. 'One does these things in a frenzy of enthusiasm. All gardeners over-plant, and change their minds. We are only in the early stages, but I must think about not making it labour-intensive. I don't want it to be a garden. I want it to be an island with lovely things on it.' Such as ferns. Ferns have been planted in little clearings and under shrubs all over the island. Testimony to the fact that every introduction to the island is accounted for and watched over is the sight of Jane all of a sudden, and for no reason I could see, struggling painfully to get down low enough to rescue what turned out to be a colony of candleabra primulas being strangled by the indigenous undergrowth. Giant hogweed, teasels, hollyhocks and *Acanthus mollis* are used as exclamation marks, and lichen-spotted branches and logs in what could be artless piles – though I doubt it – are strategically placed along the route for impact. They remind me of the nature-sculptures Andy Goldsworthy creates out of whatever he finds lying about in the forest.

Best of all, perhaps, the massive corpse of a fallen willow, sheathed in ivy, and festooned with clematis and climbing roses, has been propped up to form a bridge across the path. Ivy grows up anything it can. Apparently, bees love ivy nectar; nor is it harmful to trees, according to Jane – or rather, according to Sir Humphry Repton who once delivered a paper to the Linnaean Society on the subject. In her anthology, she writes: 'He argued what has frequently been proved since but done little to correct the prejudices of foresters and gardeners, that far from hurting trees ivy is helpful to them by keeping them warm during severe weather.'

We touch on the problem of how to deal with pests, and the rampant nettles. The answer lies in letting nature deal with them. To this end, she's built a house for bats, which feed on mosquito larvae, and feeds the birds, which feed on the slugs and aphids. Roundup is banned, and over time the ecology has balanced itself: 'It takes about five years, but eventually it does. It's really quite unnecessary to keep spraying things, and it means there's food for everybody.' In any case, they all serve a perfectly good purpose: 'People always think of creatures in relation to themselves, not in relation to each other. I mean wasps are very, very useful.' Spiders, she reckons, are the equal of Indian vultures in their relative capacity to devour what would make us all jolly ill if it were left lying around to decompose.

The circuit complete, we cross back over the bridge and walk along the riverbank to the house for lunch. Lunch over, we say our farewells in Jane's study where a little lift has been installed, and her last words before it whisks her up to her bedroom are to tell me I can snoop around as much as I want before I leave. I spot some embroidery on the sofa by the fire being worked in exquisite *petit point* and idly turn it over. The reverse is predictably hardly less exquisite, but what I really want to be doing is to get back to the island, and once there to ponder a passage that had struck me when reading her memoir. In it, she recalls being about eight years old, and how impressed she had been at the time by her perceived wealth of experience, and decides to update her childish list: '. . . I would say, "You've written twelve novels and as much again in other forms, you've travelled to seventeen countries, and you've planted nearly a thousand trees."' But her final judgment on herself is horribly harsh, and all too painfully reminds me of old school reports. 'I am,' she writes, 'less impressed, because I know I could have done much better and more.'

In fact, Jane's life's work is still very much in progress: her tally of novels written continues to rise, and all remain in print – a considerable achievement in itself, I understand from my bookseller. As well, most have been, or are in process of being, turned into television plays; the number of trees planted also continues on an upward curve. Only the number of countries visited is not increasing, but that must count as a virtue if the natural world Jane Howard does her best to cherish is to survive our tread. Dostoyevsky wondered whether perhaps 'the only purpose which mankind aspires to in this world is the perpetual process of achievement, in other words – not any specific goal, but life itself.' I ponder all this as I walk as lightly as I can around her enchanted island, imagining myself a monk – a pagan monk, I suppose – pacing this natural cloister round and round, for ever.

# Penelope Lively

## WRITER

P enelope Lively was perfectly willing to be interviewed about her gardening life, but felt she should warn me that she is now an ex-gardener: the onset of severe arthritis in her spine eight or nine years ago precluded any further activity in the garden, and in 1998 she decided to sell the family home in North Oxfordshire following the death of her husband, the academic and political theorist Jack Lively. These days she lives exclusively in London, and although the house has a small garden she is obliged to employ outside help to maintain it. So much upheaval and loss so matter-of-factly recounted made the final paragraph of her letter all the more poignant: 'I often think that if I hadn't ended up writing I should like to have been a proper gardener, instead of a spasmodic and dilettante one. But gardens and gardening have always been an abiding interest, in every sense'.

And in the process of researching my subject, I spotted an article by the writer expressing just such a yearning: 'In another incarnation, I should like to be one of the Great Gardeners – A Gertrude Jekyll who leaves her mark on the nation's gardening habits for a generation.' Which is why, in spite of her expressed fear that I might feel 'short-changed' by our encounter, I arrive at her terraced house in one of Islington's prettiest garden squares, on a murky November afternoon, full of high hopes and expectations – expectations that are given a further boost as I make my way upstairs to the drawing room and catch a glimpse through the landing window of a shrub with a distinctly metallic sheen to its multiple branchlets so that it is literally aglitter in the dank semi-darkness of the small paved garden at the back of the house. Mrs Lively identifies it for me as *Corokia contoneaster* – the wire-netting bush – a present from her daughter Josephine, about whom I would be hearing a great deal in the next couple of hours. Otherwise, the planting was largely of the handsome evergreen, architectural foliage type, with a couple of rampant climbers for the walls, such as you would expect to see in a small city garden – apart, that is from a vagabond clump of the pretty little daisy, *Erigeron karvingskianus*, that has managed to insinuate itself into a crack in the pavement right on the writer's front doorstep. Its serendipitous arrival is, as it happens, a wry reminder of her old gardening life because it is a plant – a Jekyll favourite incidentally – she never could persuade to settle in her Oxfordshire garden: 'I used to take little roots from Somerset and put them in places I thought they would do, but they died within a fortnight. I think one thing you do have to learn is not to fly in the face of nature.'

Mrs Lively had suggested in her letter that I read the two memoirs of her childhood, because gardens feature in both – which is how I learned that Somerset is where her maternal grandmother lived and gardened for the greater part of her life, where Penelope Lively also lived during the second half of her childhood following her parents divorce in 1945, and that the family still retains a 'toehold' in the district in the form of her daughter's cottage a few hundred yards down the lane from the old house. In the preface to *A House Unlocked*, which deals with this period of her life, she writes: 'It has always seemed to me that one effective way of writing fiction is to take the immediate and particular and to give it a universal resonance – to so manipulate and expand personal experience that it becomes relevant to others. This book is an attempt to do the same thing not with a human life but with the span of one family's occupation of a house.' And its garden: using as her springboard some specific plants and stylistic effects deployed by her grandmother, she proceeds to launch herself into a concise history of English gardens and gardening leading up to and including the Edwardian era: 'The family's gardens reflect a hundred years of garden taste. My grandmother's first garden at St Albans had long walks with clipped hedges, island beds in which standard roses were underplanted with white alyssum, formal rose plantings and lawns. By the time she got to Golsoncott [the Somerset house], Robinson and Jekyll had stepped in: no more bedding out, with roses as the central feature of a paved and sunken garden brilliant with primroses and jonquils in spring; elsewhere there are informal Robinsonian walks, swathes of snowdrops and bluebells, a tumbling-stream garden with bull-rushes and yellow flag irises.'

In *Oleander, Jacaranda,* she focuses on recollections of the earlier part of her young life: Penelope Lively was born (and lived until the divorce when she was twelve) in Egypt, and she describes, *inter alia*, the garden of the family home outside Cairo, both from her own childish viewpoint, and as factually as she can with the help of old photographs. This garden too, despite its location, paid its dues to William Robinson 'by way of a wild and shady water garden with bamboos, papyri rushes, irises, arum lilies. But there were also geometrical arrangements of beds near to the house, with roses and seasonal plantings'. And daffodils. Daffodils in the desert! The other ex-pats were terrifically impressed. Both her mother in Egypt and grandmother in England employed a number of gardeners, indoor servants, and, of course, nannies, and neither pursued a career, because in those years before the Second World War women didn't – not if they were 'gentry' – so the writer hardly seems fair on herself when she compares her own horticultural efforts with theirs thus: 'By the time the addiction got to me, standards had slumped.'

Her novels too, as she suggests in that preface, make imaginative use of her own diverse experiences and interests: Egypt and the West Country, archaeology, the historical past, chronology and, of course, gardening. For example, *Moon Tiger*, which won the Booker prize in 1987, is set mainly in Cairo and the Western Desert during the Second World War; *According to Mark* is a novel about a young woman who owns and runs a garden centre in Dorset, and has a love affair with a writer down from London researching a biography of her grandfather; and *A Stitch in Time* (a children's story for which she won the Whitbread in 1976) describes the adventures of a bunch of children who spend their summer holiday fossil-hunting in the undercliff at Lyme Regis.

Her poignant letter and that article I'd chanced upon beg two big questions: could she tell me what it is about gardening as an activity that leads her to believe she would have enjoyed making it her life's work. And, I hesitate, searching for a way to ask her about the double loss of her husband and her garden, 'about not . . .' She helps me out: '. . . about not gardening now? Right,' she says, brisk and to the point. 'So, a two-pronged answer. First, why would I have liked to be a gardener? One, I think it is simply the activity itself. I loved getting my hands dirty. I liked all the operations that go with gardening. I would have liked to have the time – if I hadn't had another compelling occupation – to do it full-time like my grandmother did. It was really her main occupation. She was of the generation, and well enough off, to have help, yet every afternoon she worked hard herself for a good three hours or so, as all the proper English gardeners have always done.'

But we are soon blown off course, or rather I steer us off it because mention of her grandmother's avocation reminds me that in her letter Mrs. Lively said that she thought there must be a gene for gardening, and that this gene generally runs, at least in her own case, down the female side of the family – a family she describes as hailing from 'southern gentry' stock. A far cry, then, from the northern working classes that have always tended to breed largely male gardeners, wouldn't you say? 'I think you are quite right' she concedes: 'My husband had a whiff of it, yes certainly. His father had been a passionate gardener – a very typical working class gardener. He had his allotment and he had his little garden behind the council house in which everything – he would never have bought a plant – everything would have been acquired from friends, neighbours, a slip from so and so, a root from here, although he would have bought packets of seeds. My husband said he even made a lawn from little bits of grass that he pulled up from the roadside. Yes, gardening is very much a working-class men's thing. The allotments, and the extremely skillful growing of one particular species; I love the way you discover that the national collection of something is in somebody's back garden. There's a prime example of that: I think the national collection of auriculas is – or was – in a council house garden somewhere.'

Whoever or whatever is responsible, the Lively's daughter Josephine is herself a qualified gardener, having made time she didn't have (she is Professor of Oboe at Trinity College of Music, and has a family) to obtain two Royal Horticultural Society diplomas for the pure pleasure of acquiring knowledge. When Penelope Lively talks about her daugher's achievement she sounds at once proud and a little wistful: 'I think I would have liked that. Neither Jack nor I became knowledgeable in anything like the way my daughter is. We were distinct amateurs, we messed about, and I now wish that I had either done the sort of course that she did, or had put time aside and boned up more. I used to be much impressed by another Penelope in the book world – Penelope Mortimer – who lived not far from us, at Chastleton. She came to gardening very late, in her sixties when she bought this house with a *tabula rasa* of a garden. There was nothing much there at all and she really went into how to garden and taught herself the basics. I admired her very much. She became a distinct plantswoman, like my daughter.'

Acquiring a passion for gardening in one's sixties is leaving it rather late, but in fact neither of the Livelys, nor their daughter (despite her likely double dose of the putative gene), showed any interest in the subject when they were young, and Mrs Lively believes – as I do – that this is the norm: 'I think it comes absolutely with owning your own garden. Certainly that happened to Jack and myself. I don't remember having the faintest interest in gardening before we moved into our little semi in Swansea, and suddenly we found ourselves with this area of earth that was ours and then, obviously, a tendency we both already had came showering forth. After all, it doesn't happen to everybody does it? You've only got to look at the number of neglected gardens you see from trains . . .' I wasn't so sure about this last observation, not these days. It might be better for the planet if one did, I grumble. My point is endorsed. 'The rape of the landscape! Seashore pebbles being tipped all over people's gardens. They have a lot to answer for, frankly, these makeover gardeners. I think what I most dislike about it is that behind it all is the dark shadow of property values. It's been brought to people's attention that if you have a nice garden it sends the value of your property up, which allegedly it does.' A cynical perception that leads us, bird-lovers both, to lament the urban sparrow's decline, and from there to other garden-associated ecological matters such as the Lively family's refusal to resort to 'savage' chemicals, however tempted, but a resolution not easy to stick to in London: 'London is snail heaven. Paradise. After a nice rainfall in the summer the whole place is heaving with them so when I still could I used to pick them up, put them in a plastic bag, and suffocate them.' Which, as a way to die, is probably no worse than being pecked to pieces by a thrush.

Gardening, Penelope Lively believes, creates a powerful bond between couples. But equally, I counter, the garden can be a minefield for the married. Not in her own experience: 'So I've heard. I've read that it can be divisive, but the hours you spend discussing whether to plant one seed rather than another, or pouring over seed catalogues, or discussing what to do with that bed next year. Oh, we would sometimes disagree, yes. Jack did have slightly different tastes – he probably liked stronger colours than I did. We used to open the garden, and there was always a last minute crisis and Jack would go out and buy some sort of vibrant annual and push it in. I can still see those things that didn't fit in. But on the whole we liked the same sorts of gardens, only he was infinitely more interested than I was in the grass and the hedges.' I persist: 'But men are so competitive – massive marrows, dahlias the size of dinner-plates . . .'. 'Yes, they might be,' she acknowledges politely, and proceeds to expose my shameful generalisation by adding, 'but Jack certainly was never like that. He did do quite a lot of the veg, but I did most of it, rather oddly: the usual division of labour in a family is that the husband does the vegetables and the wife does the flowers, but in fact it was rather the other way round with us. No, the main difference as far as I am concerned is that men are obsessed with grass, what the lawn looks like, and the mowing, and women, frankly, don't give a hang. I never did. I liked it daisy-speckled.'

Another generalisation: gardeners never sit still in their own gardens, I moot, and in this instance get away with it, although she does describe a delightfully civilised ritual for being in the garden without working that she and her husband evolved: 'Every summer evening we would round the garden, drink in hand. I think there were seven different seats in the garden. Jack called them the Stations of the Cross and we used to stop off at each one and sit for a bit and talk – it might well be garden talk – and then we'd move on to the next one, and about halfway through he'd get us another drink and then we'd fulfill the last three Stations, by which time it was often getting dark. Of course I'd be cooking the supper so I always had to dash in to put something on the stove or take something else off, so there was a good deal of coming or going, but we'd be out there for an hour and a half or so.'

To be able to get out into the garden and dig for a bit is good therapy for a writer, the ideal antidote to the stressful effects of long hours tapping away at a keyboard or slumped in a library, but in Penelope Lively's case the activity had an added attraction, engaging her as it did in another abiding interest: archaeology. 'I was always enthralled by what I was finding in the soil. The house had been built in 1620 and continuously occupied so it has a wonderful garden archaeology. I was always turning up not just blue and white china but earlier stuff – seventeenth-century stone-glaze and bits of clay pipe. The additional pleasure was what was going to turn up next. There was one particular glazed saltware dish which from the few little bits I found must have been an extremely shallow, wide dish and it was that sort of gingery-coloured stuff with zigzag stripes on it you see in a lot in museums. It must have been a treasured article, I imagine, and I was always hoping I'd find enough to put the whole thing together.' As a history student at Oxford, she even applied (unsuccessfully owing to the stiff competition) for a place on an archaeological dig during her summer vacation, and the professor in charge kindly told her to write to him again when she had finished her degree, if she decided she would like to make a career out of archaeology. In the end, she never wrote that letter: 'Instead I took a rather dead-end job in research, and got married very young – but that was a path I could very easily have taken, and fetched up as an archaeologist.'

It is plain from her writing that Penelope Lively enjoys unearthing facts in libraries, and rummaging around in the dusty attics of her memory piecing together fragments of her childhood as much as she enjoyed digging actual soil for new potatoes or slivers of saltware. In fact, she was pre-eminently well-suited to be a writer: as the only child of an emotionally distant mother, educated at home alone by her nanny until her parents divorce had her back in England and bundled off to boarding school, where she felt horribly out of place, she learned to exercise her imagination: 'The storytelling was a way of providing companions, but I also think there was probably something innate to it. I was an obsessive reader from as soon as I could read and I have never known any writer who was not an obsessive reader.'

She is fascinated by why people choose to do what they do with their lives: 'I have always instinctively felt that we have certain innate capacities but then contingency – what happens to you fortuitously – nudges you more in one direction than another, so it's a mixture of nature and nurture: it's not so much that there is an apposition between nature and nurture but that there's an interesting fusion between them.' Her latest novel *Making it Up* explores this very subject: what if her character had taken the other fork in the road, and not the one she chose? And if she had, how might her life have panned out? Her publishers chose the title – Penelope had wanted it to be called *Confabulation* because, she explains, confabulation is a technical word psychiatrists use to describe people (often, but not always, elderly) who sincerely believe they've done something they have not.

Writing and gardening have something in common: they are both essentially solitary occupations, for which again her childhood has left her well prepared: 'I'm quite good at solitude. I don't often get lonely. Obviously I am very lonely without my husband, and I miss family when I don't see them, but it's not the loneliness of needing to rush out and find someone to talk to. I think perhaps if you are an only child you may be better at solitude.' Equally, both activities require long periods of consecutive time devoted to them exclusively for there to be any appreciable signs of progress, so however did she manage when the children were little, and she had no help, indoors or out? (Her daughter had already told me over the telephone that her mother was never at her desk when she and her brother were around, and that she believes her mother's gift for compartmentalising her life and for being very well-organised is how she managed it.) Penelope Lively herself reckons there was no other option: 'I would prepare things in advance so that I could work while they were at school. I mean you can't say to children I'm awfully sorry, there's no dinner tonight because I've decided I'm writing this evening. It doesn't work, so you very quickly learn to do your writing when they are not there, and to be totally available when they are.' But there is another reason: unlike that other acclaimed children's writer, Edith Blyton, who was allegedly a monster mother, Penelope Lively really likes children: 'They have been hugely important to me. I enjoy children and find them extremely interesting. We didn't do a lot to that garden partly because we felt if you had children of that age – and there were always tons of village kids in the garden as well – you couldn't actually have a meticulously planted garden. It was unimaginatively planted, I now realise, but it was a wonderful garden for children.'

Josephine perceives her mother as having been an instinctual gardener, and someone who would always rather enhance the *status quo* than interfere. She gives the example of a pair of double-flowered, candy-floss pink cherry trees in the garden her five-year-old self thought the absolute acme of chic, and her bewilderment over her mother's half-despairing jokes at their expense. Forty years on, Penelope Lively has forgotten the offending trees ever existed, but confirms she would never gratuitously destroy a healthy plant, particularly a tree.

In 1977, when the children had grown up, the Livelys moved to another house in another village: their chance to make a 'proper' garden at last. Yet still they felt no compulsion to stamp their own imprint too forcefully on their new territory, never contemplated altering the garden's basic structure, or even its planting, so that 'unless anybody has interfered massively since, there'll be some shrub roses, and there'll be the leucojums the previous owner planted at least fifty or sixty years ago, and lilacs. She knew what she was doing although, like my grandmother, she was an amateur gardener.' The 1992 edition of *The Yellow Book* describes the garden under the Lively's aegis as an 'Informal half-acre cottage garden, surrounding listed C17 farmhouse with dovecote, streams, yew hedges, shrub roses.' She beefs this description up for me a little: 'It was a hillside garden with wonderful advantages: it had two streams coming down through it, and [the previous owner] had done all the right things in that it wasn't all that enormous but she'd divided it into discrete spaces so it seemed bigger than it actually was.'

Under their guidance the garden did evolve – of course it did – but subtly: 'There was quite a lot of self-seeding and we let the things that did well spread. I've always been a great believer in that – that you discover what does well.' And again, she pays homage to her daughter's superior expertise: 'Josephine knows what's what. I mean – she does a lot of impulse-buying too; I know this because I am frequently with her and we spend a lot of time in garden centres in Somerset, but she also will have decided very precisely what she wants for some particular site, which I think in a sense is the hallmark of the professional gardener. Jack and I were much more serendipitous about it.'

For someone as intellectually curious as Penelope Lively, *The Yellow Book* is a godsend: 'A splendid opportunity', she writes somewhere, 'to inspect gardening as a social and cultural phenomenon.' Now she tells me pretty well any garden will do: 'I like going to the big grand gardens in Somerset – we've got quite a few; we've got Hestercombe and Knightshayes – and to some of the smaller ones. What's that wonderful one that's a nightmare to find down endless little lanes over in East Somerset – The Margery fish garden? [East Lambrook Manor]. Fascinating. We go there at least once a year when we are down, to see it in different seasons, because it's so clever the way it changes.'

Margery Fish wrote a hilarious account (*We Made a Garden*, 1956) of the stresses and strains of creating a garden with a partner whose aesthetic and method did not chime with her own, so invoking her name could have led to further discussion about couples gardening together, but it doesn't apart from a vague 'Yes, they quarrelled, didn't they?'. However, mention of a 'proper' gardening book led on to the subject of the sad decline of quality in most modern publications, and an invitation to inspect her own now much-reduced collection (mainly of books she has reviewed and liked enough to hang onto: Jane Brown's *The Pursuit of Gardening* – a social history of gardens and gardening; a few classics, including Gertrude Jekyll's *Home and Garden*, and a treasured early edition of William Robinson's *The English Flower Garden* that had been her grandmother's bible) arranged somewhat forlornly on one small shelf in the spare-room. From there to the basement to contemplate with a fair amount of shared contempt a number of newly-published gardening books sprawled across a sofa visibly sagging under their weight. These had been sent over by the

*New York Times* at goodness knows what cost, and the writer's task is to select for review any, or all, that appeal. Few do: 'I once wrote a slightly savage review about "bookmaking". I mean these great slabs of books that are really just vehicles for state-of-the-art photography. Some are so heavy I can hardly lift them. Completely useless.'

They certainly look very out of place in the old-fashioned, country-style kitchen where Penelope Lively's helper, in faded pink-and-green flowered cotton pinny, is seated at a large scrubbed pine table placidly polishing the silver. It is fanciful, maybe, but there is a strong 'whiff' (a Lively word) of Somerset in that kitchen – Somerset in the 1940's – and I remember how in *A House Unlocked* she describes her childish dilemma over which is best – town or country: 'Shunted between my London and Somerset grandmothers, I knew where I was I was best off. Never mind that a small voice whispered sedition about the city: interesting, it said . . . busy, bright, bustling, it said . . . shops, cinemas, people, fun. But right-minded folk settled for country life, didn't they?'

By now I have long forgotten that we haven't dealt with the second half of my first question, and have to be reminded: 'What was it? Oh yes, what do I miss, not being able to garden any more?' A vase of florists' flowers catches her eye: 'I am reduced to bought flowers, which I much resent: after a lifetime of having a proper garden where I could go out and pick some.' Her anguish was awful in the early days: 'There was a point when I was first garden-deprived, and which I've now grown out of, when I used to watch all the gardening programmes. It wasn't that I wanted to see or listen to Alan Titchmarsh and the rest of them, I just wanted to look at the plants.'

However, by far the worst deprivation is not being able to handle a spade anymore: 'I miss it inordinately, yes. I loved the business of getting the beds ready, that digging over of the vegetable beds. We had the most beautiful, rich soil because it had had three hundred years of being a farmyard and of course we made our own compost anyway, so it was productive to a degree.' The vicarious pleasure she derives from her daughter's achievement must be – and is – her consolation: 'In a way, it's a wonderful kind of fulfillment. She's done what I would like to have done.'

# Beth Chatto

## NURSERYWOMAN

*If anyone is facing the need to begin a new life-style I hope they may find encouragement in the pages that follow, to take the plunge with their particular inclination or talent.*

*Beth Chatto's Garden Notebook* (1988)

Beth knew whereof she spake when she wrote the above because she had taken her own spectacular plunge into a new lifestyle back in 1967, since which time she has been communicating all aspects of her experience in her enchanting books and those inimitable catalogues of hers. Beth was forty-four years old when she decided the time had come to test the skills she had acquired as a full-time housewife and keen amateur gardener by starting a small nursery propagating largely species plants that were little enough known at that period – and not at all available commercially – to justify naming her nursery 'Unusual Plants' (later to become known as The Beth Chatto Gardens). Unusual, yes; difficult, not at all: 'Most of them are tough as old boots' she insists, and for the very practical reason that there would be little sense in selling anything that would likely perish under the care of a less experienced gardener.

What makes Beth's story so encouraging, for women especially, is the fact that she emerged from the chrysalis of her old housewifely self as the butterfly that is Beth Chatto, Officer of the Order of the British Empire, recipient of the Royal Horticultural Society's Victoria Medal of Honour, and of the Lawrence Memorial Award for best display in any one year at any Royal Horticultural Society show, gardener, nurserywoman, writer and public speaker – without sacrificing her persona or causing her family grief. Her children were grown, her husband comfortably retired, and all of Beth was somehow absorbed and recycled: all her accumulated knowledge and acquired skills; all her natural gifts; all the goodwill and friendship of people she had encountered along the way. But if she were to aspire to the ambitious standards she sets herself in everything she undertakes she would also need another, at the time undiscovered, gift: a good head for business. No, two: and an aptitude for man-management. Today 'bits of Beth', as she likes to think of the plants she has grown and sold in unimaginable quantities over the intervening period, are proliferating in other people's gardens around the globe.

Beth's life and her work are indivisible, as is her home from her staff offices and the house from the garden: with its enormous plate-glass, floor-to-ceiling windows, and the climbers festooning the outside walls threatening to force their way in like triffids, it is quite hard to tell where inside ends and outside begins. In the summer, when the windows and doors are all open, birds fly in and out of her living room at will. Unfortunately, in the winter they sometimes try the same trick and fly headlong into the glass.

The day of my first visit, almost before we've shaken hands, Beth takes me to see the rainfall chart for the previous winter period pinned to the back of a handy kitchen cupboard door to prove her off-lamented point that however wet it has been everywhere else – which it has – not much rain had fallen on Elmstead Market. From the kitchen we go straight into the open-plan living room where she indicates the proofs of the book she is working on strewn over the dining table. It will be called *The Woodland Garden*, and her aim is 'to entrance people who have shady gardens, but no woods'. A year on from that encounter and her book since published, I happened to be talking to a painter friend who was born, like Beth in 1923, and learn that he had just bought the book for the very reason Beth hoped (my friend's garden is shady all right, but since it measures roughly one hundred feet by forty and is situated close to London's Brixton market, a wood it ain't.)

Entrancing people is Beth's great gift. In fact, walking round the garden after home-grown, home-cooked lunch, I am so entranced myself I only half take in the way visitors stare so longingly in her direction, hoping for a chat. She is thoughtful, informative, questioning and coolly critical, passionate, dispassionate and compassionate in equal measure. For instance, spotting some vagabond campion among a clump of erythroniums one of the gardeners is supposed to have seen to, she acknowledges how difficult it must be for anyone new to the garden to know if a plant has put itself in the wrong place, especially when campion, to name but one, is actually encouraged in the woodland beyond the culti-vated areas. Just as with children, she points out: 'You have to learn when to say no to them. If we didn't restrain them, they'd become weeds.' Next, a clump of 'naughty' matteucas – the fern commonly known as the ostrich or shuttlecock that is always going walkabout – also apparently over-looked. 'Interesting to see if he'll move them,' she murmurs. Moments later, we bump into the very man, and stop for a chat. I wonder, will Beth say anything? Not a word.

To reach the woodland area we have to cross a grass-covered bridge over what was once her garden's famously described 'soggy, boggy hollow' area – now a series of ponds surrounded by her collection of damp-loving plants – and in so doing come upon a dead moorhen spread-eagled on the path. A dead anything, especially in my own garden, can send me into paroxysms of grief but Beth is not sentimental: picking the creature up by one leg she chucks it without ceremony onto a nearby compost heap and carries on with her story about a pair of swans that had taken up residence on the dam not so long ago and whose droppings 'as big as cowpats' had made the grass too slippery for her visitors to use. Recounting the episode reminds her of how moved she had been by a production of *Swan Lake* danced entirely by men: 'You know how strong a swan is – so masculine and fierce – and that's what they were, these virile men with their feathers, and so beautiful. There was nothing camp about them.'

We approach what she describes as a 'fagged-out' border begging to be revitalized and, eyeing some conifers ponders: 'Out, or not? You can look for years and not see it. I am having a new learning experience after forty-five years: how to renew and refresh the garden. It never finishes. A garden is like a quilt, it wears out in places and needs patching.' But with both her shoulders themselves badly worn, her quilt's demands are exigent: 'I can't,' she demonstrates, 'lift this arm up.' Wincing, she tries the other one: 'This one will go up a bit better; the washers have gone in my shoulders through working like a man, heavy trundling of barrows and trolleys and digging up things too big for me and all that nonsense because I couldn't wait for somebody else to come along and do it for me. It's my own fault. My father thought I was making a rod for my back. Now, I can't dig a decent hole to put a plant in, which is awful for me, certainly not if the ground's hard, it just does hurt. There's no cartilage left, but I can still plan.' So, Beth makes her list, someone collects the stuff from the nursery, she places it all, and someone else plants everything: teamwork.

One day, when the garden's insatiable demands had temporarily overwhelmed even Beth's courageous spirit (and which gardener doesn't know that feeling?) she asked a party of visiting horticulturists what they would do: 'To start with, I said, How many of you has made a garden for forty years? Nobody had so I said: "Well, what would you do if you stood in my shoes?" Somebody from the back yelled out "Sell it!". Very practical, the person who said that, but I couldn't! I mean there are times when I admit it gets on top of me, especially in the winter when I think of all that's involved in running it, although I'm not running it on my own by any means. And it's not just one or two people taking responsibility. We try to train everybody to be responsible for something or some area. We are all links in the chain.'

I wondered if there were a future Beth lurking among her staff? Apparently not: 'Unfortunately, I am still the captain on the ship. It wouldn't go without my staff, but I still paint the picture.' And if that looks like a mixed metaphor Beth would not allow in her writing beyond the proof stage, it is in fact the case: she is both at the helm and painting her canvas. When I comment on what a rare ability this is, she is matter-of-fact: 'I suppose it was perforce, in a way. I suppose if I hadn't got certain qualities – the determination to get up and do something . . .' she trails off. Grappling with my notes at home later, I too trail off at this point in the story to go in search of sustenance, and come across a review in the newspaper of a book with, in the circumstances, the highly appropriate title *What Shall I Do About My Life?* by Po Bronson. The reviewer quotes Bronson – 'We need to encourage people to find their sweet spot. . . . Productivity explodes when people love what they do.' – and ends with an observation of his own: '. . . it's impractical to settle for less than a life we love.'

But following one's heart, as had become clear in our conversation, has its price. Beth's two daughters recognized this cost early on, she recalls: 'When I was starting to make this into a business they were still at home and they couldn't see any fun in taking on a life where you have to work as hard as I did.' Even a small boy who had escaped his parents one afternoon and is watching her digging could see as much: wistfully, he tells her he would like a garden like hers one day, but he supposes it must be a lot of hard work. Beth answers him with a question: 'Do you like playing cricket?' she asks. 'Yes!' 'Well,' she tells him, 'I should hate it, but I love doing this.'

I wondered about the circumstance that had led to Beth beginning such a demanding new life when she was no longer young, and the clue, I felt, lay in one word in an article I came across that she had written many years ago as a tribute to her friend and mentor, the artist-plantsman Sir Cedric Morris. Here she is, describing their first encounter:

> I took a deep breath and listened, feeling incapable of any worthwhile contribution. I was the wife of Andrew Chatto, fruit farmer and grandson of the publisher. Andrew's *real* [my italics] interest and lifelong study was finding the origins and natural associations of garden plants so that we might know better how to grow them. I was also the mother of two small daughters; much of my time being spent teaching myself the art and crafts of homemaking. I was already influenced by Andrew to appreciate species plants as well as cultivars, but my knowledge was very limited. . . .

And she goes on to explain how she learned her future trade on the hoof: 'I taught myself to propagate plants from the precious screws of paper full of seed, berries or cuttings I have been given by Cedric as well as generous earthy bundles of roots, tubers and bulbs.'

At the same time – according to Sir Cedric – she was 'soaking up Andrew like a sponge'. Unfortunately, however, her husband's unworldly, scholarly nature was not suited to a life of business, and since his heart was not in his work he became ill. 'I've had enough of business,' he told her, and while she recognised her husband's exhaustion – his 'right to be tired', as she puts it – she wasn't tired herself: 'I wanted to do something!' And so Andrew's illness became Beth's opportunity. Some of her friends later wondered if he might have been jealous of her success but that, she reckons, was not to understand his character in the least: she doubts he even noticed. In any case, her success was built on the back of all he had taught her.

She had long been worried about his health, as a matter of fact: 'Bless his heart! I was terrified of losing him to cancer, and from time to time I'd try to make him give up smoking and he would try now and again, but it was hopeless, and one day he said to me – and I never bothered him again after that – "I will give up smoking if you will give up work". In those days I didn't go out to work, but work is me. I can't sit still for five minutes. I'm up and doing things: Oh! I must go and do the flowers, or the vegetables. Do this! Do that! Do the other! He would say "For God's sake, sit down!" We both achieved something,' she reflects. 'I got up and did, and he sat down and thought. He was very good for me.' She shows me photographs of the two most important men in her life: 'I mean,' she exclaims, 'look at Cedric's trousers! Look at the knees! He always looked such a gentleman, tall elegant, wavy hair, the set of his head, but no pretensions whatsoever, and of course Andrew was the same although he was a different physical type altogether – dark and slight. Here is Andrew at eighty; for twenty years we had a family lunch party, and there he is, always standing at the table waiting for something, waiting for someone to put something on his plate!'

At which point we turn our attention away from Andrew – who died aged ninety in 1999, and his important but as yet unpublished work on the subject of the ecology of species plants and their natural habitat – and back to Beth and her writing method: 'I don't use a computer, it's all done by hand. I make notes over a period of years' – which she keeps in neat, chronological order – 'then my editor Erica Hunningher takes my bagful of pieces and puts it together like a patchwork quilt so that it reads seamlessly, and yet she never changes my writing. Some editors do.' But when I mention my appreciation of the way she puts so much of herself into her writing, she seems perturbed: 'The fact that I come over as such and such a person worries me a little bit. I mean do I give too much away? I do need to keep something, an inner core . . . those famous people who let it all hang out . . . I don't know how much of my inner self I do give away but anyway I can't help it.'

The difference between Beth's generous sharing of herself and a sad celebrity's needy outpourings hardly needs emphasising, but there is a passage (goodness, there are hundreds) in her last book but one, *The Gravel Garden*, which to my mind illustrates what makes her writing so special. She is considering a problem she is having with her leylandii hedge, and turns it into an absorbing human story by telling us what she went through emotionally in her vain efforts to restore it to health, including utter despair and, eventually, gratitude to the chance visitor who succeeded in solving her problem where all her own efforts, and the Royal Horticultural Society's doubtful advice, had failed.

For anyone uncertain about their ability to write she is cautiously encouraging: 'If you can write a letter you can write, but people don't realise that it doesn't matter whether we are writing or gardening, it doesn't just spill out of us like turning on the tap. I wear so many hats I find it quite difficult to change from one to the other. When I first start writing, when I haven't done any for a good long time, I'd say it's just like rusty water coming out of the tap. Its rubbish! I try very much to make it sound like me speaking, and sometimes people say its so easy to read I can just hear you, but its not the same because you notice, if you are recorded, you are full of "ums" and "ahs" and you forget to make adverbs out of adjectives and do all sorts of silly things. Also, I love alliteration and I love repetition and at the same time like to vary the length of my sentences. I know nothing about the art and craft of writing, but reading teaches you.' When she and Christopher Lloyd worked together on *Dear Friend and Gardener*, she saw for herself how the words seemed to flow so effortlessly out of him and on to his computer. 'How annoying!' I mutter. 'It is rather,' she replies.

But however hard come by, good writing does appear effortless on the page, and Beth's imagery, like her plant associations, can be sublime. You can dip into any of her books and pull out a plum: 'Salsify slides out of its black skin as white and slippery as a baby in the bath' for example, or the yellow-leafed Creeping Jenny sprawls across the path 'like spilt sunlight'. And blue tits 'bounce like clockwork toys' across her terrace. Flat, grey wintry skies are her bane, and she describes somewhere how 'a dustbin lid of cloud' hanging over the garden is depressing her. In one letter to Christopher she ascribes her melancholic mood to dreary weather 'overcast it seems, as the bottom of the sea'.

Beth will live on down the generations through her writing, but she will also be remembered by everyone who saw them for her displays at the Chelsea Flower Show that won her ten gold medals on the trot in the late-1970s to late-1980s. She was the first exhibitor to bury her pots to give the impression her plants were growing naturally, and was not bothered if a suitable plant for her design was not in flower: 'If I wanted a spire, or spikes, I would have camassias just in bud, or just starting to break. On a bulb stand, anything not in flower would lose them the gold medal.' She also – shock! horror! – put *Helleborus foetidus* on the very first stand she ever did for the RHS in one of its Westminster Halls, and was told off by the judges for displaying a weed. And so, as well as changing forever the way nurseries – other than the alpine growers – mount their displays stylistically, Beth was also among the first to exhibit species plants, and to assemble them according to their growing requirements. She is modest: 'I mean, in a way, there's nothing clever about it – if you read William Robinson, he was aware of it. You put plants that like shade in shade and plants that like hot sun on the sunny side of your house, but when we first start gardening it hasn't occurred to the majority of us that plants, just as people, don't like being put into the nearest available hole.'

She still remembers the pain of setting up her stand – all the getting up and down off her knees day after day after day: 'You see, sometimes I was on that damned road, and the last big stand I did seemed to be the size of a tennis court.' But that was not her prime reason for deciding enough was enough, although it played its part, she admits: 'Suddenly I thought, I've had enough of this. I loved doing it, but I was beginning to have pain in my shoulder and neck and I thought what do I want? More gold medals? No, I want to improve the garden.' She ponders the question in her *Garden Notebook*, arguing reasonably that there is a limit to how many plants her existing customers can fit into their gardens, but on the other that Chelsea is the best way to make contact with future clients, and personal contact with her old ones. The RHS of course had recognised the much-needed shot in the arm her arrival on the scene had provided during a dismal period in the Society's financial history, and when she announced her intention to quit, invited her on to Council.

Her refusal was unprecedented: 'Bill Ingwersen wrote to me in horror saying, "You can't refuse; it's just not done! It was a summons!" So I wrote to Lord Aberconway to whom I was indebted because he treated me extremely well: I was his little blue-eyed girl – I mean, four times he presented me to the Queen, so I was grateful to him for that, but not so starry-eyed that I could accept something that I knew I couldn't cope with. I said how much I appreciated his kindness to me and I would have liked to return it, but my circumstances would not permit it: my husband is ill; I have a family to look after, and a business to run on my own. I cannot, I said, accept honours without being aware that they are also responsibilities.'

In other words: thank you, but no thank you. She demurs, smiling: 'Well, it was partly ignorance: I wasn't aware that it was like refusing the Queen!' Council took its revenge by not awarding her the VMH until 1988, long after it was due, but when it did finally get around to acknowledging her contribution to the cause of horticulture, and consequently its debt, it made amends by awarding her the Lawrence Memorial Medal in the same year. This medal is her most treasured accolade, but she reckons going to Buckingham Palace with her daughters to receive the OBE from Prince Charles may turn out to be her most treasured memory, family events excepted.

My notes do not reveal why Beth suddenly tells me this, but it's a Beth gem: 'I had,' she said, 'one of those ridiculous questionnaires arrive the other day about what is your favourite flower and so on. "How can you have a favourite flower?" I say to myself. "It's like asking if I have a favourite child!" Well, I sat and spat blood and thought, "How ridiculous! I don't see myself as a rose or a lily or a dandelion," but then suddenly I did have an idea and I thought, "Yes! I could be represented by the dreaded bindweed: persistent, persevering, coming up through concrete, as bindweed does."' She didn't mention the fact, but the bindweed's pure white trumpet flowers can be included in a list of nature's most elegant designs. What's more, the smallest bit of root is all that's needed to start a new colony.

Although she consoles herself with the notion of bits of herself in all our gardens, in one or other of her books she points out firmly that, of course, there is no such thing as a Jekyll plant, or a Cedric Morris plant or a Beth Chatto plant. But when she saw how soon after Cedric died his garden at Benton End was dug over, the thought that he and his creation would live on through the dispersal over the preceding years of bits and pieces of its contents is a comfort. As for the future of her own garden, although she knows it could revert to wilderness in a matter of months, she hopes it won't disappear too soon after she's gone, for the sake of all the people who love it and visit it, and her staff who rely on it. 'I'm not fussed about it being retained in aspic,' she says. 'People can do what they want, but what I wouldn't like is if it were turned into a pig farm.'

# Donald Waterer

## NURSERYMAN

'Saw the thing, squeal of brakes, snip of the secateurs, straight into the spongebag.' The 'thing' Donald Waterer spotted when he was touring south-west France sometime before the Second World War was a honeysuckle growing wild in the Pyrenees. Today it is listed in the Plant Finder as *Lonicera etrusca* 'Donald Waterer', thanks to his lifelong friend Graham Stuart Thomas exhibiting the propagated plant for him under that name at one of the Royal Horticultural Society's Westminster shows, and despite Donald himself having suggested the more modest *Lonicera etrusca* 'Castelnau'. Now approaching ninety, he still keeps an eye out for any interesting-looking natural hybrid seedlings.

It is in his blood: Waterers have been nurserymen since the mid-eighteenth century when they began hybridising what were known at the period as 'American' plants on the bleak and barren land around Woking, where the family had been established at least since Tudor times. Rhododendrons and azaleas in particular thrived on the hundreds of acres of sandy but moisture-retentive soil on which the two nurseries – one at Knap Hill, the other at Bagshot – were situated, and still are, although both establishments have long-since ceased to be family-run or even owned. (At the last count, *The Plant Finder* listed well over sixty columns of rhododendron and azalea hybrids and species, of which more than a few bear the name of one Waterer family member or another, and many the letter 'K' after a variety. 'K' indicates a deciduous azalea bred either at Knap Hill or Exbury.)

Deep roots in Surrey notwithstanding, in 1976 Donald and his wife upped-sticks for Somerset, and a bungalow on the steep, north-facing slopes of the Quantock Hills overlooking the Bristol Channel. The last

Waterer to live on Waterer land and work in the family business had made a timely exit: more changes in commercial nursery methods took place between 1950 and 1970 than had evolved over the preceding two hundred years, and the money now lay in selling pot-grown plants in the new-fangled garden centres. The era of the land-owning nurseries was over, as were the days when the goods trains would leave Woking station in the autumn filled with elegant (and returnable) willow baskets packed with plants for Waterers' customers. And the days when gypsies and East Enders would descend on Knap Hill to dead-head the mile-long 'Waterers Walk' before moving on to the Kent hop fields were long gone.

The Quantocks are not the ideal situation for growing rhododendrons, but Donald Waterer isn't really bothered – he is more absorbed in researching his family history these days. In any case, his wife Rozanne has only allocated him a narrow strip of garden out of 'her' fields, where she keeps horses. Actually, it appeared to be one big field when they bought the property, although the foundations of a greenhouse were still just discernible. But old habits die hard, so the kitchen window has to do when something worth propagating turns up.

And some years ago something did when, most unusually, *Geranium wallichianum* 'Buxton's Variety' flowered in Donald's garden at the same time as its neighbour, *G. himalayense*. Curious, he took time off from his archival studies to germinate seed from the inevitable union and got a result: one seedling came up markedly different from the rest, and in due course *Geranium* 'Rozanne' was unveiled at Chelsea by Blooms of Bressingham, amid much brouhaha.

Instinctive and intrinsic skills notwithstanding, the fact remains that Donald's seedling having turned out to be one of those 'must have' plants which appear on the horticultural scene from time to time is at least in part due to his networking skills. First of all, he showed it to Graham Stuart Thomas who liked what he saw, and urged his friend to get in touch with the authority on primary hybrid geraniums, Dr Peter Yeo, who also gave it the thumbs up. Now what? Blooms, Donald decided. Adrian Bloom was as impressed as the academics had been by the plant's qualities (extra-large, iridescent violet-blue flowers, long flowering period, vigorous yet compact habit) and sent a car down to Somerset to collect the plant for breeding purposes, though not before Donald had managed to negotiate a 'small rake-off' for himself on every plant that finds its way on to the market, which is not by any means usual practice when someone markets something someone else has bred, or collected from the wild.

Unfortunately, he didn't manage to get to Chelsea to witness the great unveiling, or watch Roy Lancaster singing his geranium's praises to camera on Channel 4, which is a shame because he cherishes his memories of manning the Knap Hill stand at the Show in the old days, and of hobnobbing with his peer group. Unfortunately, he thought (mistakenly, as it happens) I was expecting him to drop some glamorous showbiz names from the old days, and not wanting to disappoint me, he dutifully dredged his memory. Laurence Olivier and Vivian Leigh: would they do? Or what about the aristocracy? Lady Northampton for example? Apparently, as a very young man he had got in a fearful flap trying to get her order down in the – then as now – Chelsea crush and she had suggested imperiously he might do well to learn shorthand. Or Robert Morley? Robert Morley had been his schoolmate at Wellington. He was struggling: these were not the types in whom Donald had ever been much interested.

On the other hand, where stories about the great and the good in his own *milieu* are concerned he has only one problem: how indiscreet can he allow himself to be? So I goad him: Vita Sackville-West, had he known Vita? (Vita liked rhododendrons, but Harold Nicolson did not. 'Rosiedendrons' he called them, believing them to be hatefully suburban, and quite unsuitable for planting in their precious Kentish landscape.) Indeed, Donald had known her, but the meeting he ruefully recounts has nothing to do with rhododendrons and everything to do with networking: Vita wanted an introduction to Collingwood Ingram (the epicurean, and authority on ornamental cherries who happened to live near Sissinghurst Castle), whom Donald knew well, so she invited him to tea in her tower to discuss strategy. On the appointed afternoon, as he approached the castle gates, Vita appeared accompanied by a huge, unleashed, and ferocious dog.

Donald was convinced he was about to be 'eaten alive' but heroically stood his ground while she stood by and let him suffer.

An invitation to tea from Lady Anne Palmer had, conversely, turned out to be the opening move in what was to become a long-standing friendship, despite an almost equally inauspicious beginning: the creator of Rosemoor was engrossed in her weeding when Donald and his wife arrived, and continued to be so. Feeling foolish, the couple hung about for half an hour or so, and were about to creep away utterly humiliated when they were spotted, and bellowed at. They weren't the only ones: one afternoon Donald was over at Rosemoor watching Geoff Hamilton making a *Gardener's World* programme when a large party of Germans materialised. Dragooned into looking after them for her, he was obliged to dredge up the pidgin German he had picked up during the years spent in Stalag Luft 111, from which The Great Escape took place, although Donald wasn't among the ones who tried to get away, owing to a gammy leg. As it happens, he has a gift for languages and when one of the party – the epitome of 'the cruel Hun', according to Donald – asked him 'ver' he had learned his German there was nothing for it but the truth: 'In POW camp because I bombed Germany'.

One of the more spectacular plants in flower in the garden at the time of my visit was a sizable clump of *Trillium chloropetalum* var. *giganteum*, grown from seed handed to him by Lady Anne years ago with a command: 'There! See what you can do with this!' He hadn't a clue what she'd given him, but enjoyed the challenge and patiently nursed whatever it was for years before it did anything interesting, such as flower. Unfortunately for Donald, the day dawned when his friendly protagonist decided to abandon Rosemoor to the care of the Royal Horticultural Society, and went off to live in New Zealand, vowing to give up gardening. This proved not to be the case, but when he reminded his old friend of her oath she had an answer: 'It's in the blood, you know.' He knew.

Rosemoor is much changed since Lady Anne left, and Donald takes a dim view of the changes: 'They have made it into such a tailored affair. When the tide turns against gardening, and people get fed up with Alan

Titchmarsh, they'll have a problem to maintain it. They'll have to cut back. Rosemoor is marvellous, but it doesn't appeal to me nowadays, not now they've put down bark chips against weeds, and there are no more seedlings.' Ah, seedlings! Searching for a Turkey oak at his local nursery/garden centre recently, he spotted one that had not come true. At an experienced glance he could tell it was a natural hybrid of *Quercus cerris* and *Q. ilex* so, out of habit more than anything, he bought it without saying a word, grafted it and sent bits to Rosemoor for trial, out of love. Trees grow too slowly for there to be any money in them in any case.

On our stroll round the small garden with the spectacular view it becomes clear most of the flora has been raised from seed, or brought along as a cutting from Knap Hill, and I conclude a plant's sentimental associations are paramount to the man at this stage in his life. He brought with him most of the 'family', for example: *Rhododendron* 'Gomer Waterer' AGM (his father) and *R.* 'Alice' AGM (mother); *R.* 'Mrs. Anthony Waterer' (cousin) – all of whom were looking distinctly unhappy perched 900 feet up and exposed to salt-laden winds. Donald too has his namesake: at his birth, his father whimsically decided to hybridise 'Gomer' and 'Alice' to produce *R* 'Donald Waterer'. The shrub won its AGM in 1917, but Donald reckons if the botanists had realised the sentimental, unscientific reasons behind its breeding they would have been appalled.

My guide begins to spit out Latin plant names and fascinating snippets of gossip in a tumbling torrent, so it wasn't until later when I decoded my notes, with the aid of *The Plant Finder*, that I realised almost all the names I'd jotted down have, or once had, the Royal Horticultural Society's Award of Merit and that I was wrong: for a man who's family have been nursery-men for 250 years, a plant's garden-worthiness beats sentimental attachment every time, and so *Viburnum* × *carlecephalum* AGM; *Betula medwedewii* AGM; *Cistus* × *skanbergii* AGM; *Picea breweriana* AGM; *Prunus serrula* var. *tibetica* AGM; *Acer rubrum* 'October Glory' AGM, are all there; even that tricky-to-kick-start trillium has the award.

But many years ago Donald did try to grow one shrub at his nursery that was a very bad doer indeed – in fact it died, and he's never seen another anywhere. This is (or was) *Berberis gyalaica*, which he'd felt obliged to purchase when Collingwood Ingram took him to visit a nursery owned and run by a woman whose methods and way of handling her staff impressed the great collector. He found himself being nudged into buying a plant to please the lady, and cast around for something unusual enough to be worth forking out for. Since *The Plant Finder* does not list it, I contacted the holder of the National Collection of Berberis, who kindly checked a 1961 *Survey of Berberis* to verify its provenance, and the spelling. It exists all right – in south-east Tibet – but my friend from the NCCPG had never seen an actual specimen.

So much mention of award-winning plant material reminds me of the supreme accolade the horticultural establishment can bestow on human beings: the Victoria Medal of Honour. There is one for each year of Queen Victoria's reign. Sixty were minted in 1897, and by the time she died that number had increased to sixty-three, where it remains: a holder must die before anyone else can be anointed, as it were. Many legendary names in the nursery business – Russell, Hillier, Slocock, Veitch, Ingwersen – appear again and again, generation after generation, like kings. But the *über*-dynastic Waterer name is missing. Which is puzzling, in view of the fact that the Royal Horticultural Society used to be known as the Rhododendron Hybrid Society, and that by the end of the nineteenth century everyone had gone – as Donald has it – 'berserk' about rhododendrons. And then too there is the significance of that letter 'K' to consider.

Looking at the facts, however, only two Waterers apart from Donald were ever eligible, one being Anthony Waterer (1850–1924), who'd inherited Knap Hill from his father, also Anthony. Anthony *père* spent his life hybridising and selecting azaleas to form the group known as Ghent Azaleas, destined eventually to be identified by that famous 'K', but he died in 1896, a year too soon for the award. Anthony *fils* could have won it – he had inherited his father's instinctive flair for breeding good plants – but as his father's will had left him a rich man there was little incentive to market, or even exhibit, his beloved azaleas, so he didn't. He died a bachelor in 1924, and in its ever-so-faintly-patronizing obituary the RHS magazine

*The Garden* described him as being just like his father – 'not excelling in the arts of politeness, but of sterling integrity', adding somewhat ominously that 'he was rarely seen at exhibitions or horticultural meetings'. So much, then, for Anthony Waterer's chances in the VMH stakes.

Donald's own father, Gomer (named after the Belgian horticulturist the Vicomte de Gomer) was born in 1867 but he was a 'Bagshot Waterer', that is to say, from the branch of the family whose fortunes had waned by the late 1880s – due in great part, my source informs me, to the Waterer penchant for breeding very large families and making very bad wills. However, Gomer understood all too well the potential of the unmarketed – and mostly unnamed – azaleas languishing at the by now run-down and under-capitalized Knap Hill nursery. In 1931, at the age of sixty-five, in partnership with Lionel de Rothschild and a young man called Captain Robert Jenkinson, he managed to buy the business off his American cousins who'd inherited it, the idea being to provide an inheritance for his son.

Unfortunately for his chances, and his son's future, Gomer really rather preferred playing golf, and Captain Jenkinson was a rich man who showed even less inclination for hard work. Add to that the fact that this was the depressed 1930s and another world war was waiting in the wings to finish off what the first one – and Anthony Waterer's benign neglect – had not: Knap Hill Nursery Ltd was in jeopardy, and only kept on the rails with the financial support of the bankers N.M. Rothschild. From the young Donald's point of view at the time, the most rewarding aspect of his father's friendship with Lionel de Rothschild had been the odd invitation to himself to stay at Exbury: '1908 Cockburn port, a top grade cigar *and* a fire in my bedroom!'

Gomer died in 1945, and Donald – once he had been rescued from Stalag 111 – returned to Knap Hill and business as usual scouring the nursery for commercially viable seedlings. One such turned out to be a natural hybrid between *Prunus subhirtella* 'Autumnalis' AGM, and *P sergentii* AGM, eventually named *Prunus* 'Accolade', and likewise awarded the AGM – another winner for Waterers!

As we stroll on and I continue to puzzle over the missing medal – the Waterer family's eccentric behaviour and independent attitude notwithstanding – Donald tells me more about the old Waterer hybrids, most of which are, apparently, 'deeply unfashionable' these days, except in Germany where their extreme hardiness is an asset. We stop to consider *R. augustinii*, whose mauve flowers he likes, but of which some say pityingly, '*so* like ponticum'. Telling me this reminds him of the occasion when Jim Russell asked the members of the RHS Rhododendron Committee for their opinion on which was the most popular rhododendron species. 'Ponticum!' shrieked Donald, convinced he was right (he still is). 'That could be why he didn't get the VMH,' murmurs his wife. Apparently Donald's mother had wanted him to be a career diplomat. Fortunately, her son was self-aware enough to know he wasn't suited.

Poignantly, almost everyone of his acquaintance, certainly everyone he mentioned, has won the medal: Lady Anne Palmer, VMH; Collingwood Ingram, VMH; Lionel de Rothschild, VMH; Graham Stuart Thomas, VMH, Jim Russell, VMH, though not Vita, interestingly. But these are my musings: although Donald still manages to take care of the garden, 'hanging on to the push-mower as though it were my Zimmer frame' while keeping an eye out for anything unusual nature might throw up which he could possibly turn to his advantage, he does not waste precious energy in fruitless speculation. In any case, far more painful than any possible oversight on the part of the Royal Horticultural Society is the fact that, almost unbearably for a man so keenly attuned to nature, he used to be able to detect the slightest variation in a bird's song (apparently birds have accents, what Collingwood Ingram pedantically described as 'dialect variation according to their place of origin'), and who enjoys a chat more than most, he has lost his hearing. A real loss, this, but one he somehow manages to mourn cheerfully.

Donald Waterer and his wife died in 2006 within a few months of one another, both aged ninety-three. They managed to stay in their house in the Quantocks, and look after themselves and the garden to the end.

# Anthea Gibson

## GARDEN DESIGNER AND GARDENER

Garden designer Anthea Gibson comes from a long line of amateur gardeners and botanists of some skill and renown on both sides of the family, including her own mother who, Anthea acknowledges, was a keen and knowledgeable gardener 'But only,' she adds with a barely concealed sniff, 'in the way that lots of ladies are.' Indeed, the thought of becoming a gardener 'in the way that lots of ladies are' never did hold much appeal for Anthea, nor was she overly interested in botany: too much of her childhood had been spent trailing around the Cotswolds looking for wild fritillaries and Pasque flowers behind her keen older sister and her sister's even keener fourteen-year-old friend, Iain Prance (better known today as the eminent botanist Sir Ghillean Prance, former Director of Kew and advisor to the Eden Project). What Anthea wanted to do when she'd finished bringing up three children was write, or at least to be involved in the literary world, although her actual destiny had in fact already been uncannily forecast years earlier when as a teenager she had filled in some magazine quiz about what job would best suit her gifts, and it had come up with the startling advice to become a landscape architect. 'Phooey!' she thought, and took herself off to university to read history of art and architecture without giving the matter another thought.

The gods, however, had other ideas, and I am curious to find out when we meet what the catalyst had been that had set someone with so little interest in horticulture on her true course. It turns out that the garden of the house in Buckinghamshire the family lived in when the children were small happened to have been professionally designed, and to an eye trained to understand spatial concepts this fact signified one thing: there was, or could be, more to making a garden than planting out an herbaceous border. On the strength of this revelation, and once the children were off her hands, Anthea signed on for a short course at the Inchbald School of Garden Design where she was encouraged to look, to think about what she was looking at, and to read widely, which is how she came to be interested in the work of Dame Sylvia Crowe, and to decide once again to thwart her destiny by reverting to her original game plan: she would become a publisher, and reprint Crowe's book *Garden Design* (conveniently, Anthea's husband, London art dealer Thomas Gibson, owned a high-quality publishing company with not a lot to occupy it apart from printing his gallery's exhibition catalogues).

But reissuing *Garden Design* turned out to be her first and last foray into the publishing world: when an old friend asked Anthea to design her London garden for her, she agreed, and when a friend of that friend wanted hers done too . . . Twenty-six years on, that is still how it works, and she has amassed an impressive client list in the interim, including Lord and Lady Sainsbury; the Earl and Countess of Drogheda (a.k.a. the garden photographer Derry Moore); Lord and Lady Faringdon; Sir Peter Osborne, father of the Tory politician Charles Osborne; and Peter Herbert, the owner of Gravetye Manor, who asked her to restore and replant parts of the garden in the style of its original creator, William Robinson.

Anthea never advertises, and has never succumbed to the siren call of the television gardening-programme-makers because she reckons the medium is simply not suited to conveying the essence or spirit of any garden (and, I suggest, quite spectacularly unsuited to communicating the elusive atmosphere of a Gibson garden: it is, after all, a brave film director who attempts to nail Proust.) As it happens, the structural elements in Anthea's work do have a strong contemporary feel about them, but there is also a pervading sense of timelessness about her gardens because, paradoxically, she manages to capture all that is ephemeral – scents, sound, movement, memory, shadows: all that is, well, Proustian.

Her palette is cool: white; all greens, though fresh spring green is favourite; pale mauves and yellows, and that really rich blue you find in aconites and *Anemone de Caen* 'Mr Fokker'. And while Anthea does not consider herself a true plantswoman, she deploys a wide range in her designs and although she admits she has strong favourites she tries to resist using them everywhere by deliberately placing different 'people' in different parts of the garden. I jotted down a few of their names: *Anemone rivularis*, all erythroniums, most bulbs – fritillaries more than most, the balsam poplar (*Populus balsamifera*), *Hydrangea quercifolia, H. aspera* Villosa group, *H. aspera* 'Grandiflora', and *H. arborescens* 'Anabelle'. As well, a couple of unusual species from the Argentine: *Maytenus boaria*, from the cold south, which looks a little like an evergreen willow, and *Myceugenella apiculata*, another evergreen that is not reliably hardy, although it has survived seven winters at Westwell Manor, the Gibson family home in the Cotswolds, where it can get very cold indeed. With its reddish bark that turns silvery in patches on mature trees, its elegant form, its tiny, dark green leaves, small white flowers, and black berries the little tree so closely resembles *Myrtus* (or *Luma*) *apiculata*, it could be the same 'person' under an assumed name. Either way, it's a beauty.

You will not find any thugs in any scheme of Anthea's – no phormiums, for example. But what if the client likes them? All she reckons she can do is aim for what pleases her, although just occasionally an irremediably urban potential client does pose a problem: 'Because you have to have been brought up in the country, or spent time in the country in this climate to appreciate a bare tree. To some people they just look boring and grim and it is only when you've spent time with them that you begin to appreciate their winter aspect.' So, if a client expects everything to be in flower all year round, and is baffled by herbaceous plants, or has ideas Anthea feels are too far removed from her own, she turns the job down with a graceful 'I don't think I am the right person for you'.

Only once she didn't, and fifteen years on still rues the day she accepted the prestigious commission to design a garden within an existing garden for a Government-funded establishment (that's all I'm allowed to reveal) whose gardens are open to the public. She found herself obliged to work with unionised 'jobsworth' labour, comply with exhaustive Health and Safety regulations (no gaps wider than the width of a tennis ball between railings – that sort of thing), and, possibly the most difficult of all, be answerable to a committee. Her design and her nerves in tatters, she realised too late she only works well with a small team, and with people who have a let's-get-on-with-it attitude: 'I find a few people can achieve an awful lot with very little money if everyone is keen and has the same idea about what they are after.' It is a shame 'amateur' has such a pejorative connotation today: where plants are concerned, the dedicated commitment of the true plant lover must surely be a *sine qua non*. Indeed, Anthea reckons too much hard-nosed commercialism is what lies behind the 'smudgy glamour' of the Chelsea Flower Show these days.

In keeping with this attitude, her designs are hand-drawn (she only uses the computer as a database and for emails) and she has no secretary – although she does have 'people to do the house things', plus, it must be said, three full-time gardeners taking care of her own garden's seven acres. In fact, much of the actual design work goes on in her head because it is hard to pin down that 'gasp of nature' which is all she needs to refresh her imagination: 'You know how when you come round the corner in a garden and it looks just right and you aren't quite sure why? It can be a funny shape that shouldn't feel comfortable, but somehow it does. Of course,' she adds, 'I do like the formality of clipped hedges, and while everyone has a different ratio of wild to formal, the wilder the garden, the more you need hedges.'

She shares a liking for muscular hedge structures with the Dutch designers Henk Gerritsen and Piet Oudolf and their acolytes, but not their planting style. The 'grassy lot', as she calls them, favour rusty reds, dark greens and 'goldy' ornamental grasses planted within borders that peak in late summer and are expected, once planted, to get on with their lives pretty well unaided. Anthea plants her own grass-free borders in an intricate tapestry of cool-coloured, fresh-looking herbaceous perennials, that couldn't look after themselves for much more than a week. She does, however, allow regular grass to grow long in parts of the garden, and not only the meadows and orchards; for example, the edges of formal lawns are left unmown and planted up with bulbs, cow parsley, woodruff, and aquilegias. She treats gravelled areas in the same way, so that the rather austere aspect of the north-east-facing façade of her own home, with its large expanse of unadorned gravel forecourt, is softened by a screen of long grass, bulbs and foaming cow parsley planted under the surrounding chestnuts.

Vagabonds are equally welcome, at least they are if they choose to settle themselves where Anthea deems appropriate; if not . . . well, there's a lot of time-consuming difference between a seemingly natural effect, and chaos. *Alchemilla mollis* is allowed to drape itself wherever it likes over the miles of limestone paths and steps at Westwell, and almost any aconitum (except the bi-coloured varieties, which offend her aesthetic) is welcome, as are campanulas – *C. persicifolia* and *C. lactiflora* especially. She is constantly on the alert for what works and what doesn't, and at one point in our stroll there she is, on her knees, hauling out some buttercups that have violated the 'natural' purity of the scene which consists in clumps of *Leucojum aestivum* (a great favourite) pushing up through the short grass, with sweet woodruff in the longer tufts around the base of a pair of *Betula jacquemontii* planted either side of an old lichen-spattered bench on a small island in the middle of a drifting stream. Next moment, she is rubbing away at a too-new-looking stone statue with the same plant material she has just grubbed out, in a vain effort to help the ageing process. The problem here is that, while the old limestone paving, steps, walls and statuary at Westwell are decorated with a random patina of moss and lichen that has taken nature centuries to achieve, thieves broke in last year and helped themselves to whatever they could carry, and smashed a lot they couldn't.

Anthea has been working on the garden in this subtle way for twenty-five years now, with the incalculable aid of her head gardener David Baldwin, who has been at Westwell, man and boy, for almost forty; indeed, his willingness to stay on persuaded the Gibsons to buy the house, as much as anything: 'David knows much more about the day-to-day business of gardening than I do, but he doesn't have any pretensions to being a designer and he's tactful enough to say "What a good idea!" when I say I'd like to try this or that.' So far as experimentation goes, however, she does tend to tread very carefully, out of respect for the garden's history and the *genius loci*: Westwell Manor dates back to 1574, and was owned without interruption by Christ Church, Oxford until 1902, when it was sold to Sir Sothern Holland, who transformed part of the garden very successfully in the typical Edwardian style of the period. Nevertheless, she is trying to grow rice as a decorative feature, which *is* quite radical.

In fact, Anthea has a long-held fascination with water, and an ongoing preoccupation with finding ways of filling a pool very full without it flooding, which she finds a tremendously exciting concept – but difficult, so she works in collaboration with the stone and water specialist, Anthony Archer-Wills. The water gardens at Studley Royal in North Yorkshire were her original inspiration, and Studley Royal remains her favourite English garden, although nowadays she is more likely to be looking to the work of modern young French designers for new ideas. As for the rice, she is using the Carmargue variety, and hoping it will fruit sufficiently, if not to feed the family, at least to be self-sustaining. She loves the repetition of pale green, vertical growths set side by side and to this end has planted her rice in separate little tufty clumps in a square pool filled exactly to the brim with black-dyed water. On the wall nearby is a carved plaque by William Peers bearing the sombre warning that 'The Last Lark Sings where the Sky is Empty Blue Over a Green Desert', a poignant reminder that Anthea's green credentials are pretty good – she is a loyal member of the Soil Association, but does admit to having used Roundup to clear a field she wanted to turn into a meadow.

The dye, which is harmless to wildlife, comes from America and she uses it wherever she can. At Westwell, for example, an old grass tennis court has been dug out to the depth of about three feet and filled with black-dyed water that threatens to flood the narrow band of grass surrounding it, but never actually does. A stand of horse chestnuts behind an immense expanse of billowing box hedge bordering one length is mirrored in its seemingly unfathomable depths, while on the other, an installation designed by American sculptor Herbert George to ensnare shadows (*sic*) watches itself like Narcissus. Other than these shadowy reflections of man's art and nature's, the pool is empty. It is utterly spellbinding.

But if Anthea treads lightly in the garden, she treads even more lightly when she ventures out of it and into the landscape, which she is increasingly inclined to do now that the family also own a house with some land in the Scottish Highlands, and her husband has family in the Argentine who own property in an area where the landscape is gloriously – in Anthea's eyes – watery. The climate in that part of the Argentine is dire – strong winds, floods and droughts at any season, broiling summer sun, the soil is horrible, and the landscape virtually treeless. To compensate: the light is marvellous, the skies are huge, and the low-lying, perfectly flat land ideal for her purpose, which has been to work on mirroring that 'flat, watery feeling', and formalise it. 'There are,' she explains, 'lots of natural ponds – *lagunas* they call them – and that's what I've built on.' She shows me photographs: a line of trees planted here, a three foot high hillock thrown up in the distance there (in line with the setting sun and topped by the somehow oriental, somehow abstract outline of a fragile-seeming wooden framework designed to appear silhouetted against the evening sky), two narrow canals cut through the long grass disappearing into the distance 'like a Piero della Francesca stream', and that's it – and it's quite enough.

In the Highlands, again water captures her imagination – water and woodland: 'You've got the rushing clear water and these amazing stones covered with mosses and lichen and little wood anemones coming up in the dappled light. It just is better than any garden I've ever seen, and sometimes I think, why do I bother?' So up there, she hardly does, restricting her gardening activities to a small courtyard where she grows mostly vegetables, doing no more to the surrounding landscape than mow – or skim – a winding path through the long grass. And that, when Hepworth and Moore might have sculpted the rocks on the nearby beach, and there is a 'Coca-Cola-coloured' river running through the property, is, again, all that's needed. This minimalist approach she believes has crept up with age, and is affecting her life-style as well as her work: 'Now I can see the point of the Chinese collection being just one perfect bowl: you spend the first part of your life collecting things, and the next part of it shedding what you don't want.'

It is lunchtime, and in we go for a meal as simple and exquisitely presented as everything Anthea Gibson is responsible for always is, yet when I press her she insists she is not a perfectionist – is indeed even lazy by nature and, shock horror, rather untidy: 'You'll see, if you open my cupboards – they're full of muddle.' I must take her word for it. In any case, what Anthea seeks is peace: 'I want the effect to be tranquil. Everyone says that to me: your houses are so peaceful it must be because Thomas is so noisy. But I also think it's what I like.' (When I arrived, the haunting, plangent sound of the music by the twelfth-century Abbess Hildegard of Bingen was floating through the stone-flagged entrance hall, but was abruptly turned off when husband and son number three bounced in.) Before we can eat, the flowers she had been idly picking during the morning tour must be arranged for the table. In a flash, it's done: Anthea belongs to what she calls 'the David Hicks school of flower arranging' – that is, no vase should take more than five minutes to fix. Even so, since Westwell is where they entertain (she is trying to persuade her sociable husband that no one gives dinner parties in London any more), five minutes per vase adds up to quite a few hours work of a Friday, because every room upstairs and down must have its own arrangement. However, cymbidiums and pelargoniums and scented shrubs such as *Pittosporum tobira* and *Jasminium sambac* from the greenhouses take at least some of the strain.

During lunch, I quiz her about the French influences on her work – Pascal Cribier for example, whom she has yet to meet, but has seen a garden he designed in Normandy: 'It is modern without being aggressive. It looks exactly right in its site, which is old – not exactly a farmyard, a sort of old courtyard. Very simple. Totally right.' Then there is the work of Sonia Lesot and Patrice Taravella at the Prieuré de Notre Dame d'Orsan somewhere in the middle of nowhere south of Paris. Again, you can see why she likes what they are doing: the pair are both architects who yearn to work with natural materials, but don't often get the opportunity. Their sophisticated yet simple resurrection of an ancient monastery garden chimes precisely with Anthea's own aesthetic. Nevertheless she is not blindly besotted by the French – 'You know how they can talk so earnestly about the shape of a fireplace, you'd think they're discussing Aristotle.' – but finds this tendency preferable to the British penchant for dumbing-down. She describes an exhibit at Le Jardin Planetaire, a horticultural show staged in Paris some years ago, which she reckons avoided being pretentious: people were invited to sit in a kind of amphitheatre on simple wooden benches, and contemplate a sunken garden made from nothing but moss, and I try to imagine what the Chelsea Show Garden judges might make of such a sophisticated understatement. The late Nicole de Vésian, the ultra-stylish Parisienne who retired to the Lubéron and made a much-vaunted garden there out of nothing but stones and pebbles and cruelly close-shorn balls of drought-tolerant plants, which naturally – I should say, *un*naturally – were never permitted to flower, is another of her Gallic heroes. She even tried something similar in one of Westwell's enclosures, but it didn't feel right and the area has been allowed to return to its more disarmingly natural-looking, if less severely *chic*, state.

The paring-down and paring-down of her style puts me in mind of the maxim that art is about what you leave out. By chance, Anthea did say at one point that she thought gardening was 'not quite an art, more of a craft', but we tacitly decided not to pursue that one at the time. Later, however, I consulted *Webster's*, and it defines 'art' as meaning: 'The conscious use of skill, taste and creative imagination in the practical definition or production of beauty', which I would argue makes gardening an art, and Anthea an artist.

She does not actually do much digging and planting at Westwell because she has David and his assistants to do that, and there are twenty separate enclosures (not counting the meadow or the front drive) to be maintained so she could be digging the whole day long and have little to show for her pains. Anthea's practical contribution is to weave the low willow fences she uses to edge the flower beds, and being alone out there with the gardeners, knowing the family will be arriving later that evening, is the best part of her day: 'That's when I feel happy. I find interacting with people more tiring than whatever I'm up to in the garden.' And if she needs to get away from everyone, the garden is big enough to hide away in. If it were me, I'd head straight for the Bunny Walk, which has a ley line running through it, and the tranquil atmosphere within the long (one hundred and twenty feet), narrow (eighteen feet) high-walled space is palpable. A now dead but once vigorous, wide-spreading cherry tree whose branches have been lopped off at the elbow, as it were, stands centre stage, and the abstract shape that act of mutilation has created is strangely satisfying.

Westwell Manor is open one day a year for the National Gardens Scheme. For anyone wishing to visit the garden at other times, parties of twenty can be accommodated so long as written application is made well in advance to: Mrs. Thomas Gibson, Westwell Manor, Westwell, Burford, OX 18 4JT. No telephone calls, no faxes, no emails, please.

# Dan Pearson

## LANDSCAPE DESIGNER

Shyness is one of the things that made me solitary as a kid but then
when I suddenly found I was getting all this attention it changed everything, and I realised I didn't need to be shy any more . . .

Dan Pearson

The setting for my first ever interview with Dan Pearson had been his
plant-packed roof garden tucked in among the chimneypots of London's
Vauxhall. That was in the summer of 1995 when the charismatic young
garden designer with the looks of a pagan god was thirty-one years old
and when I knew little more about my subject other than that he had a
reputation for beguiling shyness, that he wrote a regular gardening
column for the *Sunday Times* and that he had already designed three
Chelsea Show gardens which had caused quite a stir at the time, Dan being
among the first to demonstrate how effective the judicious use of perennial grasses in the border can be, and to wean us all off pink and onto the
more extensive deployment of the darker end of the colour spectrum in
our planting schemes.

Now, Dan had agreed to talk to me about his life since that first
encounter – an encounter, I remind him when we meet, that had taken
place at a portentous moment in his career. He has not forgotten: 'I
remember you saying I'd got a guiding star. You didn't say "You are
lucky," but it's what you meant. I don't remember your exact words but I
remember you saying it quite vividly, actually. That was years ago and I
was on an ascendant wasn't I?'

He was, and for some years after that his trajectory into the media strat-
osphere continued, until one day in the late 1990s when he had what he

describes as an 'epiphany' – the moment when he knew absolutely that he must get back to earth before he found himself irretrievably lost out there. I remember watching him in orbit at the time and being fascinated by the fact that the slightly-built, quietly-spoken, intensely private person I felt I had met appeared so at ease in front of the television cameras, and had the stamina he'd need to travel the world for one series, or labour week after week on the garden he was in process of creating for another, while simultaneously running his garden design business, and still finding enough quiet space to write his column. There was also the highly technical reference book for aspiring designers entitled *The Essential Garden* that Dan had written in collaboration with Terence Conran during this same period. Now I was curious to know if he felt in retrospect it had been worth the effort I imagine it must have cost him.

In the event, however, my first question concerns his relaxed television persona: hadn't he found it an ordeal? On the contrary: 'It was terribly easy to do. I never questioned it, actually. Now I question it but I didn't then. Somebody just said to me "Here's a TV programme. Would you like to present it?" And I said "Why not?" I remember sitting on my roof garden afterwards and realising I hadn't thought about any reasons why not, I'd simply jumped in the deep end.'

And into his element: 'I really enjoyed it because gardening can be a very solitary thing. Also, I had had a very solitary childhood – I was a misfit at school, not a geeky misfit, I just didn't really like being there and my few friends didn't like being there either so we found ways of dodging the system and that's how . . .' his voice trails off for a moment '. . . where am I going to with this?'

'To how much you enjoyed the recognition, perhaps?'

'Oh yes!' he picks up his thread '. . . and suddenly you are in this situation when you've got a film crew, you feel part of something, which you've never felt before, and there's a real buzz and a drive and an energy to it that is very addictive.'

Addictive, and dangerous: while those months at the coalface had quarried a book that sold 22,000 copies in hardback in the UK, and whose rights were taken up to translate it into half a dozen languages including Polish, its success cost Dan dear: 'It was really, really hard work and I reached overload as a result of doing that and the TV at the same time. You know, it's very flattering to be picked up by the media and have people say "We like what you sound like and we're going to give you the opportunity to talk about what you like doing, or make what you like making." But it all happened at once. It was a very challenging period in lots of ways, and it was great to have realised I couldn't carry on.'

As our conversation progresses I begin to realise that Dan himself ascribes all his success to luck, specifically to having stumbled across the right people at the right time to guide him on his way, beginning with the two lady gardeners he often mentions, Miss Joy and Geraldine, who lived in the Hampshire village where he grew up, and who encouraged him in his passion for plants and gardening when he was a very small boy. However, and notwithstanding my own endorsement of this perception all those years ago, I now moot that finding the courage to strap himself to the mast and resist the siren calls of the media has more to do with character than any guiding star, however appropriate the image. But Dan is adamant: 'I had to crash into something. I think it had to happen to help me understand how to deal with myself because I wasn't guarding myself in any way. Now I am very guarded – about my weekends, for instance; I get really depressed if my weekends get broken into. And I am now very, very wary of the media because you are dancing with the devil. You realise whether or not you're comfortable doing that kind of stuff, although I was extremely lucky because I was working with a very good production company who were interested in the people in those shows and it was a really good little team. But those things can't last forever and I think we just ran out of luck, as it were.'

Another high profile arena Dan has forsaken, at least for the time being, is the Chelsea Flower Show: since 1996 he has only designed one show garden, and for one very good reason: 'We all felt at the time that it would be nicer to be making the real thing. We felt that really strongly here in the studio, all of us, and we were all concerned about the waste, much more than we had been.' He corrects himself: 'much more than *I* had been. It didn't seem to make sense any more: with the same amount of energy you have to put into something that's going to be there for five days you could make a garden that might be around for ten, fifteen, twenty, even fifty years, if you're lucky. I'd much rather be doing real spaces that you can walk in and be in – spaces that will change, evolve and live.'

I remember very well that last garden, with its deceptively simple planting of the achingly lovely species tulip, *T. acuminata*, spread quite sparingly, but – like Mozart's notes – in just the right amount, through a patch of long grass and how satisfied I had felt standing there contemplating such, well, such purity I suppose. But the Royal Horticultural Society judges had evidently not shared my experience and only awarded it a silver-gilt medal. So I was curious to know whether Dan believes it is the RHS who insist on its show gardens being, I would argue, overplanted, or the designers themselves who over time have set the standard? 'I think people,' he replies carefully, 'are afraid of there being nothing to look at, which is a complete nonsense. Some of the most magical gardens in the world are about space and placing something within the space that makes perfect sense of the light or framing a view or whatever it is.' As a matter of fact, I have often wondered about Dan's relationship with the RHS, and its with him. 'It has always been a bit odd,' he admits, hesitating, 'because um, I don't know, I was a Wisley boy – I did my Wisley [a two-year studentship at the RHS garden in Surrey] and I did well, but I suppose I've very definitely headed away from institutions. I think the RHS most probably just senses that. There's never been a falling-out or anything, but I've only once been invited to be a judge, and then they retracted their offer. I don't know why they did that, although to be honest I was relieved. I mean I'm not a rebel, but I've never fitted in.'

This would have been a good moment to segue to the subject of Dan's work for his clients, except that earlier I'd asked him if he actually enjoys the business of writing, and then forgotten I'd asked. But Dan hadn't, because he wanted to talk about an inspirational character in his troubled school days whom he rarely mentions – Miss Wiggins, his English teacher. 'She was my teacher between the ages of ten and thirteen, and she gave me this real sense of being able to do something and to do it well. She'd be very encouraging and write me great long notes on my essays. She loves gardening and I think she saw a potential with the writing, and the fact that I like to tell stories.'

As with all good stories, this one has a twist: Dan fell into bad company at his new school; bad company, and a wretched English teacher not up to the job who was tormented by his bored class, including Dan, who in his turn ended up feeling wretched and resentful and contriving to fail his best subject at O level. He passed in the end, along with the seven other subjects he'd sat, and then decided he'd had enough: 'I just didn't feel that the process you embark upon when you start your A levels suited me at all. I wanted to learn by being practical rather than learning through reading, so I slipped through the net.' These days he acknowledges with a degree of regret that his reading is restricted mainly to books about gardening – a fact that may owe something to his busy schedule but rather more to his physical type: 'If I get depressed, I go out and do something and work myself out of it that way. Some people become consumed by a depression but I'll fight my way out of it by being active. I've always used energy to get myself in and out of situations.'

All of which helps to explain why, when the *Sunday Times* approached him, he leapt at the chance to affirm Miss Wiggins' faith in her pupil, and provide his own story with an upbeat ending. Actually, it has a sequel: after a stint with the *Daily Telegraph* he took over Monty Don's slot on the *Observer*, which gave him an interesting new challenge: 'Allan [Jenkins, Editor of the paper's Magazine] said that he enjoyed my writing because I'm not afraid to express my feelings about things, so what I've got to do is work out how far I am prepared to go because you don't want to open yourself too much – your life isn't everybody else's – but you need to learn to present an aspect of it that's interesting to other people.' In any case, however he manages to resolve this dilemma, it was too good an opportunity for further personal development to pass up: 'It was very nice to think I was actually going to be engaging with somebody who enjoyed the writing, who was interested in what I was writing about and who would be pushing me, and it's been really revitalising. You get lazy very quickly if each week an editor just says "Thank you very much!".'

So one day a week, instead of cycling to his Battersea studio as usual, Dan stays home to write his piece, with the garden to inspire him if he gets stuck. Not, that is, the tiny roof garden I remember: around the same time that he realised it was time to change direction he decided it was also time to bring himself down to earth in the real sense, and moved to a house with a large-for-London garden in Peckham. Half of our conversation takes place here at the end of one of his at-home days, but as I also want to get a feel for his workplace we meet initially at his studio which lies tucked away behind solid, orange-painted double doors that manage to shut out the noise and fumes of the traffic crawling up and down the South Circular beyond. Once inside you enter another world, more south-east Asia than south-west London I feel as I make my way down a long narrow alleyway flanked by a very un-Dan-like collection of large-leaved exotic flora bearing witness to the fact that the studio's previous tenant had been Ross Palmer. (Before he decided to move to Thailand, Ross was fellow-New Zealander James Fraser's partner in the *über*-urban chic Avant Gardener design company.)

The atmosphere in the studio itself that afternoon is as serene as a monastery cloister although I fancy the plain old building with its white-washed brick walls and high ceiling had for most of its life been more used to the clatter of man-operated machines churning out widgets round the clock. Once settled in the cool courtyard behind the studio, and with Dan off making us mugs of jasmine tea, I have time to take in a plant more in sympathy with Dan's aesthetic – the sublimely scented *Trachelospermum jasminoides* – and to realise it had been strategically placed beside a small building which turns out to be – bliss! – the studio's very own outdoor privy. Then I remember: in one of Dan's stories about his childhood he mentions the family's outdoor privy and how it had been full of spiders and had its own 'lavatory lily' standing sentinel outside. I expect having an outdoor lavatory was common in an English village in the early 1970s, but in London in the twenty-first millennium it must be deemed a treasure. Either way, with its worn wooden seat and green-painted latch door, the little brick edifice looks absolutely in context with its Somerset Maughan-style setting, and Dan's own ethos.

On the subject of ethos, Dan chooses to work with a relatively small team of seven, excluding himself. 'I've got to be the person that does the conceptualising' he explains, 'and I've got to be constantly on a job, not just handing it over to somebody else, because the people who come to Dan Pearson's Studio want a garden by Dan Pearson. That's why the business is flawed, in a way.' Flawed? He expands: ' I mean that if a businessman looked at it he'd say "Well this isn't any good: if we remove you from the scenario you haven't got a business!" But,' he brightens, 'it's also rather wonderful for that very reason because I think clients do get something which has been really properly thought through – we hope.'

Nevertheless, however tightly Dan feels he needs to run his ship, if the business is to evolve as it must he needs a team as much for their complementary skills as for the manpower they provide, and bringing in new blood recently has completely changed the dynamic: 'I'd been doing mostly domestic spaces, but I wanted to change the emphasis of the business and to start creating gardens that have access for the public as well. We didn't do any advertising, because I've never done that but – I don't quite know how – within a year we had swapped the balance in the studio. It's very interesting.' As though you projected your wish into the ether and it somehow got picked up? 'Yes, maybe that was it: if you look at it in practical terms I was ready to work on a bigger scale and when the work came in we were able to take it on, instead of being frightened by it. It's a very interesting thing, the evolution of a business. It definitely has its own energy. It's like an animal that you are steering and as soon as you take your hands off the reins it wants to go off in its own direction, so if you are at the helm you have to keep it on course, or have people who know what that course is.'

This is where Dan's partner, Huw, comes into the story: Huw is the office manager and as such in a position to provide the overview Dan needs: 'We talk about every project that comes in to see how it's going to fit into the greater scheme of things and why it should be there.' He is all too aware that Dan risked slipping underneath the radar when he stepped out of the media spotlight and, as keeper of the diary, tries to restrict the invitations Dan accepts to those that will impact directly on the business. But I fear that precious weekend space does get broken into rather a lot.

The studio's change of emphasis away from designing chiefly private gardens decided Dan to bring a qualified landscape architect into the team to deal with the baffling bureaucracy involved in creating public spaces. 'I'm not very patient like that,' he confesses. 'That's one of the things I find really frustrating about doing public work. I wouldn't have wanted,' he adds emphatically, 'to be a landscape architect'.

I am none too clear about the distinction between landscape designer and landscape architect, and neither is Dan: 'I think that's a very difficult question and I'm on dodgy ground because I'm not really sure I know what the answer is. But I think basically, if you put it crudely, a landscape designer is not qualified, and a landscape architect is.' So I asked landscape architect Kim Wilkie if he thought Dan had nailed it, and he does, although he felt he should point out that Dan is an exceptional case in that he has the ability few possess to bring into his landscape designs such an exquisite sense of detail, balance, and finesse in public spaces he has been able to rely on his creative skill, and avoid taking the exams. Kim also points out that since landscape architects need to think in terms of centuries, and cover such vast areas of knowledge, the skill ultimately lies in knowing how little they know and getting the help they need, while keeping a clear picture of the overall concept.

Which is an accurate description of how Dan operates – as far as he is concerned, it's plain common sense: 'I think if you focus your energy properly you can have much more impact than if you try to apply yourself to everything. I was telling you about slipping through the net at school: I know where I am most comfortable and I know that it's not a good idea to put myself in a situation where I'm not comfortable because I don't function at all well, so I remove myself. I'm quite good at doing that.' And work? What about turning down jobs gut instinct says you should? He admits the spectre of the monthly wages bill makes this a tough call: 'It goes against every bone in my body and throws me into panic mode, so I have to be really calm about it and think to myself, if you'd taken it on you'd be working on something for months and months that would feel like an effort and an obligation and those feelings aren't conducive to producing good work. I'd much rather have a hiatus where there wasn't enough work than be doing work we don't like: we have all got to really love what we do, although it's important to stimulate your staff, to push them, and a gentle way of pushing them is to change direction slightly each time you take on a job.'

I imagine this could lead to friction on occasion but as Dan observes, this is all to the good: 'Because you need to have opinions in a creative space, otherwise everybody is letting themselves be led by just one person and very few gardens are created by one person alone – the best spaces are a collaborative effort.' I wonder if such a reserved character as his can ever really let rip but he tells me it can: 'Definitely. When I get overwhelmed, because I could actually lead a much more simple life; I could be writing my *Observer* column and only working one day a week but I'm not, I'm *driven* to do all these different things which does take its toll, because I have to rely on a network of people to make everything work, and that can be a burden as well, you know. So when I run out of energy or get depressed it feels like there's no sunshine and, yeah, I do lose the joy.'

Losing the joy is not quite what I had been hinting at, but Dan is not a celebrity chef, and the image he has to foster is very different: 'I know how important my public profile is in terms of enabling me to do what I want to do. I've got a lot of the work through having projected myself as a sensitive person, and I think the best clients we've got now are coming to the studio because they want somebody who's going to be considerate and sensitive to their needs and to the land and who's not going to be overwhelming as a character, and all those things have been communicated through a public persona which I have generated, but it's not a false thing.'

If it were, there'd be no clients I suggest, and he takes my point: 'They are coming to me because they want somebody who's going to access a piece of landscape very lightly. They don't want a great big ornamental garden, and we are relying much more on working with the land and what naturally occurs there, and finding ways to access it without making scars. The ornamental parts are often just reduced to kitchen – or produce – gardens: herbs, vegetables, fruit, orchard, and a little planting around the building to make people feel they've got some sort of domesticity that isn't dominated by nature too much, but that ornamental space is getting smaller and smaller.' Interestingly, the garden for which he is arguably best known (Home Farm in Northamptonshire) was, in his words, 'hugely plant-oriented'. Home Farm was his first major project post-Kew, although he had already begun his collaboration with its owner, Frances Mossman, on her previous garden in Barnes when he was only seventeen, and a student at Wisley. Home Farm was also the garden he worked on in front of the television cameras, and I've often wondered what happened to it. What happened was that the Mossman's sold the property a few years ago, and because Dan's bond with Frances was, and remains, so close he hasn't felt able to further develop the garden despite being invited back by its two subsequent owners, and despite this being contrary to his usual practise: he likes to keep in touch with his clients' gardens on a consultancy basis after a project is technically finished, because by definition no garden ever is.

But this low-key style of planting Dan and his clients now favour is not, he warns me, reflected in his own garden: 'You'll see that it's absolutely full of treasures, but if I were to garden in the countryside – *when* I garden in the countryside – I will have only a small area of ornamental garden, and I will be striving to be part of an environment that feels more primitive, something that has its own order, which I will access in a very gentle and elegant way, and I'm becoming much more interested in those points of access because they can be exquisitely beautiful – a small path that's in just the right place leading to a seat under a tree facing just the right direction, those things can be very profound. To be part of an environment like that is, I think, more appealing than going into a garden and finding a series of beautiful combinations, and although I'll always want to play with plants I can see that they will become less and less and less important.'

Rather to my own surprise, an image of the rigorously geometric designs of Spanish landscape architect Fernando Caruncho springs to mind, but when I mention his name Dan agrees there is an affinity. 'I love the fact that his work is so graphic and so sensual. It's sensual minimalism really isn't it? I can't stand that uptight minimalism that's all about perfection. Perfection is not beautiful: imperfection is beautiful, and I think what he does is allow things to be themselves in those spaces. Even though things are clipped, they've got a plumpness to them, and he has the bravery to do something like having a cornfield in a garden. Inspiring. I think we are both purists in a very different way, that's part of it. And I think his work is very much about the essence of a place, and that's very similar.'

I am curious to know what part of the country Dan imagines himself moving to when the time comes and he reckons it will have to be somewhere in the west country: 'Because I like land to be full – full and plump and rich. And I don't want to be living like Beth [Chatto, friend and lifelong inspiration] with that constant worry of drought, but I'm not going to be able to go north because I'm not very good in the winter. I like winter – I like the season – and I *love* Yorkshire, but that extra month of winter with that much less light would do my head in I think.'

This reference to Beth Chatto reminds me of a carefully orchestrated conversation between the pair that had taken place a while ago now at the Royal Geographical Society. The topic was 'Nature as Inspiration in the Garden', and towards the end of the evening Dan touched on the broad palette of species – or 'wild' – plants, that he knows from observing them growing in their natural habitat he can rely on to maintain the right balance in his designs. But Beth was sceptical: sixty years' experience has taught her that plants refuse to behave to order so she tries always to remember this: 'I've got say to myself it will never happen again, the whole thing is so ephemeral. It's not like a Beethoven concerto or a wonderful painting, there is really only this actual moment when you are looking at it.'

Seeing Dan's own garden with its collection of largely 'wild' perennials planted in exquisite combinations of magenta and maroon, deep reds and soft apricots, burnt orange and buttery yellows, and every shade of purple, I ask him how he might have responded to Beth's observation, if the conversation had not moved on when it did. His reply is oblique: 'I think you need a foundation of things that are more or less constant, which you then build upon. If you look at a river, for example, the rocks that emerge from the river are the things you can rely upon but the river will change, it'll be in spate or it'll be still, and those rocks will emerge or be submerged, and other rocks might emerge around them and there might be white water sometimes that could be reflective. You need to have those static things that allow the other more ephemeral moments to come and go, and I think you can learn to introduce enough of that for a landscape to be sustainable, and even in my own garden here, which is so dependent on ephemera, there's enough when it drops back in winter to hold it together.'

I try to imagine the scene in monochrome, but summer's tumult − the water as it were − distracts me. I can see at a glance the two discrete areas of decking (a surprise, that decking) set at different levels and separated by a path of slate chippings snaking its way up through the borders. And I can glimpse a pair of drop-dead chic solid slate slabs half-submerged in the two borders whose matt surfaces are reflecting the shifting patterns of light and shadow, but in winter would stand out proud − and rocklike. What I cannot spot at a glance is much plant material that might serve as honorary rocks, certainly nothing as obvious as a topiarised shape or a clipped hedge, so Dan has to direct my attention to, among other things, two large stands of bamboo which must class as boulders, never mind rocks. I have also managed to overlook − or look through, rather − the four multi-stemmed deciduous trees Dan has chosen as much for their attractive bark and interesting outlines in winter as for their summer display: the silvery-leafed *Salix exigua* spreading half the breadth of the garden; a hornbeam, placed to one side of the slate path with a lovely *Catalpa erubescens* a few feet nearer the house on the other; and, finally, hard by the doors leading from the kitchen to the outdoor eating area, a grand specimen of *Cercis canadensis* 'Forest Pansy' in a large, bowl-shaped stone container.

I also remember someone in the audience that evening asking Dan how people with small urban spaces can be expected to introduce nature into their gardens and not end up with a mess, and that he had advised sticking to one 'story'. He didn't say so at the time, but now admits how hard that is in practise: 'My own garden was the most difficult I've ever designed. I had all these different stories I could have told – wanted to tell – about the same space because if you look at gardens all the time you accumulate a huge scrapbook in your head and it took a long time to realise I must only use two or three pages. That whole idea of storytelling in a garden is really interesting: that you must reveal things slowly, and not clutter the space up with too much so you're not feeling over-stimulated, and can allow yourself to be drawn into it in a very natural way.'

I own to a fear that if I followed this wise advice I'd be left with not enough to do in the physical sense, and Dan empathises: 'It is absolutely essential that I have things to do. I *need* to garden. I've *always* needed to garden, and if I don't garden I start to feel odd and out of kilter. If I wasn't running my business I would be driven mad by the size of this garden: this is a weekend garden.' But he has found a solution: he 'rips' (his word) plants out whenever he feels the need. I question his choice of word here but he assures me. 'No, no! I am quite capable of ripping things out. Absolutely. I think there is something rather liberating in that.' That's the joy of gardening I think to myself: we can express our dark side without anyone ending up dead. Meanwhile Dan continues his train of thought: 'I am not sentimental about plants, and I have to be very, very tough with clients sometimes.'

However, there is one client who cannot respond to Dan as he could wish, and he was just about to fly out to meet him face to face in an attempt to break an apparent impasse. The client commissioned Dan to design an ecological garden covering 625 acres (250 hectares) on the side of a mountain on Japan's most northerly island, where the temperature drops to −35°C in winter, and it goes without saying that it is a measure of his reputation that he has been invited to undertake such a prestigious job in the first place, and of his character that he felt confident enough to accept it. However, seated in his garden on a lovely afternoon in early summer, with only the disturbing sight of one of his black cats casually swatting a dragonfly to mar our mood, he tries to explain something of what he's up against, and what it's taught him, for example: 'We supplied some planting plans for cherry trees which I want placed very close because I want it to look like a nuttery. But they never plant cherry trees that close so for them it's a very strange thing I'm suggesting. I think it's going to work because it's on the edge of a woodland and we are using a native tree that's wild anyway, but they'd made up their minds it's not right to put cherry trees that close.'

So the client ignored his emails, and when he did reply Dan's planting plan had been amended to suit the Japanese aesthetic. Dan duly emailed back ever so politely requesting they stick to his original layout. Again, no response. *Ergo*, confrontation avoided because, he explains, 'it's rude to say no! So you might find you've been having a conversation for five minutes a day for five weeks that's going in the wrong direction, but you don't know that it's been going in the wrong direction. You have to second-guess everything all the time, and think laterally and never assume anything. It's one of those really difficult things to apply, isn't it, never to assume anything? But such a good little rule when you do remember. It's very interesting. I like those differences. I've learnt so much through travelling to Japan and having to negotiate. Of course, I'd much rather they just said to me "Look Dan, we don't want to put any more trees in because we don't think it's right," and I could say "OK, what are your reasons?". But they can't, and as I am in their culture, I can't bully them into it.'

Which is why he decided to spend a week out there seeing if he couldn't demonstrate to his client on site how absolutely right his cherry trees will look planted in a mass. He got back worn out and ill, but successful, and I put it to him when I heard the news that whatever it costs him he has not so far been stumped by anything life has thrown at him. He laughs 'Oh I have! I just might not be admitting to it!'

Dan Pearson Studio
80c Battersea Rise,
London SW11 1EH
www.danpearsonstudio.com
mail@danpearsonstudio.com
020 7924 2518

# *Kim Wilkie*

## LANDSCAPE ARCHITECT

The most essential part of understanding place is learning how
to listen and really being interested in what you hear.

Kim Wilkie

When I walked into his office a little ahead of time, Kim Wilkie is on the telephone listening intently to whatever whoever was on the other end of the line is saying, yet at the same time managing to convey to me, whom he has never met, his unalloyed pleasure at seeing me standing there, and that I must make myself at home.

Home is the appropriate word: Kim Wilkie lives with his partner and dog above the shop. In other words, the large open-plan office in which I find myself is situated on the raised-ground floor of an end-of-terrace Victorian house in Richmond-upon-Thames that Kim bought for himself in the early 1980s, and later transformed into dual-purpose space when he formed his own landscape design company in 1989. But I could not know this, and as I inspect with interest his working environment I am wondering what I am going to do about describing his own garden, if he has one, and whether I dare ask a busy man for a second interview *chez lui* if he does.

A worryingly noisy blond Labrador is wandering about the place while, by contrast, the five members of Kim Wilkie's team are all seated around one large table in the centre of the room gazing in thoughtful silence at their computer screens. Kim is within touching distance to their left, another large table for meetings with each other and/or clients to their right. The floorboards are bare, the walls plain white emulsion, and a floor-to-ceiling, wall-to-wall plate glass window looks out over the garden – all very state-of-the-art and minimalist as befits a thoroughly modern landscape architect. However, the original marble fireplaces have been retained, and the floorboards are the old ones, stripped and polished, reflecting Kim Wilkie's ethos: respect and conserve what's good from the past and reinvigorate it by introducing the best of the new. In a pot on the floor by the window stands a fleshy, cut-leafed specimen of a plant that looks like a fancy variety of the cannabis weed, but turns out to be a fancy variety of begonia.

I put what happens next down to nervous excitement: when Kim joins me, I switch on the tape and the first words recorded are his: 'It's done! I was just up there on Monday. I'm really pleased! . . .' He is referring to a project he has been working on at Holker Hall in Cumbria for Lord and Lady Cavendish, but instead of waiting for him to tell me more, I leap in with a wildly generalised observation on the issue of conservation/preservation triggered by the memory of something Hugh Cavendish had said in a light aside some years ago now, to the effect that he doesn't keep any records or detailed plans of what he and his wife Grania are doing to improve Holker's historic garden, because bodies such as the Garden History Society and English Heritage – with which Lord Cavendish was himself, and Kim Wilkie remains, actively involved – might then be able to oblige future generations of his family to abide by them. Once upon a time, I moot, people could sweep away without a second thought whatever didn't chime with their aesthetic, or the *zeitgeist*, and I cite 'Capability' Brown as my example. Kim waits quietly until I eventually run out of steam before replying with admirable tact: 'Well, there are some very interesting aspects of that, and to take 'Capability Brown' first . . . Are you finding it too noisy?' Bless the man: dogs don't pad about on bare floorboards; they clack.

We move upstairs where the walls are also white, the plate-glass window is repeated, the old floorboards exposed, and the original fireplaces remain *in situ*, although up here the fireplaces are evidently used, and the floor is strewn with oriental rugs. The window opens on to a terrace serving as both vegetable garden (contained in two huge, waist-high copper planters) and outdoor dining room, with a table made out of a solid glass cube doubling in its turn as the light-well for the office space below. The minimalist kitchen has been built into an alcove no bigger than a cupboard, a comparably tiny glass vase of flowers containing sprigs of sweet box (sarcococca), snowdrops, stripy arum leaves, and the tiny narcissus 'Tête à Tête', sits on the dining table, and a bowl of overblown blue hyacinths on the coffee table.

Before settling down again we go out onto the terrace to look down on the garden which, like the house, serves a dual purpose – for example, a curiously curved, startlingly bright blue glass bench on the path running the length of the garden's left wall was specifically designed for Kim by Ben Barrell to accommodate at a sitting all five members of his design team, when it's warm enough to eat out. The same colour is repeated in the hard surface of the small parking space beyond the ceanothus hedge that inspired the choice in the first place. At the house end, prostrate rosemary grows on a sloping bank, and on wires and trellis fixed to the garden walls some persevering soul – almost certainly Kim himself, who is famous for his patience – has persuaded a specimen of *Vitis cognitiae* to work its way around. A narrow rectangle of lawn has been carved into shallow terraces (grass-covered amphitheatres on a vast scale, but similar in principle, are a feature of a number of Kim Wilkie Associates projects) and the grass known as Yorkshire fog (*Holcus lanatus*) sown on the slopes, with regular lawn grass on the flat areas. Four specimens of *Arbutus andrachnoides*, whose flaky, cinnamon-coloured bark and crisp, matt leaves stand in nice contrast to the shiny brilliance of the bench, complete the stylish picture.

Back indoors, and again the first words are Kim's, again they appear to be out of context, and again they reveal the man's passionate involvement with his work: 'We ripped the fence down! Bamber Gascoigne led the party and fifty of us pulled it down!' 'Gracious!' I yelp, 'You resorted to vandalism!' 'No! Volunteers! It's an Heritage Lottery Fund sponsored bid. And the view! It's just wonderful what a difference it's made. Let me know what you think.' The fence in question is, or was, a brutal-looking chain-link-and-concrete affair that unceremoniously sliced off one corner of the area of ancient common land lying between the brow of Richmond Hill and the timeless pastoral scene of cattle grazing the Petersham water meadows alongside the Thames below. Kim Wilkie and his friends are actually only the latest in a long line of local residents dating back to the end of the nineteenth century who have taken it upon themselves to try to protect the famous view from the predations of the developers or, in this particular instance, to restore the *status quo*: some greedy grandee in the past had helped himself to land to which he had no right. Months later I bump into Kim plus dog and colleagues engaged in a working stroll along the terrace in the spring sunshine, which must beat breakfast meetings in a hotel. Beaming, he calls out: 'Enjoy the view!'

His excitement is easy to understand: not only has getting rid of the fence made a huge difference, it is sixteen years and counting since Kim persuaded people that his Arcadian dream was achievable and John Gummer, the then Secretary of State for the Environment, gave government backing for an ambitious project to analyse, record and plan the future of the entire Thames landscape for the twenty-first century. And so Kim's dream got a name – the Thames Landscape Strategy, of which the successful Lottery bid (known officially as Arcadia in the City) to remove the offending fence is a small but significant part.

I would like to hear more about the Strategy, but am hoist on my own petard because Kim wants to argue the case for 'Capability' Brown: 'I think that's a very interesting philosophical point you raised. I think there's probably an unfair perception that he just swept away things without regard to what had been there before. I say this, because in the projects of his that I've been involved in it strikes me that he did look extremely carefully at the place and the possibilities of it and responded very sensitively and brought out the innate 'capabilities' of the land. But yes, there were a lot of people immediately after who attacked his quite radical thinking and gave him the reputation for being a destructive vandal.'

But people, at least rich people, I persist, could and did tear down what they perceived as out of date, or in the way, couldn't and didn't they? Kim sticks to his agenda: 'I actually believe that people have really passionate feelings about the landscape and their place in it and I think the conservation/preservation issue is an interesting one, but in many ways it muddies the water. I think what people have always done is to cherish the memory of places and those memories may not always be terribly factually accurate. It's a sense of the spirit of the place, which is to do with how people have lived in that place for a long time, the stories that go with it, the way that the land and the water and the air move. I think if the politicians were to acknowledge this they would be mining quite a rich seam of strength of feeling and passion. Sometimes it is to do with not wanting anything to change, but mostly it's because people care very much about the place that they live in. Where I agree with you is that to keep things just because they are old, and to try to restore minutely to a plan that may never have been quite implemented in the first place is a big mistake.'

Which would explain Brown's decision to sweep away the arguably inappropriate Dutch- or French-style gardens and replace them with a form that reflects the rolling English landscape, and our low light levels you mentioned earlier? 'Absolutely, and the best kind of conservation and sensitive engagement with the landscape is based on understanding what's important in the place – what the real beauties of it are, how it's used, how it works, and then allowing that to inspire the next move, so you don't keep everything. Hugh at Holker has kept a lot of things that are intrinsic to the place, but he hasn't been completely hide-bound by any single designer or any single phase, and what he and Grania have done is come up with a really imaginative long-term plan which allows his children scope to do an awful lot without binding them to minute details that would stifle any creativity.'

He cannot emphasise enough the value of the work the Garden History Society is doing in the field of academic research pioneered by Mavis Batey. Interestingly, he tells me it was Mavis Batey herself who taught him to look beyond pure academic research into ways in which that history is applicable in the future. In fact he has addressed the Society on this very subject: 'I was showing the way that Ham Lands and this area have been managed for centuries. Not only was it a beautiful and historic landscape, but also the way it was managed was immensely practical in that the water meadows absorbed all of the water so that the flooding downstream during the critical two hours of a storm was alleviated, and the avenues were perfect as dry routes through the wet meadows. I showed them that, rather than leap into greater and greater technological solutions with concrete and steel, sometimes just to go back and look at how people understood the way that land and water work gives you a solution which is beautiful, which is very practical, which is not expensive, and where nature conservation and human enjoyment and an aesthetic continuity all come together.'

He is also pleased with the way he perceives English Heritage has evolved in recent years. 'I think imagination and flexibility is what Hugh was wanting in English Heritage and I'm sure he really helped – along with Gilly Drummond [Chairman of The Association of Gardens Trusts] who has been very good at leading them along a braver route. It's much riskier if you start to make judgments as to whether it's relevant, or good, or not. But in the end you have a flexibility that keeps it alive.' He cites one of his own company's projects as an example: 'At Heveningham [Hall, a Palladian mansion in Suffolk], they allowed the demolition of Grade II listed walls and garden right beside a Grade I listed house. They said this particular Victorian garden beside this fantastic Georgian building never really worked, and in a pretty landmark decision they said, "Yes, it can be cleared away and a new design can go in its place."' I didn't think to ask him if the Victorian Society had fought the old garden's corner, but when it came to the other half of the project – the implementation of an existing but never actually executed design by 'Capability' Brown for landscaping the valley on the opposite side of the house – every local ecology group and every naturalist society and all the surrounding parish councils and every municipal body in the county of Suffolk had a point of view to express. Eventually, the design was executed exactly as Brown had envisaged it two hundred and fifty years earlier because Kim was able to satisfy them all that ultimately it was the ideal solution for the topography of the land.

But I realise not everyone shares his view about English Heritage when later I read this comment in one of the Garden History Society's newsletters: 'We consider that the scheme [for a golf resort hotel] proposed for Tottenham Park raises issues of fundamental importance for the future of major historic designed landscapes in the context of "regeneration" and "enabling" development. We are concerned that English Heritage, in a desire to be seen as "developer-friendly", is prepared to compromise too much.' So I asked the Society's then chairman, Dominic Cole, for his opinion. Dominic explained that it is the Society's prime purpose to be vigilant, and that, yes, some might call it bossy and interfering. He also pointed out that not all planning applications to develop a listed landscape can be relied upon to be quite as sensitive to the spirit of the place as those submitted by Kim Wilkie Associates, or, come to that, Land Use Consultants, the company he works for.

Kim too worked for Land Use Consultants after he qualified in 1984, but left in 1989 to start his own business. He felt he needed the freedom to take on whatever interests him, including loss-making enterprises if he wishes, and to sit on as many time-consuming committees as he chooses (the English Heritage Urban Panel, the National Trust Gardens Panel, the London Mayor's Public Realm Group, and until recently the Royal Parks Advisory Board, are only the most prestigious). I am impressed by the man's selfless dedication but he thinks perhaps I am missing the point: 'The whole idea of duty and obligation seem terribly heavy and worthy,' he agrees, 'but it's almost as though life presents you with some extraordinary opportunities and you need to pursue them for your own satisfaction, and sense of fulfilment: you gain as much as you give . . .' He hesitates, remembering the downside for a moment: 'Though there have been times . . . just getting the view cleared here has been a nightmare in terms of one or two people not wanting any change whatsoever and there are endless public meetings and you listen and you compromise and you try as much as possible to respond to the common mind – the common opinion – but there comes a point when you have to say "No! I know this is right and I trust that I can help lead this in the right direction." You can't simply be a sponge for . . . for . . .' For every negative attitude? 'Yes. It gets to you in the end.' So how do you stay sane? 'I've got a small holding out in Hampshire, and at weekends I'm farming and chopping wood and I think that contact with the soil and doing it yourself. Also, having a dog makes a huge difference.'

However, he admits he has reached his limit: 'I mean you are right, we've been handling a huge number of projects and its been really, really exciting and I wanted to be learning as much as contributing on all these different committees, but now I want to breathe so slowly, slowly I've been doing less and less committee work and gradually choosing just to go for very few projects where I really like the people – the clients. I was actually saying to Grania on the train down from Holker recently that you go through about thirty years of seizing every moment you can, but there just comes a time when suddenly you think you want to savour the moment rather than seize it, and she said "You're getting old!"' Kim Wilkie was born in 1955. You decide.

Either way, he has other plans: 'I want more time to look at farming in the rural community. It's not a priority for this government although it's one of the biggest things that's happening in Europe at the moment – how we manage our land, how we grow our food; the changes now are as great as happened in the Agricultural Revolution, or after the War.' There is also a job he has his eye on: 'What I'd love to be is on the board of the South Downs National Park, if it ever happens – or something like that.' And leave London? 'Ultimately, yes. I'm a country boy at heart. I'm not a good urban dweller.'

Maybe not, but owing to his willingness to listen to the people who have to live there he is very good at designing spaces to make dwelling in urban areas at least as pleasant as possible. He tries to find ways to balance conserving what people perceive to be worth hanging on to with state-of-the-art creative innovation. His company was involved, for example, in the regeneration of the inner city around Southwark Cathedral and Borough Market. In fact, the first time I ever heard of the now ubiquitous farmers' markets was through listening to Kim urge all present at a lecture he was giving some years ago now to shop locally and to use these markets wherever possible.

Once again, politics enters the frame: I wondered if the problem farmers face has to do with the electorate's expectation that food ought to be, to coin a phrase, cheap as chips? (As it happens, our conversation took place shortly before Jamie Oliver's heroic campaign to get the government to put more money on the school dinner tables hit the media.) But cheap food is only part of the problem – there's the deliberate decision by government to keep the price of aviation fuel low to consider: 'I don't know *how* we begin to change that, but I think the European Union, if it took it seriously, really could . . .' I suggest it might be our nomadic past that has programmed us to keep on the move and, if so, there's scant hope: 'There's partly that, but . . .', he hesitates, reluctant to let such a despairing thought go unchallenged: 'I'm not sure how nomadic we really are still, and I suspect that a lot of people would rather stay at home, or rather not go that far if the aspiration were not constantly thrown at us. I suspect that many people kind of dread going on holiday, but feel that they have to because everyone else does and how can you resist a five-pound flight to Bangkok? We think we want to travel all over the place, but actually the process of travelling is pretty miserable and when we get there it's not usually all that nice. Probably people would be a lot happier not travelling as much.' Kim believes it is only (only!) a question of people becoming more aware of their connection to where they live, to the land itself, and that in England (though not the United States, worryingly) that sense of belonging to a place remains strong.

Later, as I drove home through ancient, unspoiled Richmond Park, I remembered William Morris' Utopian novel *News From Nowhere*. Morris's hero, as I recall, lived and worked in a great city at some point in the future, when society had reverted to the barter system. If he felt the need for fresh air and exercise he would simply set off for the countryside on foot and find a farm to work on in return for his food and lodging. Morris's dream may not be a feasible proposition for the twenty-first century, but listening to Kim Wilkie it seems clear that if you believe enough in something, and have the will and the patience to see it through, your vision can be realised. Indeed, he was scheduled to address a public meeting that very evening about how the flood plains in the Richmond area can best be managed in the future – St Mary's Church Hall, Twickenham. 7.30pm. Would I like to come along? I would (but in the event allowed myself to be defeated by the rush-hour traffic on the South Circular, and felt curiously ashamed).

A suspicious thought: Is Kim paid for all the time he puts in on the Strategy? 'Not all of it, but right at the moment, yes, I am being paid. We found people to pay for it, bit by bit. I mean in the end it was never really paid for, but gradually we put it together and more and more people joined forces with it and now there's a co-ordinator who keeps it going and brings it all together. The partners are up to fourteen now, I think. It's got a complete life of its own.' I imagine that having so much paid or unpaid work on the go at once must require an ability to delegate, but that's not the way Kim Wilkie operates: 'I am not sure it's a question of delegating, I think it's a question of sharing. When it's a good idea it's not your idea *ever*. I think probably the biggest step was to realise we are part of a common mind and a common heritage and a common culture and sometimes you have the opportunity to promote an idea or crystallize it, but nothing is ever anyone's single possession. The trouble is, if you try to grasp it too tightly you'll suffocate the idea, and I think that's why it's a question of sharing rather than delegating.'

Such a wise attitude would explain the atmosphere in the office I'd noticed earlier: the sense that here was an ensemble cast at work. And indeed discover this is the case when he explains the company's *modus operandi* – how they all take a collective look at a new commission before one person assumes the role of team leader although even then 'because we are all in one room round one table it means everything is discussed all the time'. And then there's those working walks and communal lunches; they even all go on site together whenever feasible. For example the company, along with half a dozen other leading landscape design groups, was asked to dream up a new layout for the courtyard at the heart of the Victoria & Albert Museum. The competition was awesome: the iconoclastic, controversial New Yorker, Martha Schwartz, the super-cool Kathryn Gustafson from Paris (best known in England for creating the Princess Diana Memorial Garden in Hyde Park), Anna Olins from Canada, Adrian Geuze from Holland, and the many times Chelsea Gold Medallist, Christopher Bradley-Hole.

So was the brief: to create a tranquil garden that was also 'really hopping', with space for exhibitions as well as for nightlife which, he hardly needs point out, is 'an impossible combination!' Where, or how, do you start? 'You go and sit in the space, walk around, watch how people use it. We spent quite a lot of time just sitting there, and ate in the space and watched people. Very often the first ideas jump out at you immediately, and then you just need to work with them and work with them, which isn't usually the way that design is taught.' Anyhow, not at Berkeley University Environmental Design School in California where Kim studied landscape architecture, and where students were taught to dismiss their first idea, or go for its opposite – at least come up with some options – which Kim reckons may work for some, but not for him: 'Nearly always – within the first minute or the first hour – it comes to me, almost as if a place has its agenda. You just have to understand you can never recapture the freshness of that first impact. And in the case of the V&A: 'When you've got architecture that is that insistent and so many different functions to cater for you have to come up with something quite simple, so first we just looked at how the building had evolved – that big Italianate façade in the courtyard used to be the front entrance before the Aston Webb wing was built. It's a wonderfully ramshackle museum. I love the treasure trove that's there and the fact that you can get so lost. It's like getting lost in Tutankhamen's tomb.' When I congratulate him on winning he makes light of his team's triumph, reckoning that they probably won because their solution was the simplest and therefore the cheapest to implement. My money says they won because they really heard what the old place was telling them.

This gift for listening is surely the reason his team was chosen by the Prince of Wales – or to be accurate, the Prince of Wales's Charitable Foundation, in conjunction with the Mihai Eminescu Trust under the chairmanship of Jessica Douglas-Home – as the best to report on the special character and value of the mediaeval Saxon villages still intact in the Transylvanian region of Romania, and the surrounding pristine landscape. Kim speaks German, which meant he could communicate with the largely German-speaking population, and since he really enjoys 'rudimentary living', staying for a fortnight in a local guesthouse was not the challenge it might be for some.

I am very curious to know what he thinks the chances are for this ancient way of life to survive and predictably Kim is hopeful: 'You can't stop the clock, but there is something extremely special that still is important to the people there and it's a kind of essence of what's important to all of us, so it's a question of trying to find a way in which the most critical elements can be kept, and yet bring in washing machines, the internet, find ways to get to the city, and still keep that very precious relationship between man, the land and the nature conservation element. I don't know the answer, but it's contributing to the dialogue and helping to see what is so special it needs to be treated as sacred, and where there is total latitude for change.' (The Trust is aiming to use local Romanians wherever possible apparently, and that will help the people understand what's important to them about their heritage, and teach them the necessary skills to restore and conserve it.) 'It seems to be working,' he says, adding cautiously, 'Heaven knows how it will all turn out, but at least each village is getting a pride in its architecture and its landscape.' I try to remember who it was said that all it takes for evil to triumph is for a good man to do nothing as I think to myself that evil is already beginning to stalk this ancient region in the guise of tacky tourism: Draculaland theme parks and cheap motels at every crossroads is a very real possibility, and a certainty if the good guys do nothing.

Kim Wilkie can listen to what people have to say in all sorts of tongues besides German, which is a gift that would have served him well if, as was expected of him, he had joined the Diplomatic Service after Oxford. Throughout his years at Winchester and university he went along cheerfully enough with everyone else's notion of his destiny, and would probably have been in Washington by now if he hadn't at the eleventh hour found the courage to give it all up and follow his heart.

The stark fact is that at the age of twenty-one and fresh from Oxford he fell 80 feet off a mountain in Guatemala and managed against the odds to survive. The near death-experience may have been his 'eureka' moment, but it was actually only the catalyst: he had realised he was on the wrong path the previous year, when he was still up at Oxford and doing a summer job as an environmental correspondent in Iran: 'It was the year before the

Ayotollahs. Quite an exciting time. But the young people I spoke to in the British Embassy who'd just joined seemed a bit disillusioned by the diplomatic life, and I could see that as a civil servant you don't have very much latitude to be yourself, or to follow what you believe is right. But the landscape architects I met were completely enthralled by the possibilities there, and I remember saying to them "What you're doing isn't even work! It's just fantastic!"' Whereupon one called his bluff – if he imagined it was all such fun why not become one himself? Quite simply, because it would have meant throwing away an expensive education. 'So,' he concludes, 'I think falling off the mountain and realising that life could stop at any moment gave me the courage to say I'll start all over again. And of course, it's much harder work than anything else! In some ways it was very liberating because I stopped thinking "God! I've got this whole life to be sensible about." It gives you the sense that it may not be very long. At some stage in your youth I think you need to become aware that life isn't infinite.'

Kim is now working – 'all for free! My particular input is on water' – with Zac Goldsmith and John Gummer on environmental policies.

Kim Wilkie Associates
34 Friars' Style Road
Richmond-upon-Thames TW10 6NE
020 8332 0304
www.kimwilkie.com

*Indignation! The Campaign for Conservation*, Kit-Cat Books, 93 Castelnau, London SW13 9EL. Tel/fax: 020 8846 9550

# Ronald Blythe

## LAY PRIEST, POET AND WRITER

And now – the snow. And what will happen if you can't get up the road? Nothing: that will be the bliss of it. I shall drink port and read Elizabeth Taylor, feed the wrens and the vixen, should she call again – and have no end of a time.

*Word From Wormingford: A Parish Year* (1997)

How romantic! I thought when I read that passage in a cutting from *The Church Times* my sister had saved for me, and what courage it must take to live alone and all the year round in such an inaccessible spot, the kind of spot the urban-based writer might seek to rent for a few months to finish his book, and then flee. Furthermore, my febrile imaginings as to the extent of Dr Blythe's isolation were further exacerbated by the instructions I received on a postcard as to how one should approach his property. They read: 'Turn right along Lt Horkesley Rd. Track to Bottengoms Farm on left. Name on brick wall. Stop [double underline] at Sign! Very Important!!' Heavens above! What on earth lay beyond? A cliff? A bog? A raging torrent?

The icing on the cake would be a ghastly storm on the day of our assignation, but since this was scheduled for October in the warmest year for a millennium that was unlikely, and so it proved: I arrive at the top of the steeply-descending, deeply-rutted grass track on a warm, sunny, gothic-fantasy-dispelling kind of morning, and am almost tempted to abandon the car and walk the rest of the way to get at least a sense of what it might be like to live in such a remote place without one: Ronald Blythe does not drive.

But in the event, unsure of what I might be letting myself in for (a twenty-minute walk each way as it turned out), I park as directed in front of 'the Sign!' beside an appropriately picturesque old wreck of a black-painted shed at the entrance to an orchard that I must cross to reach my goal, which in the event turns out to be an ancient, cream-washed, rose-covered idyll, complete with mossy-tiled roof, whose front door stands wide open and welcoming, allowing the early morning sun to stream through into a square, stone-flagged entrance hall where a large, almost-all-white cat has his head down in his breakfast bowl. Catherine Morland might have felt a twinge of disappointment but I think I'd like to move in.

My host appears stage left. Bright blue eyes and small, lithe frame proclaim his East Anglian farming blood, shoulder-length white hair his poet's soul, and anxious concern for my welfare – about where I would like to sit, or what I would like to do, or drink before we set off on our prearranged Cook's Tour of the south-west Suffolk countryside – his solicitous nature. It soon becomes plain my host is really looking forward to being my guide round a part of the world he has lived in all his long life; less plain that he is going to enjoy being asked lots of questions.

Questions, incidentally, that were going to have to cover a bewilderingly wide range of subjects not obviously connected with gardens: my editor has asked me to get Ronnie – as he likes to be known – to talk about his childhood lived out between the wars in a small Suffolk village during the great agricultural depression that had hit East Anglia so hard – a period that the writer evoked so vividly in *Akenfield*, an elegiac, partly autobiographical account of a way of rural life that had endured for centuries, but was on the point of vanishing forever in 1969 when the book was first published. I have also been reminded that as a struggling young poet in the mid-1950s Ronnie Blythe had lived at Aldeburgh, that he had known and worked for Benjamin Britten during that period, and to be sure to get that story too.

Another friend urged me to read for my research The Wormingford Trilogy – *Word from Wormingford, Out of the Valley* and *Borderland* – since they contain a selection of the entertaining essays the writer has been contributing to *The Church Times* for the past fifteen years which are in effect his personal journals: in just 400 words he somehow manages to chronicle the minutiae of his quotidian life, to reflect lightly on serious liturgical issues and make wide-ranging literary allusions. However, this same friend also has a warning: 'He will talk more than willingly about his fascinating life with the Bloomsbury set and Aldeburgh mob, and about being chased by exotic actors.' And a request: 'But you would do us all a service if you could get him to talk about what happened to him during the Second World War: it's a blank in his life.'

My dilemma is this: if my subject is prepared to reveal to a perfect stranger what he did in the War, and vouchsafe hitherto untold tales about his poverty-stricken rural upbringing, his glamorous-sounding youth, his connection with Benjamin Britten, and his link with the Bloomsberries, would there still be room on the plate for a helping of horticulture? Perhaps best not to sit down, in the circumstances; perhaps best to walk the garden and hear its story before getting too caught up in the intriguing details of the writer's own. But in the event, the garden itself brings many strands of his life together for the simple reason that Bottengoms Farm once belonged to the artist-plantsman John Nash and his wife, Christine, who were not only part of the Bloomsbury set, and friends of that other local artist-plantsman, Beth Chatto's mentor Sir Cedric Morris, but also, crucially, close friends of Ronnie himself – so close that when they died within a few months of each other in 1977 they bequeathed him the property.

As we stroll round the garden in the warm sunshine, I hear its story and so much more. I hear how the old place had been semi-derelict when the couple bought it in 1944; how the painter had spent the next thirty years and more transforming two of the farm's original 80 acres into a plantsman's paradise based on William Robinson principles; how Ronnie had met the couple when he was working as a reference librarian in nearby Colchester's Public Library in the years after the war, and how Christine (who had been at the Slade with that quintessentially Bloomsbury figure Dora Carrington, and been her friend) had taken a shine to the aspiring young poet: 'I mean, I can't tell what really happened except that she was a tall, attractive, enchanting woman. I can't see her actually finding me, but looking back . . .', he hesitates, 'I mean, we can't tell when we are very young how attractive we are as a person, can we?' Some can, all too easily. Be that as it may, it was Christine Nash who encouraged Ronnie to think of himself as a 'real' writer – that is, gave him the confidence to quit the day job and risk half-starving to death while he found his literary feet. His mother was appalled apparently, but he was in good company: 'A lot of my friends were writers and painters and lived a kind of simplicity then which is unknown today, so in a sense we were all right. I had a pitiful bit of money and a bike, but it was tenuous.'

Back to the garden – or, rather, back to John Nash's garden, because Bottengoms remains his in the writer's mind: 'John always said he loved the house, but Christine said he loved it really because it had several kinds of soil – some London clay and that wonderful, marvellous loamy stuff where a farm has been and people have grown things for centuries, as well as some gritty bits.' I comment on the garden's spectacular display of rosehips, which reminds him, 'a lot of old English roses, yes, that's right, some of which John put in and some of which I've replaced. That's 'John Clare', a new rose. I'm the President of the John Clare Society, and they sent it. This is 'Gloire de Dijon', John's favourite rose. All his life, if he saw an empty old house he would go in and take cuttings from roses. He was incredibly knowledgeable. I've got his great gardening dictionary upstairs edited in, I think, 1895 by the Keeper of the Botanic gardens at Kew. Four volumes. A most wonderful book, with little line engravings, which he had by the side of his chair and which he read all the time. It's got all his markings in it. He used to say if he could have his life over again he would be a musician first, gardener second and artist last but that's a bit of nonsense really because he was an artist through and through.' Very occasionally, a plant that wasn't a Nash introduction catches his eye: 'That's a grapefruit which Roger Deakin, who's just died, gave me. It's about four years old. Isn't that nice? Lovely man. A great friend. He gave me a new scythe. He lived in the Waveney valley.'

If you weren't bothered about saving the seedheads, a scythe might be just the thing to cut a swathe through the mouldy detritus in the flower beds after so much recent rain, but Ronnie *is* bothered, at least moderately: 'I leave some because John saw them as part of the life of a plant. I keep the handsome ones, that's right. I began doing the autumn tidying then all the rains came so I've only done a bit so far. You really ought to see it in the spring, it's fantastic – it's a semi-wild garden with lots of wild flowers, especially in the orchard, which has lawn paths between wild flower areas. It's covered with equisetum and primroses.' *Equisetum* – horsetail, but a rare and rather lovely variety originally found in Belgium and doubtless introduced by John. Unfortunately, it's no less invasive than the type and Ronnie consoles himself in his Sisyphean task with thoughts of Mirabel Osler: 'As a devout member of the Mirabel Osler set . . .' he writes, 'I allow the garden its beautiful muddles.' Mention of my own devotion to Mirabel jogs another memory: 'She's enchanting! She came for a picnic. It was summertime and we had a picnic up the top there. Yes, that's right. I remember laying the tablecloth on the grass and we all sort of sat around – about eight people. Forgotten who they all were . . .' which in turn jogs another: 'The Nashes were great picnickers, with all their picnic baskets and things. In fact I'll show you the place where we had one great picnic because we'll be going through it in a minute, a place called Tiger Hill. A bluebell wood. In early May there are nightingales.'

The orchard introduces Sir Cedric Morris to the story: 'He was very dignified and extraordinarily kind. Yes, that's right. He put a lot of plants in this garden. That's a type of olive. It doesn't have olives, just tiny orange flowers. He gardened at Hadleigh about twelve miles from here and almost every time I came John would say, "Let's go and see Cedric and Lett," and we'd drive over there. I used to have to write catalogues – art catalogues, you know – for his exhibitions. "You're a writer," he'd say, "so write!"'

Below the orchard, the garden bleeds off into a waterlogged woodland that still serves its vital purpose: 'This is called Lower Bottoms and it's full of streams and ditches and the water for the house is pumped up. If you run a bath a tank fills up and the overflow runs back to the river again. Down there are two old horse ponds and they are full of wonderful wild flowers – marsh marigolds and such. It's a garden in a wood really, with a stream in it. Part of the river water table, that's right, yes. There are several houses like this by the river. Isolated, not on the mains. This is probably a Saxon road. Tremendously ancient. It's how they all were really until 1930, yes.'

*Ronald Blythe*

In his column he observes cryptically: 'I was born drinking from a well and I expect I'll die drinking from a stream, but there will have been a fair stretch of living in between.' A fair stretch of living of such civilised simplicity I imagine the planet has barely registered he's been on it these past eighty-four years.

*A propos*, it is 11.30 and if we were to travel to Lavenham Blythe-fashion – on foot to the main road to catch the bus that has been ploughing its way between Bury St Edmunds via Lavenham and Sudbury to Colchester since Ronnie was a child and he took it to school and back each day – we should be off, but we aren't, so there's time to do the indoor tour.

Which begins in the larder I'm familiar with from the chronicles: 'A home and away week,' he writes. 'Without thought and minus planning, I turn out the larder. It is one of those rambling rooms tacked on to the farmhouse proper in the eighteenth century. It is also temptingly accommodating, so that eventually it will contain a great many unlarderish items whose mouldy breath brings a whiff of mortality to the true inhabitants of this space – jams, wines, strings of onions, and a nice bit of cheese.' Today, I can see only unimpeachably larderish items artfully ordered: neatly labelled jars of this season's jam and pickles; the potato harvest scrubbed and sorted according to size and variety in trugs and bowls; ditto the last of the tomatoes and a few quinces; onions and garlic suspended from the oak cross-beams. Oh, and enough wine laid down to see the writer through a longish winter siege, I'd say.

And all over the house, this same careful juxtaposing of possessions I put down to his librarian's training but Ronnie reckons is about more than that: 'I think basically it's an aesthetic thing. I like the rooms to look attractive – I think that's what it is – to set off the pictures and flowers and things. I just tidy it up as soon as I get up, before I do anything else.' His friends, I learn, opted for a rather different aesthetic: 'The Nash's were amazingly untidy – mantelshelf piled up to the ceiling with invitation cards, things like that – but they had lovely food and there was no electricity, just oil lamps and candles in the bedrooms. It had a great beauty about it.' I can imagine – and the suffering in winter.

All the way up the narrow staircase as steeply raked as a ladder to a hayloft, and in all the bedrooms (now, mercifully, centrally heated), hang the overflow from the ground floor living rooms of paintings and drawings and photographs the writer inherited from the Nashes. Christine's old bedroom looking out east over the garden to rolling farmland has become Ronnie's study, and here he works at an elegant little writing desk with his back to the window, the cat's basket at his feet, and a pair of binoculars to hand suggesting he, unlike his literary hero Thomas Hardy, who never would, permits himself to be distracted by the view. He does, and by more besides: 'Well, you see, I write every day – stories, essays – so when somebody comes it's very nice really. In any case – and I'm sure this happens to you – I'm writing when I'm not writing, when I'm on my own, when I'm gardening or washing up or walking up to the post office. I'm retentive by nature so I don't have to rush upstairs and put it down.' And when the moment does come to get it all down? 'Well, some I write by hand on very nice foolscap paper, then when I've done a good bit I type it up and put it into the file and bit by bit the book grows and then when it's all done I go through it and sometimes, if I'm lazy, I'll have it professionally typed, but usually I do it myself.' A computer would in any case horribly compromise the room's aesthetic, and quite possibly the lapidary quality of his enviably concise writing style as well.

Next door, in what was once John's studio, and half-concealed behind a rail on which hang a number of austere black robes – Ronnie is a Lay Canon of the Church of England – I notice an uncharacteristically untidy pile of letters and papers that prove to be work-in-progress: 'I'm having to shape my next book from all those papers of that period and that's why they are there. Bit by bit they will be reduced but actually I don't really like reading old letters. It's rather sad isn't it? Melancholy.' When I reveal that I find much sadness in his writing, and that it is this willingness to reflect on the human condition – on death and loss and loneliness – I find so compelling, Ronnie sounds alarmed: 'But it's not pessimistic is it?' On the contrary, and I agree that solitude is what preoccupies the writer, who has many friends but has always lived alone: death and loss and solitude.

Perhaps this extract from the Wormingford chronicles best illustrates my point – and his:

> Every now and then it happens, the loner dies and the sociable are made to feel unsociable. . . . What I would like to know about all the loners I haven't known is how their years passed. There they stretch, from my boyhood on, the usually pleasant faces that might say 'Good Morning', but never 'come in'. . . . Those who ask nothing of nobody until the undertaker calls are a dreadful worry to village Christians.

Or the piece in which he muses on how artists and writers must beware the 'euphoric vision' of the countryside, and to make his point quotes the comparably compassionate, equally unsentimental Beatrix Potter's observation that 'every lamb that is born is born to have its throat cut'.

Time to be off. A hand-written envelope addressed to *The Church Times* sits on the hall table: it contains next week's episode, and we post it *en route* to Lavenham. We also stop by Wormingford church to pay our respects to Constable's 'Wormingford relations' interred in their grand tombs, and to visit John and Christine Nash's more modest resting place. We then drive slowly across the Stour Valley, down little-used lanes and through the odd water-splash and I believe we must have passed every house and every mill and every stretch of the river Constable ever painted, or his family ever owned, as well as what remains of 'Gainsborough's forest' – a.k.a. Cornard Wood.

Ronnie Blythe was born close by Lavenham, and remembers the perfectly intact – and now perfectly restored – medieval town (whose church John Betjamen deemed the most splendid of all the wool churches in East Anglia) when it was a picturesque ruin at the nadir of its once-great fortunes: 'Nobody came here. Flowers and grass grew in the streets. When we were children we walked across the fields from our grandmother's house at Acton. We used to climb the tower, enthralled by it. Moss on the ancient roofs. Higgledy-piggledy streets. Gypsies all around who wintered on the common here. To us it was like a fairy tale place, as you will see when we get into it. Now well-to-do people have done the houses up, which is lovely in a way.' In a way. As lovely as a fly in amber, say – and just as dead, I felt.

At lunch, I mention oh-so-casually that my late father-in-law was the poet and writer Alan Ross, and that I'd spotted a poem of his in one of the numerous anthologies of wartime essays, stories, poems, letters and diaries that Ronnie has edited over the years. Since Alan Ross was called up in 1942 and he and Ronnie were both born in 1922, can I assume he was also? I can, but that simple statement of fact is about all the grist I'm going to get: 'You see, nothing very interesting happened so I always leave it all out. It didn't seem to me to be important, yes, that's right.' But I want – or have been asked to get – the facts. The facts! I appal myself, but grind on grimly: had he been engaged in any actual fighting, for instance? My companion is far too well-mannered to tell me to back off, and much to adroit to feel the need to get rough: 'Actually I wasn't in combat or anything like that, no, but the war itself seemed to me far less interesting and important than my development as a literary sort of person, and making these friendships really, yes, that's right. I associate it mostly with reading, with reading Proust for the first time, with writing poems.' And before I've regrouped for a further assault he's cleverly changed tack by telling me about someone else's war: 'I didn't know Alun Lewis – you know, the poet. All those lovely letters to his wife Gweno were also written to another woman. I've just been given them. It was a revelation to me that he had this other friendship, which was a passionate friendship.'

Resisting with difficulty the lure of such tempting bait I try one last, feeble cast myself by suggesting the war must have affected the person he is today. 'Very much so!' he agrees equably, ignoring the unspoken implication that this being the case, then I need the details: 'But I didn't seem really to become me until I went off to that stretch on the Suffolk coast with James Turner and Britten and all those people and began writing properly.' Began, in other words, the process of transforming his source material – his life – into art. I would have done well to remember this extract from a speech the writer delivered recently to Essex University thanking its Chancellor for honouring him with a doctorate: 'When I was on *Desert Island Discs* Sue Lawley said, "You were hard to do." This amazed me. I imagined that a longish list of titles would have made it easy for her. My books weren't hard to read, nor easy to write.' Just so.

With mutual relief we bring ourselves back to the present by turning our attention to our food and to considering the importance of routine for the solitary soul: 'Like all writers, I just make a pattern, yes, that's right. I get up around six or half past – a wonderful time of the morning, yes. I love a walk in the garden in bare feet through the grass, particularly in the summertime. That gives me a wonderful sense of freedom. Then I sit and have tea and talk to the cat for a long time, don't do any work, listen to the news, dress, have a bath, have breakfast – the same every day: home-made muesli, thick-buttered toast, proper coffee and fruit. Slight tidy up of everything then go to my study at about a quarter to nine. I always read a bit before I work, to prime the pump – at the moment I'm reading *Swann's Way*. I read Proust right through about every five years, a few pages at a time.' Crikey! 'Yes, that's right – it always seems to be new. Like listening to Mozart. The letters come at half past ten,' he adds, reminding me that the post's arrival is a highlight of the day for the dedicated letter-writer, and what a pleasure I've opted to deny myself these past few years: opening emails of a morning just doesn't cut it.

But we've not yet reached the halfway mark: 'I have a picnicky kind of lunch, and then I garden, saw wood, or whatever, and go back to work, if nobody's about, until dinner time. But it's not as conventional a life as people might imagine, in a way – the freedom of it is that you can do what you like.' Like indulge ourselves in this uncustomary midday feast, for example, although that won't much affect my companion's evening routine: 'At about a quarter to seven I come down and have a drink – something like gin and Cinzano, nothing very much, then I cook a big meal, greedily – baked potatoes and all sorts of things, and I have a glass of wine. This takes until about nine when I listen to the radio – talks, plays, whatever. People telephone then so that's broken into by often longish talks to friends. When I go to bed – usually about eleven o'clock – I might have some whisky. I'm not,' he adds, ' a grand cook – I make it up as I go along. I make my own soups which last for several days, and cakes, but I don't do any formal entertaining. I can't cope with it really. I think Max Beerbohm divided the world between hosts and guests and I'm really a guest in that sense. I give my kind of giving but I don't give parties. I used to make the mistake long ago of inviting people for the weekend and I was exhausted by having to look after them. I didn't know what to do really. Yes, that's right. So I never do that now, except for people I know.' People such as his closest friend and walking companion, the nature writer Richard Mabey, and his partner Polly.

However, John and Christine Nash being never far from his mind, soon we are back in the old days: 'John could never be alone and I came to live with him when Christine was away – I made his bed and washed his clothes sometimes. When she died he said to me one day [change of delivery to imperious posh]: "I must have some clean socks". There was a drawer next to his bed with about fifty pairs in. She'd always laid them out for him. Can you believe it? And I always cooked – he couldn't have done it himself. He would say "What are we having tonight, dear boy?" He was wonderfully polite and appreciative, but the worst of it was sometimes he'd say it at four o'clock in the afternoon, and if I was reading or writing he'd look irritated because he'd finished painting at four and "What are we having for dinner?" meant "What are you reading and writing for? Start cooking!"'

The transfixing revelations keep coming – that the Nash's had a circle of friends who called themselves the Dear Ones, for instance – and only stop when he remembers it's John-in-the-garden anecdotes I am after, or so he affects to believe. I remind him that he has already given me plenty of those, and that it is his own relationship with the garden, with the world, that interests me. His response is utterly disarming: 'I am essentially quite a shy person. I need to be more boastful!' Short pause: 'I've just been given the Benson Medal for Literature. How about that?' How indeed – the Arthur Christopher Benson Medal is awarded for a lifetime's contribution to literature. Tolkein won it in his time, as did Lytton

Strachey in his, as have one or two of Ronnie's poet's circle from those early years of struggle.

Back to Bottengoms for tea via Long Melford – another gem of a medieval wool town whose magnificent church my guide has chosen to guide me round. I feel comfortable in Long Melford – feel its heart still beats, the sign being nets at the windows suggesting real village folk live here, and that I should watch where I try to pry, unlike at Lavenham, where I felt pressing my nose up against the mullions was my tourist's duty, so I did and then felt guilty.

Once back at Bottengoms and kettle on my host wanders around the house gathering together for my benefit Nash memorabilia, his Benson medal, a bulging file of cuttings of previously published gardening essays and photographs of his old gardening friends he's assembling for a book, as well as a rare copy of *The Aldeburgh Anthology*, which Ronnie edited in 1972, and rare because it's one of only a hundred copies the publishers had the whole gang – Britten, Piers, Imogen Holst and Ronnie himself – sign. Seeing the book reminds me we haven't covered those years he spent with 'the Aldeburgh mob', but it's getting late and he can't think of much that might fit into a story for a horticultural readership: 'Britten used to walk on the marshes with his little dog in the afternoons and the thing was not to talk to him,' he remembers. 'He just wanted to be free and think about things, that's right, yes. And none of them were remotely, at least not to my knowledge, interested in plants, but John Nash came because he was interested in the rare plants which grew in the shingle – the biggest shingle ridge other than Chesil beach – so there were all these sea hollies and wonderful things.'

The retrieved Nash memento turns out to be a tiny, bulbous glass vase: 'This was the flower's throne. When he taught flower painting John would put one flower in that and the person who did the best painting got the flower. But in the studio upstairs there used to be half-pint milk bottles – remember those little tiny milk bottles? – he used those for the thrones, but when he'd finished painting, even when they were wilting, he couldn't bear to throw them away so there were all these dead little flowers on the windowsill. Wonderful really.'

The phone rings, and rings again. My cue to leave: my subject has morphed into pastoral mode – it appears someone important in the ecclesiastical hierarchy has died and what I am witnessing is 'the Church of England bush telegraph at work'. Pure Barbara Pym. As I crunch my way back to the car through a deep litter of oak mast in the orchard I hear the plangent sound of the wind soughing in the tall trees beyond, soaring like a descant over my own earthly tread, and feel rather pleased with myself for hearing it when I recall this extract from the Wormingford journal:

> I imagine that we all get used to hearing some repeated epithet which sums up our circumstances, situation, house, etc. Quiet is the one which I hear most. It isn't exactly true, but I know what people mean. The consolatory and healing nature of quietness pours through the scriptures. Be still, be still. I hear what, presumably, my visitors do not hear, an orchestrated sound of wind in trees, Bernard ploughing, birdsong, far cries from the sports field, water flowing, walls scratching and creaking, old clocks on their rounds, much rustling.

Ronald Blythe's most recent publications:
*A Year at Bottengoms Farm* published by Canterbury Press (2006)
*Fieldwork*, a selection of essays covering the writer's life, published by Black Dog Books (2007)

# Richard Mabey

## NATURALIST

A human being is a part of the whole that we call the universe, a part
limited in time and space. And yet we experience ourselves, our thoughts
and feelings, as something separated from the rest – a kind of optical illusion of our consciousness. This illusion is a prison for us, restricting us
to our personal desires and to affection for only the few people nearest
us. The task must be to free ourselves from this prison by widening our
circle of compassion to embrace all living beings and all of nature.

Albert Einstein (1879–1955)

Six hours into our conversation, I asked Richard Mabey if there was
anything he felt we hadn't covered. There was: 'From the way our
conversation has drifted pretty much around subjects we are both interested in, it might give the impression that I am an entirely theoretical
person. And although I confess I do sometimes go out with, as it were, my
head in a cloud of contemplation of the great issues and thorny philosophical problems, I do absolutely love the *stuff* of the world. However much
I may reflect on the nature of chaos and the future of the planet, I still just
adore seeing the first primroses and smelling broom and suchlike
mundane things. Like you, I love food, so very, very simple sensuous
pleasures are profoundly important to me.' I felt responsible, but was
absolved: 'To be fair to you, if I had been setting the pace it would have
come out as well, because those are the things that intellectually interest
me. The rest, I almost take for granted.'

Most of our philosophical musings had been triggered by thoughts and
ideas expressed in the two books the writer published last year. The first,
*Nature Cure* (nominated for the Whitbread Prize), is a painful but ulti-

mately joyful account of his descent into the hell of deep depression and eventual resurrection through the support and love of a woman he calls Poppy (a.k.a. Polly, now his life-partner). The second, *Fencing Paradise*, is an elegantly written and thought-provoking account of the writer's imaginative response to whatever caught his eye as he wandered at different seasons of the year around the Eden Project's celebrated biomes. These two books between them led us all over the place, much as Richard allows his own thoughts to roam far and wide; indeed in *Fencing Paradise* he sometimes devotes no more than half a sentence to describing the initial trigger before he is off on his imaginary travels: 'Well, it would have been deeply tedious to have just written a travelogue of Eden,' he points out, reasonably, 'so I used it as a series of prompts really. I loved bringing together what seem to be incongruous elements. For example, the whole chapter about smell was something which I deliciously enjoyed doing – moving from a quote by – who was it? – yes! Coleridge – "a dunghill at a distance smells like musk, and a dead dog like elderflower", to a bit of plant biochemistry through to homeopathy and eventually to the production of oil. It was slightly mischievous of me, but I wanted to show how far you could stretch the real connectivity of things, and quite deliberately I pushed it as far as I possibly could.'

The painter Paul Klee said he created his lapidary images by the simple expedient of taking a line for a walk. That, it strikes me, is what Richard Mabey does with a thought, only in his case the thought often gets taken on a literal journey which is why, when it was agreed sometime in August that at the tail-end of November I should come down to Norfolk to meet him, I made a note to myself that I would like him to take me with him. But I lost my nerve: the writer may be able to walk in the fen – or round the Eden Project – without a notebook, pondering thorny philosophical issues while enjoying the stuff of the world, but I doubted I could. To justify such feebleness of spirit, I convinced myself his garden would be almost as wild as the fen, and therefore a stroll round it would be as rewarding, and less stressful. (Ironically, without my realising it at the time, my tape recorder chose to pack up when we were outdoors, but when later I e-mailed Richard for help his gnomic reply, while poetic, indicated little sympathy for my plight: 'Some say stones have ears, that ghosts and auras and all manner of transnatural things are stored in their very material structure. Shall I send you one from the *garrigue*?'

In truth, for this naturalist, there is scant difference between being out there and thinking about being out there, but people sometimes find this puzzling, so when writing *Nature Cure* he devised a little 'literary conceit' to separate the doing from the thinking. He had discovered that Victorian moth-hunters described the hours they spent outdoors in the dark looking for 'those ethereal creatures of the night' as 'dusking', and decided to appropriate the word for himself: 'I thought it was a lovely word for a lovely idea, and it seemed to fit with me sitting with a book in my lap in a rather dark room trying to work things out, because I see the thinking as fieldwork inside my head instead of in the fen. The two modes of getting to grips with the world don't feel different because the sensual experience seems to have ideas lurking under the surface, and I get fizzy fingers when I am reading something marvellous.'

And so, like moths after nectar, we spend most of the day flitting around in our heads in the dim light of the couple's four-hundred-year-old cottage, whose steep thatched roof looks from the outside like a giant tea-cosy pushed down low over the pot to keep its contents warm. Which was just as well: it was freezing out, and the chimneybreast in the living room where we settle now holds books. A picture on the wall behind Richard's head catches my eye. It was painted by the West Country artist Kurt Jackson, and when I get up to have a closer look I realise the artist has placed himself at the heart of a wood in winter and that the squiggles representing the forest floor are actually not quite decipherable words expressing, I imagine, the artist's feelings about being hidden in that wood quietly observing the world beyond its bare branches.

The picture jogs my memory. 'Culture isn't the opposite of nature,' the writer suggests in *Nature Cure*, 'it's the interface between us and the non-human world, our species' semi-permeable membrane.' What did he mean? 'It's a tricky one', he admits. 'It's a question that preoccupies me a lot of the time, as it does the little growing band of so-called nature writers who aren't just scientific describers because one of the base lines for talking about our relationships with nature is the idea that the development of language was the absolute, final, insurmountable barrier – the point at which the human species was alienated from nature because we could only then see things as it were through this distorting glass of image-making. That has traditionally been seen as rule one: we are estranged! Now I'm not the only one who's beginning to think this is a limiting way of looking at things. Language is, for a start, our nature. It's what developed out of cave painting.'

A book entitled *Why Birds Sing* by the American nature writer David Rothenburg is sitting right there on the table in front of us and its premise supports Richard's own view, which he sums up for me: 'Perhaps the actual philosophical agony about whether image-making and language estranges us or not is less the point than whether we can *use* language, perhaps rather like birds sing, as a way of celebrating our connections with the rest of the world, and a way of explaining to ourselves how we fit into it: to stick up for language as a special gift that humans can bring to the biosphere.'

Unfortunately this intrinsically optimistic take on life does occasionally annoy his more earnest peers, and they go on the attack. One hit him especially hard: back in 1989 the then Environment Editor of the *Independent* wrote a review of one of his books which still rankles after all this time: 'He was rather patronisingly nice about some bits, but at the same time he felt that my kind of joyous celebration of nature was, in the current status of the world, "like sending postcards from Hiroshima". The words are branded in my brain! I was fantastically hurt because I felt it was truly misrepresentative of what I've been trying to do all my life, but in the end I thought maybe that's what I would do, when the smoke's died down: pick up life and start again. I suppose the essential point is that I believe the vitality of life itself has always been, up to now, stronger than the forces of destruction. Otherwise the planet wouldn't be there.' Throughout the day the writer's hopeful spirit reveals itself, but when I, a touch breathlessly perhaps, express my admiration for his attitude he

' " have my bad nights quite often, and suffer like anyone else. You mustn't think of me as some sort of St Francis.'

Which, of course, I do. For one thing, I am hoping against hope he may have some positive ideas as to what's to be done about global warming. He does not. 'I don't,' he says firmly, 'believe in a plan to save the planet. Too complicated. If it happens at all it'll happen in one of two ways: either by the cumulative effect of lots of small positive changes, or by a major catastrophe. The idea we all had at the age of eighteen that a world council of wise men could sit down and say, "This is what we must do . . ." I mean, please!'

Buddhists, I understand, say: 'There *is* nothing to do.' Such a profound concept, combined with Richard's opinion, gives me An Idea. What, I wonder, if we are anciently programmed to respond only to immediate danger? After all, once upon a time, if we didn't deal with the lion at the mouth of our cave first, any other threat lurking in its shadow would be academic, wouldn't it? He examines the idea from all angles before concluding: 'That is a really original point! Yes, I think that we may be anciently programmed to look for immediate danger rather than the long term. A radical thought! It kind of reinforces the qualification I have to my optimism – that I suspect it will need an immediate in-yer-face crisis of global proportions before anything happens. I know this is what Jim Lovelock thinks, and I pretty much share his view on that.'

This leap to the top of the class is gratifying since I had managed to get off to an unfortunate start when I arrived. The fact is, shortly before I was due in Norfolk I had bought a hybrid car, for which Good – or Green – Deed I fully expected a pat on the back from the great naturalist. Unluckily for me, he was intrigued to know how the motor operates, and when I airily admitted I hadn't a clue he was clearly appalled: 'How passive!' was all he actually said, but it didn't take long to discover that Richard Mabey deplores unquestioning acceptance of anything. What's more, gadgets have always held a fascination for him, a trait he inherited from his father and for which he is grateful: Richard reckons his curiosity about the natural world is simply a development of that same gift. Also, and perhaps surprisingly, the writer received a science-centric education, and went up to Oxford in 1960 to read biochemistry, with every intention of inventing a new type of food to feed the world, until his grand plan hit a snag: 'I'd not done biology at school, only chemistry and physics, so I wasn't prepared for the rigours of the dissection room, nor to have to extract the contents of our own stomachs. Literally, on day two of our arrival in Oxford we had to swallow a very large polythene tube and apply a pump to it.'

So he abandoned the plan – though not the idealism, switched to reading PPE, obtained a good second class degree, and became in the process radically politicised: 'I was very much involved in the peace movement at Oxford before it became clear – or clear to me – that you couldn't separate the destinies of human beings and the rest of the planet. I felt at that point it was a choice. Then, may be four or five years after Oxford, the ecological dawning began in me as well as in the world outside that our fates were inseparable.'

He remains 'quietly' political: 'I got some raised eyebrows during the time of Live8 – Make Poverty History – when I said the slogan ought to be Make Poverty the Future!' And it really saddened him when he realised he had to explain himself. For the record, he meant: 'Of course, it's tremendously good of humans to look after their kind in peril, but as a philosophy the idea that we can in some way raise the living standards of the planet perhaps up to that of Bob Geldof is complete nonsense. It would be very interesting to ask him if he was prepared to lower his living standards to a level every living person on the planet could aspire to without wrecking the whole system. I wonder if he's thought that through?'

Before addressing other even more thorny issues (which later we do), we go for our stroll, wandering round the garden in the same haphazard way we'd been wandering around in our heads. In any case, Richard's garden doesn't dictate: it has no paths to follow, or 'rooms' to walk through; it has no architectural 'features', or vistas, just a pleasant view of sheep grazing the old common land next door. What it does have is a pond, an odd-shaped, terrifically deep pond whose banks are too steep for plant life to get much of a purchase. A large ash tree has its roots in the water. This is, or was, a working pond dug to provide the clay to build the house, and later used for retting locally grown hemp. A small cottage sits beside the pond. This is Richard's office where, ideally, he writes every morning from nine to one before clocking off to go for a walk, or better still an outing: 'I *love* going for little trips!' Once back, he aims to read in his library from four to seven, unless it's his turn to cook, and he's not up against a deadline, in which case he'll pack it in at six.

His general aim out here is to give nature a chance to claim back some territory. (In *Nature Cure* he takes issue with the way people talk about 'reclaiming' land by asking: 'How can we use that presumptuous word as if we were snatching back from nature something that was once ours?') And so, here in his own garden the old lawn is being left to turn itself back into a meadow in its own time: no drastic scalping, or plugging with selected wildflower specimens. Instead, it gets cut three times a year to weaken the rank species, and gets burnt in patches to see if that will stimulate some king of interesting regeneration of wild species. If any opportune bald patches occur they get a scattering of wild flower seed. Further back, where it bleeds into the woodland area, the once immaculate lawn now has the truly wild aspect of an old hermit's wispy beard.

An oak is busy colonising this area with her offspring, which are now being joined by a few other wild-seeded insurgents – blackthorn, hazel, sweet chestnut, cherry, ash and hawthorn. Eventually, this motley army will have to fight it out with Richard's deliberately introduced selection of larger specimens of the same native species planted because he had feared the wild bunch might not arrive in time – in his time, that is: 'We project the problem we have with our impatience on to the exterior world,' he had observed earlier, when my tape recorder was mercifully still functioning: 'Instead of saying we can't wait, we say the wood can't grow unless we help it. This is a damaging projection because it cumulatively builds a picture of nature as something that is weak and incapable of prospering without intensive care, whereas what we are *really* saying is that we haven't got the time to wait for it to be itself.' However, he and Polly have hit on a neat way to solve the problem of how to introduce a native species without actually planting it, or having to wait for one to turn up: an unloved ornamental cherry in the front garden has been cut down, and new growth from its wild root stock is already almost as tall as the one it had been forced to foster.

But a stout wall encloses the designated vegetable patch to protect its denizens from their wild, unruly relations. This is Polly's domain: 'Paradoxically Polly is the one who looks after the more ordered bits of the garden and I'm the one that looks after the wilder parts, to the extent they need looking after.' For example, the handsome herbaceous border at the front that came with the property will stay 'as long as my *slave* is willing to take care of it!' But Richard did have one go at high-maintenance husbandry: 'I wanted to try out a bit of three-dimensional, three-layered cropping, and I wanted to use the hedgerow as a model, so I built a *legume* hedge with runner beans down the middle, peas slightly lower, then asparagus peas at the bottom – a complicated kind of domed structure that was fabulous to look at, and felt terribly ecological – but in term of output it was useless because nothing had enough space to optimise its output.' Such perceived foolishness makes him laugh: 'It was a great lesson. I should have known in advance – I've preached it often enough – that there is a profound difference between the energy flows in cultivated eco-systems and wild eco-systems. The wild works fine, diversifying energy into the maximum possible number of forms, and normally the output of those forms – biomass – is quite low. Agriculture and horticulture work to exactly the opposite model – by reducing the number of energy outputs but maximising their size. That's a fundamental difference between culti-vated and wild systems. I tried to build an entirely cultivated system to a wild model and it didn't satisfy either.'

The stone from the *garrigue* Richard alluded to in his unhelpful email is a reference to a raised bed he has created in the middle of his own wet, fertile fen land, with the help of a load of lime chippings that happened to be avail-able locally. Now he can grow his favourite flora – for which '*garrigue*' is the collective name – those low-growing oily, aromatic, silvery-leafed, unde-manding species (and bulbs) adapted to thrive in the thin, dry, poor, stony soil of the Mediterranean. Basically the bed is a naturalistic arrangement of helichrysum, salvias, thymes, lavenders, *Euphorbia wolfenii*, rosemary, phlomis, and juniper. Derek Jarman's beach garden at Dungeness springs to mind – an impression re-enforced by the way an assortment of rusting bits and pieces of old farm machinery once used to grub out all the hedges in the neighbourhood is now festooned with bird feeders. Jarman's beachcombings may have been more artfully organised, but as an ironic statement Richard's gleeful juxtaposition couldn't be bettered.

Back indoors, we visit the library in what was once someone's dining room. Other than the books, and one chair and a stool, the only furniture in the room is a plain, beautifully-proportioned table about three feet square made out of naturally stained elm. Its ever so slightly tapering legs give it an ageless quality, so that it seems more likely it had been found in some ancient Celtic tomb than to have been made, as it was, a few miles down the road by furniture maker David Gregson. The books are arranged on shelves around the room according to subject: birds, trees, botanical books, with his favourite specialist writers – John Clare, Gilbert White, Ronnie Blythe – allotted their own special section.

Interestingly, with the exception of Richard's own books, and one entitled *The Mind in the Cave* by David Lewis-Williams, all the books he mentions during the day were written by Americans – and they all boast marvellous titles: *The Plausibility of Life* by two biologists, W. Kirschner and John Gerhart; *Pilgrim at Tinker Creek* by Annie Dillard; *The Singing Neanderthals* by Stephen Mitten; *The Lives of a Cell* by Lewis Thomas; *Song of the Dodo* by David Quammen (the book that beat Richard Mabey's own *Flora Britannica* to the Natural World Book of the Year prize in 1997), and – also by Quammen – *Monster of God: The Man-Eating Predator in the Jungles of History and the Mind*. All these books are as valued by Richard for the elegance of the writing as for the ideas they express.

Attractive titles notwithstanding, it's hard to imagine seeing any of them piled up in Waterstones' window, so Richard shops on the Internet, although there was a time during his depression when he couldn't because he couldn't work the computer: 'Every time one of those windows came up I completely froze. I thought, "What on earth do you do?"' Nor has this debilitating difficulty with choice altogether gone away: 'I remain intellectually bothered by it – how best to spend this moment of one's existence when there are so many opportunities available?'

Talk of choice reminds him: 'If you were to ask me the question – and I don't think anybody ever has – which is the most important book I possess, I'd say it's a book called *The Comedy of Survival* by Joseph Meeker. It is an astonishing attempt, so refreshingly and upliftingly written, to show the similarities between the way that life survives on the planet and the way that characters survive in literary comedy by ducking and diving, and not becoming tremendously ideological or self-sacrificial or making austere moral judgments. It is funny but, being the kind of writer he is, also profoundly wise.' However, for reasons too deep for him to go into, Richard's Desert Island book was, and remains, *The Wind in the Willows*.

I had been struck by the lack of media coverage *Fencing Paradise* attracted when it came out. Richard too, and he concludes that one reason was the understandable – though wrong – perception that it must have been a rushed job since it was published only months after *Nature Cure's* grand entrance; another, he suspects is plain snobbery: 'Eden's reputation in literary London is not very high. They regard it, rightly or wrongly, as being the botanical equivalent of Alton Towers, so a book that comes out with Eden Project on the spine, even though it has my name on the cover, is assumed to be a publicity document and therefore not worthy of a review in a serious paper.'

I own to those same negative sentiments about a place I've never visited, and am interested to know what Richard himself thinks about the Project, and its ethos. Well, he enjoys its atmosphere, but is not altogether happy about the Project's overall concept: 'Consciously, they say they are simply an entertainment and an educational facility, and are at pains to point out that they are not trying to present a blueprint for Utopia. But every so often you sense that somewhere in their collective subconscious this is what they are trying to do. Increasingly they are envisioning them-selves as a centre of excellence, as a kind of intellectual shrine bringing people together. In addition to the ordinary Joe Public coming in and paying their money, great professors come flocking in – which is good – and it would be absolutely in the spirit of Eden if they could find a way of bringing those two groups together. But I think it is still rather a two-cultures situation.' That could account for my own disinclination to visit the place: I'd hate feeling I was not one of us.

He is also worried by the Project's tendency to over-simplify complex subjects: 'Take sugar: sugar is a plant, therefore sugar, Eden argues, must be talked about constructively. Hence: Sugar Production Creates Seven Million Jobs Worldwide! The fact that the stuff is also a killer is not mentioned.' So, armed with statistics provided by the World Health Organisation, the writer decided to challenge the team on the basis that '400 billion dollars-worth of healthcare worldwide probably slightly outweighs seven million jobs.' But that, he fears, was an inconvenient truth too far.

Indeed, while Richard is at pains to emphasise the fact that Eden is a lot of fun, equally he has some serious concerns: 'I'm not sure they've thought through the subliminal message of the whole operation – which is that plants are a panacea to the problems of the planet – and that provided things are done with plants it's OK. They haven't thought through the issue of the conflict between the domestication of plants and the need to conserve their intricacy in the wild. Whether it is intended or not, the Project conveys the image that the proper future for the planet is the bringing in to ever more sophisticated control and domestication the wild vegetation of the earth, and my argument against that would be that we *need* wild vegetation for all kinds of reasons ranging from the ethical to exceedingly intricate practical reasons to do with systems we are not clever enough to reproduce yet.'

We segue to fear and to our species' instinctive need to make order out of chaos, which leads to an absorbing Mabey seminar on the brand-new science of canopy ecology, and the attempts being made to harness its potential in what's left of the Amazon rainforest: 'The intricacy of what's happening up there is just mind-boggling. I truly believe the planet, and we too, need chaos for all kinds of reasons, and that the way for us to learn to live with that is to understand it – to understand it as far as we can; I mean, obviously a semi-chaotic system can never be fully understood, that's what's important about it: it's always on the edge of producing new things we haven't yet caught up with, and the planet needs it because it provides all these new possibilities for a changing world. But once one can begin to glimpse the beautiful, undulating intricacy inside the chaos, then I think that's the point when you can say its not frightening, it's majestic! There is the idea . . .'

. . . And in flies Polly. Polly, a lecturer in child development, is back from a tough-sounding day in Thetford's infamous Abbey Housing Estate. Introductions over, she flies off almost at once to write up her reports somewhere else. Impressively Richard continues exactly where he left off: '. . . that one could marginally *farm* the canopy, that is, not just gathering what is there, that could be pretty destructive, but speed the whole thing up – impatience again – encourage it to grow more by doing little bits of translocation of epiphytes further along the branches. I suppose the trendy word for this is agro-forestry, isn't it?' But he has reservations: 'I mean, once you've upped the productivity the temptation is to up it a little further. Are they going to start introducing pest control? If so the entire ecosystem is going to collapse.' Finding it hard to imagine they won't, I nevertheless feel bad about expressing my cynicism. 'No! No!' he assures me. 'It's a necessary counter to getting over-enthusiastic about the idea, but it might be better to have a degraded bit of forest being used in this way than no forest at all, if that's going to be the choice, which it might well be in some places.' At which at least half-hopeful point Richards decides its time to get dinner going, since it's his turn to cook, and I trot along behind him, thinking to check a few spellings and such while he cooks, but am ordered out: the banquet he is devising requires his full attention. Polly, meantime, reappears in a cloud of Diorissima and it's time for our first drink.

The next morning I drop by again as arranged to take some photographs, but the day is dank and Richard is feeling grumpy: 'I'm not a good coper with claggy grey damp days – with the dour bits of winter. It's complex – I get it in bad springs as well. I get it *worse* in a bad spring because it kills that sense of expectation and, as I get older, the sense of opportunities to do things notching down as the years go on I find quite awful.' And since it was still early enough for him to get in a morning's writing, and for me to get home for lunch, we decide that's what we had each best do with our respective day.

To reach this part of south Norfolk by car from London entails a drive through agri-business land, but in the mist of yesterday's frosty dawn the landscape had assumed a magical disguise: each leaf – and last year very few had fallen by the end of November – of every oak and beech in the woodland bordering the route, every blade of grass and teasel seedhead in the verges, and each twig in the bristly hawthorn hedges was rimmed with hoar frost which the rising sun transformed into tiny diamonds.

The return journey in the dismal rain reveals a darker side, however: its product – great mounds of sugar beet as big and potentially lethal as cannon balls piled up at every field gate, waiting to be picked up by the lumbering lorries now blocking my road. So, to pass the time, I reread a passage in *Nature Cure* that had cheered me up first time around; perhaps it would again. The writer, on a whim, has decided to turn his back on the familiar fen and take a walk through this despised landscape. The wheat harvest is over and he imagines he'll be walking through a wasteland, but instead discovers the fields are one mass of foraging birds – enough to keep two sparrowhawks in business: 'A tiny bit of me,' he writes, 'wished they weren't here, making excuses for these spendthrift arable wastes. But that is the benediction of the wild, to see opportunity in the briefest of openings, the narrowest of windows. Tomorrow the fields would be clotted with overblown cash crops. Today they were dancing.' It is hard to have to accept that our species may well not be here to wing off a postcard when the dust settles next time around, but good to know this won't, after all, be the end of the world.

Richard Mabey's latest book, *Beechcombings* was published in October 2007.

# James Lovelock

## ENVIRONMENTALIST AND
## ORIGINATOR OF GAIA THEORY

Success is relative:
It is what we can make of the mess we have made of things.

T.S. Eliot (1888–1965)

Our rendezvous is for 8am in the dining room of an old inn situated alongside the quay of a picturesque Cornish port a mile or two south of St. Austell. The daunting hour and unlikely location almost forty miles from Professor Lovelock's home in Devon are due to his unusually hectic schedule following the publication last summer of his third book on Gaia Theory, *Revenge of Gaia*, with its apocalyptic vision of what will become of our species – all species – if we don't stop burning fossil fuels in the very near future, and to the fact that he will be staying at the hotel following an evening spent at the nearby Eden Project exchanging ideas with the naturalist Richard Mabey about what our species might conceivably make of the mess it has made of things.

In the event, I am on my third cup of coffee by the time the Professor and Sandy, his stylish American wife of almost twenty years, come down to breakfast full of apologies for being late: they had been in London all the earlier part of the week promoting the paperback edition of *Revenge*, and yesterday evening had not ended after audience questions but continued convivially on in a local restaurant with Richard and Tim Smit and friends, until one-thirty in the morning. Such a rigorous schedule, and yet the eighty-seven year old Cassandra *de nos jours* is buoyant as he settles down to tea, toast, bacon, tomato and a banana he divides with his wife – with whom he shares everything including each and every day and an e-mail address.

This evident zest for life I am now witnessing I first registered back in 1991 when I heard him on *Desert Island Discs* telling Sue Lawley with infectious enthusiasm how he always follows his heart and obeys his instincts, and had been inspired to rush out and buy his book. Even today, when his prognosis for our future is so bleak, what must be innate optimism keeps him cheerful: 'I have nine grand children don't forget. I always say to them on the rare occasions that I see them that they are just like I was in 1938: there's World War Two looming and what do you do? When people – women mainly – said I'm not going to have any children in a world like this I said Don't be daft! The future lies with your future. And I say the same now. I once put it: If you have a diagnosis that cancer's going to kill you in six months it doesn't stop you going to the dentist to have your tooth fixed.'

My own instinct had been to disregard Richard Mabey's well-meant email warning me not to read *Revenge of Gaia* in case I found its message too unbearably grim. And then, having read it, to write at once to the Professor requesting an interview on the assumption that he must have a garden and that there'd be some horticultural hook – or thorn – I could hang our encounter on. Instincts are one thing, assumptions another: Jim Lovelock does not have a garden – a detail he failed to mention when agreeing to our meeting at some future, unspecified date – and I'd reached page 319 of his 400-odd-page autobiography, *Homage to Gaia*, before learning that he had handed his land back to Gaia over thirty years ago by planting 20,000 native trees on its 35 acres. Nor had he ever thought it up to much as a passtime. 'Indeed,' he writes, 'I detest gardening' (an aversion he shares with Richard Mabey).

So a seaside hotel in February is as good a place as any to hear about my subject's ingenious attempts all those years ago to feed his then young family off the land without recourse to a spade: 'I had some really daft Dark Green ideas at the beginning,' he recalls 'and one of them was being semi-self-sufficient. But I'm too lazy to garden and I read somewhere you could grow things by just laying a black plastic sheet on the grass and the grass would die off underneath and you had an almost ideal situation: you didn't have to dig, just plant potatoes and cut a little cross in the plastic on top so its shoot could come up. I thought: "Great! I'll try this." And it worked like a dream, all these healthy looking potato plants coming up. Then came the time to lift the plastic to harvest them and I discovered I'd created a nice little eco-system: underneath it was seething with adders! The mice had come in to get the potatoes and the adders came in to get the mice.' There were others – for example, lettuces grown in long plastic tubes from seed to maturity and into the shops without being touched by human hand. (Don't ask.)

I did rather wonder why, in the circumstances, Jim Lovelock had agreed to meet me; but, as I was only too pleased he had, decided not to enquire. Nevertheless, I did also rather wonder what, his publishers' demands aside, drives the man so hard now that he is retired. I also imagined that with the scientific community having at long last recognised Gaia Theory he would consider his work done. 'Retired? I'm still not retired!' he splutters. 'And in answer to your second point, I think there's an awful lot of closet nay-saying going on.' One week later I watch on television a gang of out-of-the-closet nay-sayers – mainly right wing politicians and American climatologists – telling us it's only the sun up to its old tricks and we'll be back in another Ice Age before we know it. In other words, not our mess after all. Dangerous stuff, to be sure.

What the Professor had actually announced in his autobiography, and I had misinterpreted, was a plan with his wife to celebrate the new millennium and his ninth decade by walking the 680-mile coastal path round Devon and Cornwall. Now, what with the book and all, I wondered if he'd ever managed to fit in that hike? His face lights up: 'Oh boy! Yes we did!' he rejoices, triumphant. 'It becomes a pilgrimage, and you don't give a damn about the weather or about anything, and you get such a sense of achievement and satisfaction and boy is it hard! It's 91,000 feet of climbing!'

I had, of course, been at Eden the night before and been struck by the fact that Gaia had not been mentioned by name by anyone. Why? 'I know. It's a sad business. It never does. It's a dirty word to most scientists. You see when the biologists attacked the hypothesis during the 1970s they attacked dirtily: they associated it with the New Age, so scientists just shied away from the very concept of the thing. I think there were 1,200 scientists signed a petition in Amsterdam in 2001 stating that the Earth is a self-regulating system that regulates climate and composition and it's composed of all life including humans, the air, the oceans and the surface rocks. Well, that's Gaia! But they weren't going to call it Gaia. They called it the Earth System.'

Gaia is what the ancient Greeks called their goddess of the Earth, which is why, back in the mid-1960s, the distinguished writer William Golding proposed it as an appropriate name for his friend's embryonic hypothesis. If I remember my mythology, those Greek gods could be pretty brutal when the mood took them, couldn't they? 'That's right. I've said: Gaia has got no more sentiment than an inter-continental ballistic missile on course to its target, it's as pitiless as that. It's the very opposite of the kind of doting mother those silly people of the New Age want. Their feminine images of gigantic overweight women with enormous bosoms holding the Earth I find revolting beyond belief.'

As it happens, the biologists' attack on the hypothesis had been as irrational as their perception of it: 'You see,' he explains, 'before I came along the geologists were happily saying: "We can explain the Earth and its evolution. Biology is just a passenger. We don't need biology." And the biologists were all saying: "Yes, the geologists are right. Biology's got nothing to do with the Earth – that's their subject across the quadrangle: life just adapts to the Earth the geologists describe." And that was the set-up, a very nice set-up: a nice division of territory. The beautiful agreement, if you like. You can just imagine two great nations, powerfully armed, living side by side, taking one another's product, and getting along very well together. Then along comes this fool saying: "No! No! No! It's really only one subject. You ought to be united." Oh boy! I mean, did that cause trouble!'

One biologist even went so far as to call Gaia 'an evil religion'. 'They are as bad as the Taliban!' he laughs, amused at the irony, but warning me – just in case I take him literally, I suppose: 'I wouldn't push it too far because they'd never start shooting or wielding knives!' Although he could be forgiven for thinking it a distinct possibility: the mighty sword of truth the leader of the pack, the evangelical atheist and formidably articulate biologist Richard Dawkins wields is a fearsome weapon. I long to know: has his old adversary ever apologised? 'Not really. The nearest he got to it was when we were at a meeting on evolution in Oxford and we both said our pieces but the audience got restive and said, "Why aren't you two disagreeing with one another?" And Richard piped up: "Well it's like this, I've got my disciples and Jim's got his, and it's the disciples that quarrel!"'

But now that Gaia Theory is widely accepted, even if under an assumed name, Jim Lovelock can afford to be gracious: 'In retrospect, I'm always grateful to people who force me to think, even if they annoy me at the time. I thought Richard went over the top, but he always does about everything. I also think biologists have made a fundamental mistake by attacking the Creationists. You see, I know lots of good physicists who, when they come across a Green muttering about earth forces and ley-lines and waving crystals around, just shrug their shoulders, think they're mad as hatters, and leave them to get on with it. The biologists enter into the argument, which is silly because they are in a battle then, and it's made the Creationists far worse than they would have been.' Doesn't that suggest all biologists are the same? 'They are!' he laughs, and proceeds gleefully to recite a poem by Ogden Nash to make his point:

> I give you now Professor Twist,
> A conscientious scientist
> Trustees exclaimed, 'He never bungles,'
> And sent him off to distant jungles.
> Camped on the tropic riverside,
> One day he missed his loving bride.
> She had, the guide informed him later,
> Been eaten by an alligator.
> Professor Twist could not but smile
> 'You mean,' he said, 'a crocodile.'

The tribal aspect of human nature interests him greatly, and he quotes the biologist E.O. Wilson, who some years ago asked the question: Is humanity suicidal? And went on to conclude that it is a pity the first intelligent animal on Earth had to be a tribal carnivore. But last night Jim Lovelock pointed out the other side of our predisposition to annihilate the perceived enemy: our willingness to make huge personal sacrifices in pursuit of that aim, and again evoked the Second World War as an example, concluding: 'So one of my hopes is that when climate change gets really bad, as I'm afraid it's likely to, it will bring back that kind of response among people. One is nowhere near so selfish under those sorts of circumstances.'

And if it doesn't, and we carry on as we are, like some rogue virus hell-bent on destroying its host, and so itself, what then? The professor is sanguine: 'Usually, under natural selection, a successful virus comes to terms with its host. I think,' he continues, 'the Earth will go up to the hot state and I would think at least 90 per cent of us will be killed. I don't usually use that figure; I say 80 per cent because a) I'm not sure and b) it's too terrifying altogether to think of the human species being virtually wiped out. But a few breeding pairs, that's enough to carry on: we are a very tough animal. We'll fight our way back. But think of the selection that happens: the survivors will be the ones with the nous, the sense, the ability to survive under adverse conditions. I mean, there are some that say our intelligence is developed during those interglacial jumps.' *Force majeur?* 'Yes, that's right. I mean we're up against it every time or we get stuck in the mud of endless peacetime, getting more and more liberal and more and more silly. I'm aware that it's all coming unstuck, but I think the ultimate future may be a better type of human coming from it all.' Again, this positive slant that makes his message bearable: All shall be well and all shall be well and all manner of things shall be well.

As it happens, last summer I heard the Professor address an audience in St Paul's Cathedral, and express his fervent hope that science and religion may start working together again, as they once did. He pointed out that very few scientists are full-on atheists (always excepting the biologists), because this would imply certainty, and that as an agnostic himself he doesn't worry about what will happen to him after death because he puts his trust in Gaia: 'I become part of the Earth: I offer Gaia as a way of life for agnostics.' This morning, he goes further: 'I mean, if people want to treat Gaia as a religion I can see no harm in that, because people want faith and they want to believe in things, and Gaia is like the old goddesses: just, but very, very brutal.'

In any event, Armageddon isn't expected here in the British Isles quite yet, and the subject the scientist and the naturalist had been invited by Eden's Friends to consider was Our Countryside in the Twenty-first Century. Marvellously, they managed to end the first part of the evening on an up-beat, with Richard telling us about the great swathes of East Anglia that are already being strategically restored to fenland, and how the sea is being allowed to reclaim stretches of its old territory along the Norfolk coast to the benefit, he argued, not only of wildlife and delicate wild eco-systems, but also of the local community that has suffered so long under the yoke of agri-business. He finished with a defiant challenge: 'I would say that we probably will all go under and the water will be over our heads in perhaps fifty years but I think it would be good to try to make the first thirty worth living.' To which Jim responded: 'I'm not going to add to that: it's perfect! It's what I mean by sustainable retreat.'

In *Homage to Gaia*, the professor evokes a poignant image of the ravages we've inflicted on 'our countryside' over the millennia: 'We took the breath-taking beauty of our land as much for granted as would a peasant farmer that of his young wife,' he writes, 'and we expected it to work for us, not realizing that a life of drudgery is incompatible with beauty.' And in *Revenge of Gaia*, having suggested that the humanist concept of sustainable development and the Christian concept of steward-ship are flawed by 'unconscious hubris,' he evokes another: 'We are no more qualified to be the stewards or developers of the Earth than are goats to be gardeners.'

Richard Mabey, incidentally, decided early on in the evening to turn the title of their discussion from a statement into a question: 'Whose

Countryside?' he asks. The irony is inescapable: by enriching its soil we impoverish the Earth. And he spelled it out: 'Rich soil is basically the enemy of a healthy planet. We should be beginning to think about three-dimensional farming – forest farming – systems of agriculture that would not rely so much upon cultivation of the soil but on allowing complicated eco-systems to develop from which we then gather crops. Wheat in my view is the most dangerous plant on the planet!' But if Richard the naturalist sees our assault on the Earth as beginning in earnest at the dawn of civilisation around ten thousand years ago, Jim the scientist dates it much earlier: 'Well this is why I said last night – and I meant it very strongly – that we fell from grace, to put it in religious terms, the moment we started using fire; indeed there's one or two scientists who really think that we started changing the climate of the earth long, long, long ago – way back in our history, hundreds of thousands of years.'

In any case, as he told the audience last night, he and Richard perceive life from two quite different, equally valid viewpoints: his own, the holistic overview: the Earth as observed through a telescope from outer space; Richard's, the fine detail obtained by peering into a microscope. And although they agree that a large proportion of our countryside must be returned to its natural state of predominantly broad-leafed deciduous woodland, their solutions for a sustainable *modus vivendi* in a newly restored landscape were markedly different. Jim Lovelock's, for example, depends on our having found a way to keep the lights on and civilisation up and running without burning the planet to a crisp in the process (he favours the nuclear option, but didn't say so for fear it would high-jack the evening), and is geared to supplying the needs of a vastly inflated population once the desertification of Europe begins in earnest and these islands are one of the few inhabitable places on Earth: pack us hugger mugger into high-rise apartment blocks, Hong Kong style, and synthesise our food. A grim-sounding scenario, which led someone in the audience to say Something Must be Done! about the unsustainable growth rate of the population, and Jim to point out that something was indeed being done, though not by us – eugenics having proved a non-starter politically – and to ponder our arrogance: 'Any biological species that overpopulates and starts using its resources faster than they can be supplied crashes. Why our species should be exempt from that I just don't know, and I think we are due a big crash.'

You could have heard a pin drop. At breakfast, I ask Jim what he felt about Richard's review of his book in which he'd praised the scientist's prescience, but feared he was not a good psychologist. 'I'm not!' he agrees, unperturbed: 'I don't work out how to influence the opposition. I'm only interested in the evidence and what's going to happen.'

Richard's own strategy for our long-term survival suggested, but didn't spell out, that this crash had already taken place: he pictured a return to a hunter-gathering lifestyle living in and off the fruits of the forest and farming the wild deer who'd share it with us. It was only when another member of the audience pointed out that a hunter-gathering lifestyle in Plymouth may not be an option that he managed to conjure up an image for city folk William Morris would have appreciated: urban residents growing grapes and melons and figs vertically up their properties' sun-baked walls, allowing their gardens to revert to the wild state – a Utopian vision that had Jim Lovelock asking wryly how many he thought such a system could sustain.

As for the decision not to mention nuclear for fear it would disrupt the evening, Jim's advocacy of it as the only way forward in the short-term means he has put himself beyond the Green Pale. But then the Greens have put themselves beyond his; he thinks them 'silly' – unrealistic in their aims, smugly middle-class in their attitudes, and worse: 'They live in a dream world, a rather nasty dream world in a way because they are not taking account of ordinary people's lives.' Earlier I had asked him if, as an independent scientist working alone, he sometimes felt isolated from his peer group – his tribe, as it were – and he had been adamant: 'But they are not my tribe! I don't belong to any scientific tribe. I always see myself as a lone scout going up on the hill and looking ahead and then coming back and saying Hey! There's something terrific up there and they say "No!

No! Go away!" and they don't believe you.' He decides his natural constituency is probably the intelligent working class. Which makes sense: somehow Jim Lovelock's story reminds me of Dickens' – what with their shared relish for undertaking prodigious walking feats, and the fact that his highly intelligent mother was sent at the age of thirteen to work in a pickle factory in the East End of London, where she was born. Jim himself was brought up in Brixton, where he learned early on in life what burning fossil fuels does to the atmosphere when the winter smogs Dickens evoked so vividly brought on his asthma and nearly killed him.

Meanwhile, Sandy has begun sending out unmistakable signals from the next table to which she's tactfully withdrawn for the duration, so I start to sort my stuff out from the detritus of breakfast, and her husband to fold his napkin as carefully as if he were at home, while we swap Buddhist concepts and he tells me how proud he is of the way he ended his first book on Gaia: 'So what's the recipe for living with Gaia? I ask, and answer: There are no recipes there are only consequences. And that's very Buddhist, of course.'

*The Revenge of Gaia* (Penguin/Allen Lane, 2006, paperback 2007)

*Gaia: Medicine for an Ailing Planet* (Gaia Books, 1999)

*The Ages of Gaia* (W.W. Norton, 1988)

*Gaia: A New Look at Life on Earth* (Oxford University Press, 2000)

*Homage to Gaia* (Oxford University Press, 2001)

# Lucinda Lambton

## WRITER AND BROADCASTER

O n a cool, blustery evening in the Chelsea Physic Garden early last
summer I watched Lucinda Lambton being presented to members of
the Garden History Society as its prospective new President, and was
impressed by her (apparently) cheerful willingness to clamber onto the seat
of a non-too solid looking kitchen chair and to remain there, teetering
slightly in her peep-toed, wedge-heeled sandals and flimsy frock, smiling
bravely down on us all while the Society's new Chairman delivered his
own speech at not inconsiderable length, and the wind whipped at her
ankles.

Lucinda Lambton's name is possibly not the first to spring to mind in
the context of gardens, yet in 2006 she had delivered a lecture cheekily entitled *A Compendium of Architectural Delights: with a Garden or Two Thrown
In* to the Royal Horticultural Society, no less. Perhaps it was this talk that
had attracted the attention of the GHS, who were on the hunt for a star
performer to take over the role from Sir Roy Strong. And if her rousing
speech to us that evening is anything to go by, it looks as though the Society
has found itself a modern-day Boudica prepared to lead her troops from the
front against the enemy, in defence of our beleaguered heritage. In the faint
hope of capturing Lucinda's inimitable delivery on the page, the italics in
the following extract from her opening salvo are mine:

> If I may, with this first talk to you all, [I will] throw my hat into
> the ring by making a plea that we put cemeteries particularly high
> on our list of areas in need of our nurturing and care.

For, throughout the cities of the *world* and so often amidst the *grimmest* surroundings, there are these *enclaves* of nineteenth-century Elysian Fields. Great *tracts* of planting at its most picturesque; landscapes that set off to *perfection* an architectural Utopia in miniature – with classical temples and columns, domes, canopies and obelisks, gothic pinnacles and gables, all presenting a showpiece of the architect's, sculptor's, stonemason's and letterer's art; in other words, nineteenth-century cemeteries are places of *breathtaking* beauty and interest, that are so often *bewilderingly* neglected today.

Time and *again* I am bashed in the head with bewilderment, when driving through some densely built-up area, and suddenly spotting, through a gateway, a *swathe* of landscaped grounds, *filled* with sculptural splendours, with locals walking by, harassed by urban life, and seemingly unaware that the *Garden of Eden* is but mere feet away. Yes, cemeteries, situated as they so often are, amidst dire surroundings, are greatly in need of our help.

Thank *God* they have not yet been designated as brownfield sites – as far as I know, that is – although even that may only be a matter of time. We will be on to it with a vengence if they do.

Captivated, I wrote to Lucinda begging an interview and my request triggered a phone call challenging me to tell her why, pray, she had never heard of *Hortus*, but full of the news that now her husband, the distinguished journalist Sir Peregrine Worsthorne, was alert to its existence he had only the other day spotted fellow members of the Garrick Club *poring* over it, so that was good, wasn't it? And yes, let's make a date to meet at her home in Buckinghamshire.

Home turned out to be an old Victorian rectory set halfway up a more or less perpendicular wooded hillside that rears up from the floor of a secluded valley in the Chilterns. A tangle of vegetation, overgrown yew and a pair of imposing, solid metal gates decorated with appliquéd dogs' heads and a frieze of *bas-relief* gothic arches guards the property, and screens it from view from the single-track lane that is the only feed into and out of a now wholly gentrified picture-postcard village that at ten-thirty in the morning was wreathed in blessed silence.

Until, that is, I manage to breach the gates, scale the ski-slope of a drive and provoke a huge and boisterous lurcher and his low-slung, white-haired accomplice into paroxysms of frenzied barking. They have me covered between them until Lucinda's secretary Claire emerges from her office in a converted garage hidden in the woods nearby, and calls them off. Some time later, Lucinda herself materialises out of the sombre recesses of her Pugin wallpapered, lily-scented entrance hall to enquire, in an unsettling opening gambit worthy of Pinter: 'Do you wear Crocs?'

Our morning together is destined to be spent in a spacious light-filled conservatory whose exterior imaginatively replicates down to its last finial a Victorian Gothic church, or private chapel perhaps since it is attached to one side of the house. However, as it boasts four separate points of access, two from the house, two into the garden, instead of being a tranquil sanctuary it is in fact a major thoroughfare, or stage, on and off which throughout the morning – this morning at least – a cast of characters engaged in some mysterious sub-plot would be making their exits and their entrances in an endless search for one another.

But first, as Lucinda has gone in search of a pair of Crocs for me to try because she believes I'll end up a martyr to my feet if I don't overcome my vanity and wear the brutes, I stray out onto a narrow terrace strewn with pots of *Lilium regale* and some highly desirable cast-iron Victorian gothic garden furniture, down steep steps smothered in lady's mantle and *Geranium endressi*, and out onto a lawn separated from the rest of the rectory's sprawling acre by Piranesi-scale crenellated yew hedges. I am examining her collection of domestic animals constructed out of chicken wire and box growing within this space when Lucinda reappears: 'I do feel,' she informs me, 'that this is the pauper's answer to a *grand* and *individual* garden. It *must* be! It's not expensive and you could have anything.' 'Here,' gathering pace as she gets into her stride, 'there are two chickens in the trees and a rearing pony out there and then there's a goose and a squirrel and a rabbit and a pig and a dog chasing a cat and a cockerel and a cow and a bull and calf and a sheep and a ram and a lamb.'

Back inside, we settle ourselves at a round table littered with the remains of breakfast, the post, today's *Guardian* newspaper and a vase of sweet peas. If there hadn't been so many bizarre artefacts – Lucy's toys as they are known in the family – lying in wait like sirens on the shore we'd be all set, but one succeeds: 'This is a really exciting piece. It's part of the fence of the government house in Benares and it's of Queen Victoria when she was young as seen by an Indian artisan. Queen Victoria never went to India, but there she is by an Indian. She looks Indian doesn't she?' She does. Determinedly, I open at random *The Oxford Companion to the Garden*, which I've brought along for reference, and ask Lucy if she has any particular garden, or garden designer, or period style that might get us started. 'Blank! Blank!' she yelps. 'I'm trying to think. I mean garden history's thrilling in terms of realising there was a summerhouse here or a temple there, and whenever there's a building, my pulse quickens. Would you mind if I did something a tiny bit rude, but not too rude?' And she's gone again, this time to fetch her nail varnish. I seem to remember it being lots of fun trying to assemble together blobs of mercury spilt on the science lab bench at school, but quite impossible.

While Lucy, head between her knees, attends to her toenails, I mention that the dictionary actually defines a garden as a plot of cultivated land attached to a dwelling, so there's bound to be a building involved. 'Oh good, yes. They're part and parcel. Siamese twins.' And then the *Companion* fulfils its purpose: 'What's that book? How lovely! Look! Painshill! But it's all because of the buildings. Grottos too! Leeds Castle with its *sensational, sensational* grotto buried in encrusted subterranean passages. That is absolutely *extraordinary* and there again why on *earth* isn't there more beautifying of sensational gardens going on to attract people to statelies, rather than [turning them into] a theme park? Restoring these buildings in the grounds would seem to me to be – *is* in fact – a way of bringing people in.'

At which moment, Lucy's husband, an exquisite apparition in faded pink from head to toe, enters from the house. He is looking for Claire and, introductions over, exits again, this time into the garden. Dazzled by his casual elegance, and curious, I wonder if Perry, as he is always known, shares Lucy's passion for Victorian Gothic? 'No! He hasn't got any sensibilities of an aesthetic nature, but makes himself look quite wonderful, which is interesting – very interesting. A beautiful *rainbow* of clothes.' Clothes maketh the man, I muse. 'I suppose they are more reflective of self rather than my outside interests. Yes, that's a very good explanation.' One might imagine that someone equally at ease on a rickety platform addressing erudite members of the Garden History Society, in front of the television cameras entertaining a mass audience, or even from the pulpit of St George's Hanover outlining to a well-heeled audience the purpose of the recently-formed Old Rectory Association, let alone prepared to take Prince Charles to task for not spending enough time showing her round his garden at Highgrove, must be an out an out extrovert. But is she? I ask, and am rebuked: 'Well, I'm both,' she answers, reasonably. 'I work alone for hour upon hour upon hour, week upon week, month upon month and then . . . I don't want to go on talking about that, I'm feeling too self-centred suddenly . . . I've done terrible things with this Stain Devil. I must have done it with too much vigour. It's taken all the skin off my hands.'

Chastened, but recalling roughly where we'd got to when life intervened, I mention the ongoing restoration work to the long-abandoned eighteenth century wilderness garden that had been left to moulder quietly away in its combe at the back of Hestercombe House in Somerset, while the Lutyens-Jekyll creation at the front was drawing all the crowds. Lucy is predictably as unmoved by the latter – 'All those marching cubes and pergolas' – as she is captivated by the Picturesque and we are back on track: 'I'm entranced by the idea of those eighteenth-century pleasure grounds – Vauxhall Gardens, all of them. *Very* interesting, because they lower the taste, don't they? They are early theme parks. I know another. It has a hermit and hermitages and very steep walks up and down and rocky glades and pastoral views, like being on a roller-coaster. What was it called, though?

It turns out she has two distinct gardens in mind, and all we have to go on is that one is in Shropshire, the other in Yorkshire. Fortunately the dogged hunting down of obscure facts in books, on the internet, in the recesses of her own memory, and of anyone else's who comes within striking range is a challenge to be relished – her laptop was her Desert Island luxury, for heaven's sake. And with the help of the *Companion* we manage to pin down the Shropshire garden (Hawkstone), largely because after some frantic cudgelling the first half of its name pops into her head. The name of the other does not, so when Perry reappears, still – or again – looking for Claire, he is put on the case because Lucy has remembered it belongs to a friend of his, 'a *highly* cultivated master of foxhounds, always entertaining,' she urges and off he goes to scour Debrett's and his address book, but in vain.

Crucial names and pertinent facts needing further research are beginning to accumulate, and it is clear we'll need another day together or I'll end up with a rag-bag of sumptuous scraps. I fear this turns out to be the case, although at our follow-up meeting she does snare her Yorkshire prey by making her way inch by inch up the MI on an AA road atlas: 'Hackfall!' she announces, triumphant. Google reveals that Hackfall is now in the hands of the Woodland Trust – which would explain why it is not listed in Debrett's as her husband's friend's home address – and that it was created by John Aislabie, the disgraced eighteenth-century politician best known in the horticultural world for designing the classically formal water gardens at his home, Studley Royal, and its celebrated wilderness walk that culminates in a view of the very last word in romantic follies, the monastic ruins of Fountains Abbey.

Meantime, back in the present, Lucy has to provide lunch out of a bare cupboard for the cast, and as she scurries about the rectory's cavernous kitchen in search of ingredients I decide to read out loud to her what the *Oxford Companion* has to say about Cetinale, her late father Viscount Lambton's celebrated garden in Tuscany, but can't because it's too dark. In any case, far better to hear her own response to what he and his companion Clare, a notable plantswoman, achieved over the thirty years they lived there together. 'It's sensational! It moves me!' she yells above the noise of running water. 'It moves me so much I want to *scream*,' adding resignedly, 'but after you've screamed once that's no good any more, so I walk round shaking my head in disbelief.' In mitigation, she recalls Virginia Woolf wrote about the difficulty of expressing the beauty of nature, but can't quite remember what she said, or in which book she said it: 'Remind me what her books were called. I'll have to look it up.' It's my turn to go blank. *Mrs Dalloway* . . . *To the Lighthouse* . . . In any case, with a mob to feed and a suitcase to pack and a journey to be embarked upon by two-thirty latest, there's no time to start trawling through her oeuvre, much as she might be tempted.

I remember a question I'd been meaning to ask all morning. Which actual gardens had Lucinda managed to muster for her talk to the RHS? Daft question. 'Conservatories, of course! That's where the two worlds meet isn't it? *Vast* and great conservatories! Flintham is one I showed. I can't remember what the others were.' The Flintham property in Nottinghamshire that she devoted a whole chapter to in her book, *Lucinda Lambton's A to Z of Britian*, has been in the Hildyard family since medieval times, and is not open to the public, but its conservatory, which clearly owes a debt to Paxton's Crystal Palace, features in any book on the subject of glasshouses.

Actually there is one real garden that came up in our conversation and which she could well have included in her talk – Waddesdon's 'full whack' recreation of a Victorian-style planting scheme: 'I think it's *horrible*, but it's interesting because that's how the surroundings of the house were conceived. *Hideous* but dead interesting . . .' And for contrast, she might also have included a charming garden she'd stumbled across when researching her book, *Old New World, The Old-fashionedness of America*: 'I'll tell you a magical example of garden history I discovered. In the 1800s, Thomas Hughes, who wrote *Tom Brown's Schooldays*, founded a commune in Tennessee for the younger sons of English nobility where they could learn a decent trade. But it failed entirely, this Utopia, because these second sons were all so hopeless and when the last one went it closed. Rugby it was called, and I found this *extraordinary* lending library that hadn't been changed since the day it was built – in 1880, I think it was – the smell, the books, everything.' The survival of such a treasure in the heart of the Appalachians is surprising enough, but there's more: direct descendants of the plants Hughes' ancient mother had brought with her from England have managed to endure the hostile climate all these years, and are thriving: 'I found primroses and scillas and jonquils growing there. Suddenly in the mountains of Tennessee there was this *tiny* little garden round a house. The absolute magic! *That* is another interesting thing I hadn't thought of until this moment: that particular survival was evidence that the nineteenth century still lives in Tennessee – lives, *lives!* Those same plants. Isn't that thrilling?'

Before too long we are back to grottos and pondering Lucy's unquenchable curiosity about the past: 'It's entrancing to know – anywhere you go, it's entrancing to know what's over the wall, it's so much nicer *knowing* than *not* knowing. God, do you know about Mrs Delaney who made grottos? She was renowned in the 1700s, and she was the Duchess of Portland's great friend and together they worked on a shell grotto and many other things, so that acre up there would prove the richest, *richest* historic excavation for the artist and the gardener, excavated and researched and studied. I mean it's just a great corporate *lump* now.' She's lost me. What is? 'It's called Bulstrode. It was built by Benjamin Ferrey [architect friend of Pugin who Lucy believes, but to her annoyance can't prove, may also have built her rectory since he designed the church it once belonged to somewhere up there in the woods above our heads, and Bulstrode is only a mile away]. 'The house is pretty ugly but I like the whispers of history around the place. I'll have to go and get my book if you want the facts. It hasn't got a garden, but [the old house] had Mrs Delaney there making all her grottos.'

'Only', she despairs, remembering, 'they are no longer there!' This appalling thought triggers a full-scale lament: *'That's* a very sad thing. The ephemeral nature of gardening is exquisite pain to me – that's *really* exquisite pain, it *almost* makes me perversely determined *not* to love it.' As if on cue, a butterfly starts beating its flimsy wings against one of the conservatory windows close by, reminding Lucy that she once kept a butterfly alive one whole winter: 'We put honey in flowers and if I'd been out all day I used to rush home to make sure my pal was still here.' What happened to it? 'It disappeared one day.'

No time left to meditate further on life's transience, the unbearable fact of, and as we wander over to Claire's sanctuary in the woods to scour the diary for a free morning for a return match Lucy tries but fails to convince me that I have witnessed an unusually fraught day in her life. However, I do believe her when she says that what she really likes is having 'frenzied plans, and then suddenly they're all cancelled. Oh, that's so lovely.'

My next visit two weeks later starts off in much the same way as the first, only this time Claire isn't there to administer the necessary first aid, and Lucy isn't waiting in the wings for her cue or, rather more worryingly, even in the theatre. An hour or so goes by – clearly I've hit another day of diary overload – before hysterical barking heralds her return. When she learns that I was about to leave she is genuinely amazed: 'Were you really going? Was there really any fear of your running away?' – and gratifyingly penitent when I say I was, though not for long – 'But I'm not too sorry, because it's a lovely day to be sitting here. *Please* do stay for lunch. What we've got to do is look up those things you said.' How does the song go? *Beguiled again. Something or other again. Bewitched . . .*

And so, I find myself on the shady terrace drinking *vin rose* and chatting idly to Lucy's urbane husband, while she is busy ferreting out facts in her study, or foraging for food for us all in the kitchen. 'Perry,' she announces on one of her fleeting appearances, 'is as informed as a dog on matters of gardening. Ask Rastus [the low-slung one]. He'll give you better information on gardens than Perry,' and is immediately contrite, demanding to know: 'Why is it that the only person I am ever nasty to is Perry?' He consoles her: 'You're never nasty, Lucy. Maddening, but never nasty.'

The terrace overlooks the site of the old (as in original) rectory, and a four-hundred-year-old yew, unclipped and immense, still marks the spot Lucinda unsurprisingly longs to excavate. It strikes me as verging on the miraculous to have found a property so close to London so ideally tailored to her tastes and interests – to her entire persona – but divine intervention had nothing to do with it, only nerve and sheer bloody persistence. Her game plan was simple: never compromise. 'Bette Davis [in *Dark Voyager*] said, "Don't let's ask for the moon. We have the stars." Well I looked for the moon, and got it. For about twenty years I looked for a gothic house in a village within twenty-five miles of London – sixty things in the post every morning, year after year after year. All around here it's *beautiful* – and it's magical when you go for a walk and come across a wooden signpost saying: To London.'

I have a postcard – black background, white lettering – which I keep pinned to my kitchen dresser to remind myself: 'Never, ever, ever, ever give up' is the message.

Lucinda's forthcoming book is on the subject of buildings in the Caribbean and Britain financed by 'sugar money'. It will be published in 2009 by Merrell Publishers. Information about her other published books, along with more facts in connection with all the people and/or historic gardens mentioned in this piece can be obtained by 'googling' the relevant name.